ULTIMATE GUIDE
TRIMWORK

CRE▲TIVE
HOMEOWNER®

ULTIMATE GUIDE

TRIMWORK

CREATIVE HOMEOWNER®

ULTIMATE GUIDE: TRIMWORK

CONTRIBUTING WRITERS	Neal Barrett, Steve Cory, Phil Schmidt, Jay Silber
MANAGING EDITOR	Fran Donegan
JUNIOR EDITOR	Angela Hanson
PROOFREADER	Sara Markowitz
PHOTO COORDINATOR	Mary Dolan
DIGITAL IMAGING SPECIALIST	Frank Dyer
INDEXER	Schroeder Indexing Services
COVER DESIGN	David Geer

Current Printing (last digit)
10 9 8 7 6 5 4 3 2

Manufactured in China

Ultimate Guide: Trimwork
Library of Congress Control Number: 2009932394
ISBN-10: 1-58011-477-6
ISBN-13: 978-1-58011-477-6

CREATIVE HOMEOWNER®
www.creativehomeowner.com

Creative Homeowner books are distributed by
Fox Chapel Publishing
1970 Broad Street
East Petersburg, PA 17520
www.FoxChapelPublishing.com

Safety

Although the methods in this book have been reviewed for safety, it is not possible to overstate the importance of using the safest methods you can. What follows are reminders—some do's and don'ts of work safety—to use along with your common sense.

- Always use caution, care, and good judgment when following the procedures described in this book.
- Always be sure that the electrical setup is safe, that no circuit is overloaded, and that all power tools and outlets are properly grounded. Do not use power tools in wet locations.
- Always read container labels on paints, solvents, and other products; provide ventilation; and observe all other warnings.
- Always read the manufacturer's instructions for using a tool, especially the warnings.
- Use hold-downs and push sticks whenever possible when working on a table saw. Avoid working short pieces if you can.
- Always remove the key from any drill chuck (portable or press) before starting the drill.
- Always pay deliberate attention to how a tool works so that you can avoid being injured.
- Always know the limitations of your tools. Do not try to force them to do what they were not designed to do.
- Always make sure that any adjustment is locked before proceeding. For example, always check the rip fence on a table saw or the bevel adjustment on a portable saw before starting to work.
- Always clamp small pieces to a bench or other work surface when using a power tool.
- Always wear the appropriate rubber gloves or work gloves when handling chemicals, moving or stacking lumber, working with concrete, or doing heavy construction.
- Always wear a disposable face mask when you create dust by sawing or sanding. Use a special filtering respirator when working with toxic substances and solvents.
- Always wear eye protection, especially when using power tools or striking metal on metal or concrete; a chip can fly off, for example, when chiseling concrete.
- Never work while wearing loose clothing, open cuffs, or jewelry; tie back long hair.
- Always be aware that there is seldom enough time for your body's reflexes to save you from injury from a power tool in a dangerous situation; everything happens too fast. Be alert!
- Always keep your hands away from the business ends of blades, cutters, and bits.
- Always hold a circular saw firmly, usually with both hands.
- Always use a drill with an auxiliary handle to control the torque when using large-size bits.
- Always check your local building codes when planning new construction. The codes are intended to protect public safety and should be observed to the letter.
- Never work with power tools when you are tired or under the influence of alcohol or drugs.
- Never cut tiny pieces of wood or pipe using a power saw. When you need a small piece, saw it from a securely clamped longer piece.
- Never change a saw blade or a drill or router bit unless the power cord is unplugged. Do not depend on the switch being off. You might accidentally hit it.
- Never work in insufficient lighting.
- Never work with dull tools. Have them sharpened, or learn how to sharpen them yourself.
- Never use a power tool on a workpiece—large or small—that is not firmly supported.
- Never saw a workpiece that spans a large distance between horses without close support on each side of the cut; the piece can bend, closing on and jamming the blade, causing saw kickback.
- When sawing, never support a workpiece from underneath with your leg or other part of your body.
- Never carry sharp or pointed tools, such as utility knives, awls, or chisels, in your pocket. If you want to carry any of these tools, use a special-purpose tool belt that has leather pockets and holders.

Contents

Introduction

TRIMWORK HAS THE ABILITY to change the overall character of your home. It not only provides a practical service by covering the rough edges and seams between different building materials but also adds a distinctive touch that gives a home architectural detail and character. All of the major design movements—from Colonial days until the middle of the twentieth century—have been associated with a particular trimwork style. However, many of the homes built in the years since the end of World War II lack distinctive molding and trimwork treatments that home builders of an earlier era automatically included in the houses they built. Where molding is used, it is often small and plain. *Ultimate Guide: Trimwork* shows you how to reverse that trend and use trimwork to add character to your home.

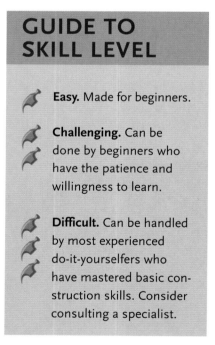

GUIDE TO SKILL LEVEL

Easy. Made for beginners.

Challenging. Can be done by beginners who have the patience and willingness to learn.

Difficult. Can be handled by most experienced do-it-yourselfers who have mastered basic construction skills. Consider consulting a specialist.

Even casual living spaces benefit from trimwork. Note the ceiling beams and cornice treatment.

There are many ways that you can improve your home by upgrading the existing trimwork. Because window and door casings are the most visible uses of molding and trimwork, they are a good place to start. You can replace the thin clamshell or Colonial moldings with larger, more interesting profiles.

Enhance walls by replacing existing base trim with a built-up assembly that provides a substantial foundation for the entire wall. Install a chair rail or wainscot mid-wall, and add a distinctive cornice treatment where the wall meets the ceiling.

But those ideas are just the beginning. *Ultimate Guide: Trimwork* will show you how to add wall panels, ceiling beams, columns, fireplace mantels, and much more.

Wall panels, left, can help turn an ordinary room into a more formal living space.

The cornice below includes picture rail molding, wallpaper border, and crown molding.

The first part of *Ultimate Guide: Trimwork* provides design information and step-by-step projects for adding trimwork to your home. Chapter 1, "The Power of Trimwork," shows the part that trimwork has played in residential design since Colonial times. It will help you determine what trimwork styles will work best in your home.

The next seven chapters present trimwork projects, including window and door casing; base, chair rail, and wainscoting; wall frames; crown and cornice molding; beams, columns, and pilasters; staircases; and mantels. A detailed tools and materials list, step-by-step how-to photography,

and clearly written instructions accompany each project. In some cases, detailed illustrations show you how the trimwork pieces go together to form a distinctive design. Each project provides the information you will need to install trimwork like a professional carpenter.

Installing trimwork is popular do-it-yourself activity, and "Part II: Fundamentals" will help you acquire the basic skills needed. The chapter "Trim Materials" will aid in your design and purchasing decisions. The chapter "Tools and Techniques" not only covers tools but also illustrates installation techniques used by the pros.

Painted wainscoting and chair rail, opposite, provide a firm foundation for this wall.

Textured molding profiles painted white, above, complement the blue of the walls.

In this room, right, window casing, chair rail, and base molding form a cohesive design.

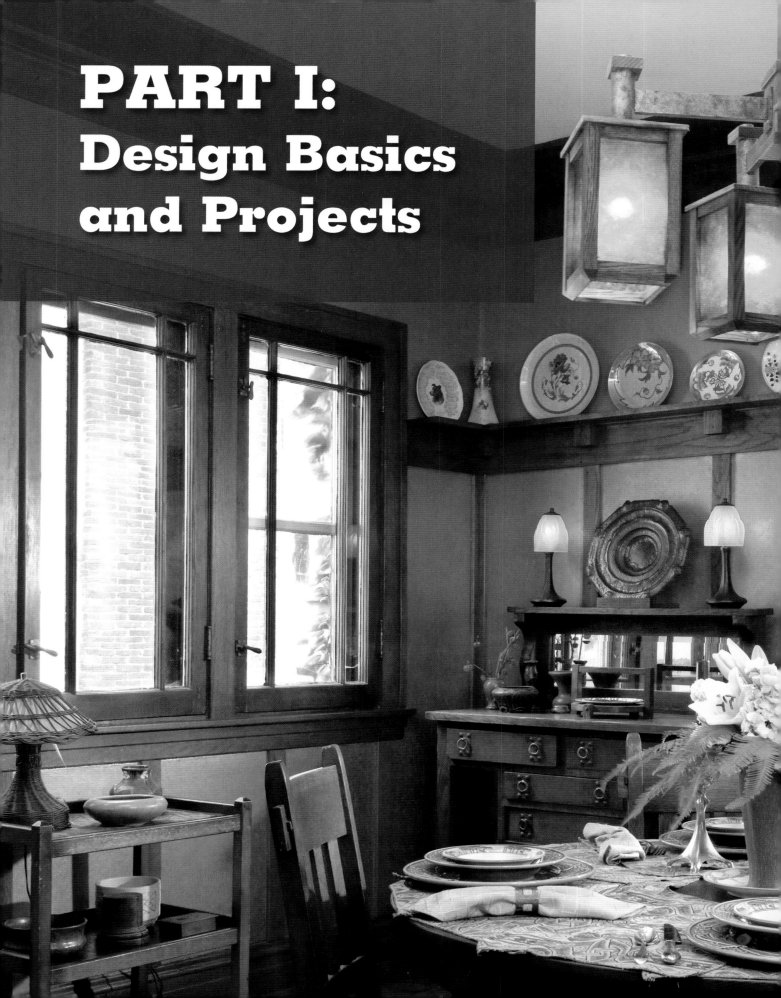

PART I:
Design Basics and Projects

the power of trimwork

1

MOLDING AND TRIMWORK can transform a room from an empty box to a richly textured living space. In the past, homes contained a wealth of architectural trimwork that lent character, beauty, and substance to their interiors. But the trimwork used in most modern homes serves to hide joints between surfaces while providing little in terms of ornamentation or style. This book will show you how trimwork can transform your home. Trimwork—door and window casings, crown molding, wall treatments, picture rails, base trim, and the like—can completely alter a room without changing its basic structure, giving your rooms the warmth, harmony, and sense of completeness trimwork alone can impart.

CHANGES IN HOME DESIGN

Until the mid-twentieth century, the use of decorative trimwork was standard in the construction of new homes. Most new houses incorporated trimwork that reflected the interior design style of the day. The early colonists brought with them a taste for dark, formal wood paneling of England during the seventeenth and early eighteenth centuries. By the mid-1700s, classical details such as pilasters, arches with keystones, and doorways with pediments—all elements of the English Georgian period—began to find expression in American homes. Heavily influenced by both archaeological and architectural discoveries of the time and by the English masters, America's own Federal style evolved during the early nineteenth century. Federal style also relied heavily on classical architecture and motifs, in particular those of ancient Greece. But it was heralded for its lightness and grace. Toward the end of the nineteenth century, the Victorian style took root, and Victorian-era houses usually displayed ornate, intricate door and window casings, elaborate baseboards, and elegant crown moldings.

Trimwork, such as crown molding, wall frames, and chair rails, was once standard fare in home design.

The Power of Trimwork

While modern architecture lends a sense of space to a home, it also sacrifices the warmth and intimacy of the traditional approach.

In the early twentieth century, architects, builders, and homeowners reacted against the perceived excesses of the Victorian Era, opting instead for the cleaner, simpler lines and square profiles of the Arts and Crafts movement. Influenced by the Arts and Crafts movement, homebuilders in the 1920s abandoned elaborate cornices and instead used small picture molding where walls and ceilings converged; doors and windows were cased out with flat boards usually about 4 inches wide. The subsequent Modern movement espoused that all ornamental features should be stripped away so that only a pure statement of function, process, and material remained. This took home design further away from the use of architectural trimwork.

But even if evolving tastes gradually rejected more ornate styles, trim remained a standard feature of new homes during the first half of the twentieth century; chair rails and crown moldings, though simplified, were still being installed, and carpenters didn't ask whether you wanted architectural trimwork in your new home—they just asked what style you wanted.

Vanishing Trimwork

The postwar building boom of the late 1940s and 1950s radically changed homebuilders' attitudes toward trim. When World War II veterans returned home and started families, demand for housing skyrocketed. Builders realized that if they reduced the amount of trim in a house to the bare minimum, they could build faster and cut costs. By using a simplified molding to cover the gaps around the window and door frames, and between the wall and the floor, builders saved on both materials and labor. This molding, called ranch or clamshell molding, was designed to have a streamlined profile that was consistent with the minimalist interiors of the new ranch and raised ranch houses. More recently, so-called Colonial trimwork has come into vogue for window and door casings as well as base trim. Colonial casings, like clamshell, are 2¼ to 3¼ inches wide but are milled with a more complex (though still simplified) profile. They are designed to look more at home in traditional settings.

Today many new houses are built with a minimal amount of simple trimwork of the clamshell or Colonial type. In some cases, the homeowner and architect look to the past for inspiration and incorporate some of the beauty, warmth, and character imparted to an interior by the use of more-ornate architectural trim designs.

TRIMWORK AS A DESIGN TOOL

With the trend toward simplicity has come both a loss and a challenge. Most homes built today lack the ornamental details that provide a space with architectural character and identity. Rooms are often plain and featureless. Open floor plans commonly seen in contemporary houses create large, undefined areas and undifferentiated spaces.

This is where architectural trimwork comes into play. Installing decorative molding not only adds beauty and substance to a plain home but also is a superb—and often simple—solution to the design challenges posed by many contemporary houses. The versatility of molding makes it adaptable to a variety of design treatments.

Without trimwork, as shown in the before photo, opposite, the front door of this house looks too small for an entry with a vaulted ceiling.

CASING DEVOLUTION

THE ELABORATE CURVES AND BEVELS of Victorian-era casings gave way to square, flat profiles of the Arts and Crafts movement in the early twentieth century. During the building boom of the late 1940s and early 1950s, the plain clamshell casing emerged and continues to be widely used today.

3-PIECE VICTORIAN CASING

CLAMSHELL CASING

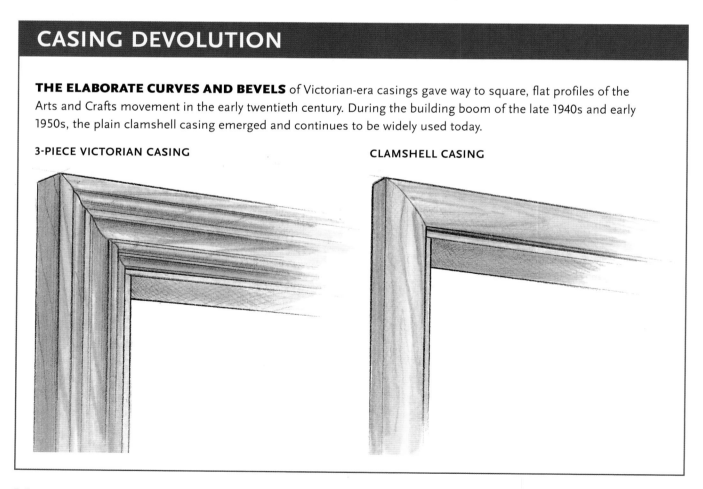

Trimwork Solves the Empty Box Syndrome

Rooms owe their architectural identity to their basic size and shape, the balanced placement of windows and doors, and the trimwork on the walls and ceilings. In most well-designed older houses, elaborate, built-up molding treatments lend character and beauty. Today, most houses continue the minimalist trend discussed above. Decorating them usually involves "applied materials"—such things as window treatments, wallpaper, and paint—that homeowners can apply or remove fairly easily themselves.

The applied-materials approach goes a long way toward improving the appearance of some houses, but it has its limitations. This fact becomes especially clear when you're faced with the "Empty Box Syndrome"—walls and ceilings that are as featureless and nondescript as the inside of an empty box. You can dress up rooms with curtains, paint, and carpeting, but stark and sterile walls will remain the dominant feature of a room's background. If you are surrounded by plain white walls in your home, consider them a blank slate upon which you can create beautiful rooms with fresh architectural identities.

Without resorting to major reconstruction, such as moving walls and windows, the best way to enhance the character of a house architecturally is to install or upgrade the trim.

AFTER

BEFORE

The Power of Trimwork

The Challenge of Open Floor Plans: Tripartite Walls to the Rescue

Modern architecture introduced the open floor plan to American home design, but with it came new decorating challenges. In this type of layout, rooms are not separated from each other by walls with cased-out passageways. Instead, they flow freely and openly from one area of the house to another. In addition, ceilings are often raised, creating what are known as vaulted or cathedral ceilings.

When people began to live in these houses, they realized that areas that are physically open to one another had to share the same or similar wall treatments. But if they did, where did one room begin and another end? What if the homeowner wanted to use a different color palette in the family room from the one in the kitchen? Did an open plan preclude using more than one wallpaper pattern in the public areas of the house? With no differentiation of space, the easiest decorating solution for these rooms is either to paint them the same color or to wallpaper them with the same wallpaper.

The alternative, using architectural trimwork, is much more creative, especially when you consider incorporating

The addition of stately columns helps delineate space while preserving an open, airy feeling in this handsome room.

the tripartite wall. It is a three-part horizontal treatment of wall surfaces consisting of wainscoting (panels or wall frames) and a chair rail on the lower portion of the wall, a cornice at the top of the wall, and the field between them. The tripartite wall evolved in response to the most common decorative treatment of wall surfaces during the mid-1800s, which was to cover them, top to bottom, with a single pattern of wallpaper or decorative paint.

The tripartite wall is an ideal decorative solution for the enormous walls created by cathedral ceilings. Installing raised-panel wainscoting or a wall-frame treat-

ment at the bottom of the wall, plus cornice or panel molding just below where the ceiling begins to depart at an angle, transforms the entire character of the room. Not only that, the trimwork effectively changes the perception of the space. What may have felt cavernous before feels cozy now.

Another solution to meandering open-plan layouts is to build partition walls with cased-out passageways. Extra-wide passageways outfitted with pillars resting on podiums are also quite attractive and dramatic. Installing pilasters is an elegant design alternative to consider.

A three-part, or tripartite, design consisting of wainscoting, wall area, and crown molding creates a classic look in any home.

Trimwork can make a small space seem larger. This plain entryway, below, opened up dramatically once the chair rail and wall frames were installed, right.

AFTER

BEFORE

Trimwork Makes Rooms Appear Larger

As you consider redecorating, you might be concerned that extensive trimwork will make small rooms feel even smaller. In fact, however, the opposite occurs. Through a phenomenon known as "geometric illusion," trimwork often makes a room appear larger and wider. Long horizontal lines, for example, can make you perceive that a room is longer and wider than it really is. Likewise, long vertical lines can make a low ceiling appear higher than it actually is.

MOLDING TYPES AND FUNCTIONS

With the proper tools, an understanding of some design basics, and knowledge of how trimwork is applied, most homeowners today can install and enjoy architectural trimwork. Between standard stock items and custom-milled possibilities, the choices available to you are nearly endless. Although the most popular types and their use are described here, you can also find cross sections of all of the common moldings displayed on a molding board at most lumber supply dealers.

Molding used to trim doors, windows, and other openings is called casing. (See Chapter 2, "Door and Window-Casings," page 38.) Casing is also commonly used for chair rails, cabinet trim, and other decorative purposes.

Base trim protects the bottom of a wall from wear and tear and hides irregularities where the wall and floor meet. A shoe molding is installed along the bottom front edge to hide unevenness in the flooring and give the baseboard a finished look. Other moldings can be used to enhance a wall, including wainsoting and chair rails. (See Chapter 3, "Base, Chair Rail, and Wainscoting," page 72.) Wainscoting can impart a country look to kitchens and bathrooms or a more formal appearance to living or dining rooms.

Wall frames look like a series of empty picture frames running along a wall. (See Chapter 4, " Wall Frames," page 106.) Painted in the same color as the surrounding walls, they lend a sculptural quality to a surface. Painted to contrast with the surrounding wall, they can create a striking three-dimensional appearance of varying depths.

Different molding types include: (A) cornice; (B) door casing; (C) chair rail; (D) subrail; (E) wall frame; and (F) baseboard molding.

The Power of Trimwork

Cornices create a decorative transition between walls and ceilings and work especially well in rooms with high ceilings. (See Chapter 5, "Crown and Cornice Molding," page 138.) Crown molding, the most popular type of cornice, has a profile that projects out and down and gives a rich appearance. Cornices are also used in combination with other moldings to form decorative mantels and frames.

Pillars, with their massive presence, are useful as a way to define space in an open floor plan. Fluted pilasters are elegant architectural elements that can enhance any room.

(See Chapter 6, "Beams, Pillars, and Pilasters," page 164.)

You may think the elegant staircase is a thing of the past, but the application of trimwork can improve any home's main staircase without extensive construction. (See Chapter 7, " Staircase Details," page 184.)

The same is true for fireplace mantels. The popularity of wood-burning and gas-fired fireplaces has made these appliances popular for additions, renovations, and in new construction. In most cases, the embellishment of the area around a fireplace is left up to the homeowner. (See Chapter 8, "Fireplace Mantels," page 196.)

A curved doorway and passthrough share the same casing and pilaster treatments.

Stock versus Custom Milled

The moldings just described typically come from stock profiles available in lumberyards. If you install these profiles properly and give careful attention to the design elements of a room, they offer very satisfactory results. Yet the look you wish to achieve may not be attainable with stock profiles alone. Single-piece stock moldings may be too small or too thin, making them appear insubstantial in their surroundings. In such cases, your best choice may be to use built-up, or multipiece, moldings, made by combining various complementary profiles to produce what appears to be a single piece of molding. You can combine different pieces of stock molding, although this can be tricky because stock molding is not designed for this use. Or you can combine single-piece stock moldings with custom-milled profiles—an easier way to achieve attractive multipiece profiles.

Obtaining custom-milled profiles is less costly than most people believe, and the results can be markedly superior. Small woodworking shops can create built-up molding components at a reasonable price and will work with you in achieving your specific profiles design.

The Power of Trimwork

Trimwork that caps a paneled wall serves as a display area for a collection of goblets and steins.

GAINING CONFIDENCE USING TRIMWORK

Redecorating with trimwork gives you a chance to create new warmth and beauty in the home with which you originally fell in love. To do so with confidence, you'll want to make design choices appropriate to your space and decor. In some contemporary homes, for example, elaborate molding treatments could be out of place. But don't make the common mistake of underestimating the amount of trim that rooms can tastefully accommodate.

This book will guide you through the process of planning, designing, and installing both simple and more complicated trimwork. Throughout the book, photographs of trimwork provide ideas and inspiration you can draw on in developing your own plans.

In addition to dozens of trimwork projects, you will also find help in selecting materials and in using the tools that are designed for trimwork applications. While each project covers the basics of cutting and installing trimwork, the appendix, "Tools and Techniques," page 246, provides more detailed information to achieve professional-quality results.

A pillar standing on a podium lends a touch of distinction to a simple open passageway and helps to delineate space.

The Power of Trimwork

TRANSFORMING A ROOM

BASIC TRIMWORK

A dining room in a typical house built today will be trimmed with ranch, or clamshell, molding around doors and windows and at the base of walls, creating a sterile, empty box of a room.

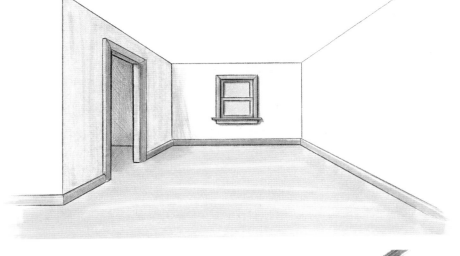

ENHANCED TRIMWORK

Installing crown molding at the top of the walls, a chair rail around the perimeter of the room, a more substantial baseboard, a wall panel under the window, and wider window and door casings lends architectural character.

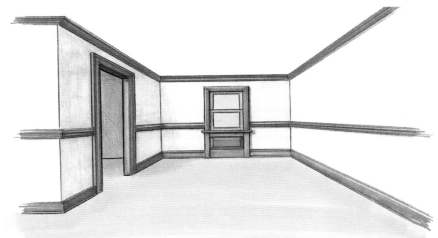

COMPLEX TRIMWORK

Installing beams, a framed opening, wall-frame wainscoting, built-up base molding, and substantial door and window casings transforms the empty box into a room that looks more spacious, warm, elegant, and complete.

MODERN AND TRADITIONAL TREATMENTS

Before you can decide how to proceed with your trim projects, you need to know a bit about your options. While you don't have to feel locked into following any particular style or design tradition, it is helpful to have an understanding of the historical trends and elements that define some of the predominant design trends. Then you can create the trim details to suit your taste using features that resonate with your own aesthetic sensibility. If you are thinking about mixing specific trim details from different periods or disciplines, you might consider borrowing a technique from professional interior designers. Try creating a small

sample board for your project, with all of the decorative elements for a room displayed together. Then you can better see how the moldings, colors, and materials affect one another and avoid a costly design mistake.

Learning from the Past

Architectural embellishments have a long and rich history. Carvings and sculptural details were used from ancient times, with the most opulent examples used for public buildings, religious centers, and the homes of the wealthy and powerful. Many of these features were carved in stone

Simple designs fit the contemporary space above.

Painted molding, above right, complements the decor.

Paneled pillars, right, flank a decorative railing.

Elaborate profiles decorate a grand room, opposite.

and have survived to this day, still valued as artifacts of a treasured artistic heritage. If you look to ancient Greece as one example, you'll find that structural members of public buildings were treated as decorative elements. Columns adhered to strict principles of design; most were fluted and were adorned with carved bases and capitals. Friezes on buildings featured figurative details, often based around the exploits of heroic or mythic characters, and these could be capped by a molded cornice. Many of these elements have been borrowed, in greatly modified form, as inspiration for some of the predominant architectural styles still visible in many public and residential buildings in our country.

Of course, most of the residential detailing in the United States has been fashioned from wood and not stone. And our homes are usually quite a bit more modest than the ancient Greek temples. But the desire to establish a style

and make a personal statement about our environment is linked to those ancient roots. Design inspiration can come from many places, and historical precedent is a reasonable place to start.

Modern Designs

By the middle of the twentieth century, housing demand in the United States was growing at an unprecedented rate. As soldiers returned from World War II and the country returned to a peacetime economy, financial optimism was growing. Almost overnight, the dream of home ownership became a real possibility for a generation of people. Government-subsidized mortgages for veterans and a growing economy provided fuel for the housing boom. And to fill the need for housing stock, builders around the country sprang into action turning old farmland and vacant properties into residential tracts.

The Power of Trimwork

Colonial

Early settlers in our country brought with them established tastes and preferences in architectural styles. As the colonies developed, it is not surprising that many of the earliest cultural influences came from throughout Europe. The *American Colonial* style was the first manifestation of a particularly American aesthetic by the new settlers of our land, although it drew freely on a variety of established styles, predominantly *Georgian*. (See page 30.)

In the earliest period of settlement, colonial homes were largely frontier structures. Simple log structures or half-timbered huts were the first individual dwellings. As regions started to become more developed, larger, more elaborate homes appeared and attention was directed to-ward a more refined interior. In the more public areas of a home, plaster walls were common, and whitewashed finishes were popular. Often, on upper floors, the structural framing was left exposed. Baseboards and cornices, as well as plaster ceilings, started to be used by the early 1700s, and decorative wainscoting was common in the formal rooms of a home.

Fireplaces were a focal point of any home, particularly in the parlor or dining room. Sometimes the walls around the fireplace were paneled, first with plain wooden boards and later with more ornate treatments. Decoration around a fireplace could be as simple as a molded lintel across the top of the opening or complex, featuring pilasters and carvings of classical designs. Floors were often wide pine boards.

Exposed beams, opposite, are a favorite Colonial detail.

Rough timbers, above, add character.

Open fireplaces, above right, add visual interest.

Distinctive molding, right, enhances a hearth.

Modern Interpretation. As Colonial style is inter-preted in modern homes, it is most often the less orna-mental elements that have survived, such as an open fireplace with simple millwork, built-in china cabinets or hutches, and simple trim details. Baseboards and casings tend to be flat boards with the addition of a simple back-band or shoe molding. Ceilings can be accented with cove molding and rustic beams. Wainscoting is frequently used, but it tends to be constructed with beaded tongue-and-groove boards rather than more formal panels. Some-times, Colonial style is blended with a farm-style Country aesthetic. Furnishings might include floral-, fruit-, or check-patterned curtains, handmade quilts, simple rustic furniture, or braided rugs.

Georgian

Georgian style developed in England in the early eighteenth century, and it relied heavily on elements from classical Greek and Roman architecture: symmetry, regularly spaced windows, and elaborate molding details. Columns and pilasters were used as decorative elements, and definite rules of proportion were strictly obeyed.

Early Georgian interiors may have featured full-height wooden paneling with a painted finish, but later plaster or stucco walls were often covered by paper or fabric with applied molding such as *wall frames*. Both wood and plaster ceiling moldings were used, and the cornice treatments were often quite elaborate. As trade and immigration increased between England and the American colonies, Georgian style made the cross-Atlantic voyage, and many pattern books and architectural manuals were printed as reference for carpenters. Furniture of this style is best represented by the designers Chippendale, Sheraton, and Hepplewhite.

Georgian Today. Today, Georgian-style interiors are characteristically elegant but uncluttered. Walls in formal rooms are often divided into three sections, with a decorative frieze and cornice at the top, a center field with paint or wallpaper finish, and a paneled wainscot with chair rail at the bottom. Classical motifs such as urns or acanthus leaves occasionally appear as decorative elements. Wall frames are sometimes used instead of paneling or wainscoting, or in addition to these elements. These lend themselves to a variety of paint and wallpaper treatments that can impart a more or less formal feel to a space.

Georgian-style interiors, right, grew out of designs developed in early eighteenth century England.

An elaborate cornice, opposite top, complements the mantel moldings.

Wall frames, opposite bottom left, are often found in Georgian interiors.

Integrated trimwork, opposite bottom right, ties the elements of this Georgian-style room together.

The Power of Trimwork

Federal

The *Federal* style became popular in the years following the American Revolution. This style was initially based on the work of the Adam brothers from Scotland, but builders in the newly formed United States soon put their own mark on the genre. Details from Greek and Roman buildings were freely borrowed as ornamentation, and features such as curves, ellipses, and elongated windows were used to modify rectangular Georgian homes. Many Federal-style homes have an arched Palladian window above the front entry.

Curves figure prominently in Federal-style designs, as shown in the curved room at left.

Greek and Roman themes, below, play a large part in the molding and trimwork selected for Federal-style rooms.

Greek Revival

After the War of 1812, affection for British influence in design started to fade. American designers, most notably Thomas Jefferson, became influential, and an offshoot known as *Greek Revival* started to spread. Contributing to the popularity of Greek Revival design was the fact that it referred back to the ancient democracy as the roots for the new democratic nation. In fact, this style resonated so successfully with the American spirit that it became known as the "National Style." These buildings feature elaborate cornice trim with wide friezes, columned porches, and gabled or hipped roofs. Interiors tend to be less ornate than in either Federal or Georgian styles.

Greek influences are obvious in the bathroom shown at left. Note the elaborate cornice treatment.

Understated details, below, became a hallmark of a style that came to be known as the "National Style."

The Power of Trimwork

Victorian

Victorian style takes its name from the reign of Queen Victoria of England, who ruled from 1837 to 1901. This genre covers a variety of individual movements, including *Gothic Revival, Italianate, Queen Anne, Stick, Eastlake,* and *Shingle* styles. Each of these fashions has its particular characteristics, but all are marked by an extremely ornate sensibility. Spires, towers, spindled porches, decorative brackets, and patterned shingles were commonly used elements, and as a result, the tendency toward overwrought excess has become synonymous with Victorian sensibility.

Victorian Trim. Interior millwork featured moldings layered upon one another in elaborate combinations. Images could be carved into the surface or applied to almost any millwork item or combination of items. Often, these decorative elements did not even mirror or respond to similar moldings elsewhere in the room but instead provided a general sense of complexity and ornamentation. Doors and windows were trimmed with pilaster casings that included plinth and corner blocks. Elaborate apron panels under windows and architraves over doors added other decorative elements.

Elaborate casings, opposite, convey the Victorian design sense.

Stone and metalwork, above, were often combined with elaborate moldings.

Mixing design details, right, is common in Victorian-inspired designs.

Patterned wallpaper, bottom, supports the elaborate mantel trim.

The Power of Trimwork

Arts and Crafts

If the Victorian style was a celebration of the fruits of the Industrial Revolution, with its mass-produced ornament and overwrought excess, the *Arts and Crafts* style developed as a rejection of those same values and tastes. In England, William Morris and John Ruskin set the tone for this movement, promoting an ethic of simplicity in design and rejection of the industrially produced aesthetic. Their philosophy incorporated more than purely visual ideals. They spoke broadly of the effects of the home environment on quality of life, and they related design principles to hygiene, sanitation, and a general sense of right living. Before long, American designers picked up this theme, and Arts and Crafts design flourished in a variety of separate styles like *Mission* and *Craftsman*. Despite its elaborate appearance, much Victorian furniture and decorative elements were not particularly well made. And in their effort to develop a new design philosophy, the Arts and Crafts designers placed great emphasis on the quality of construction.

Trimwork Evolution. Trim systems in the Arts and Crafts style are typically rectilinear and angular. The decorative motifs that appear most often are derived from medieval, Japanese, and Persian influence. Wide, flat casing, baseboard, and friezes are often used, as particular value is given to the decorative grain of the wood. The millwork is generally finished to allow the wood grain to be seen, with warm reddish brown or dark brown stains most common.

Your Style

Of course, the design of interior trim does not always adhere to any of these particular design disciplines, and the above list is not intended to be a comprehensive catalogue of historical trends. But by examining these concepts of style, you can get a sense of how trim details evolved. You can also see how each of these approaches relates to one another. Sometimes one style grows organically from a prior fashion; at other times, a new form is the result of a strong reaction against a popular trend.

Built-ins, opposite, are favorite design elements.

Flat casings, left, provide strong visual lines.

Beamed ceilings, above, decorate public rooms.

Natural wood, below, is a common design theme.

door and window casing

2

THE TRIMWORK, OR CASING, YOU SELECT for the windows and doors in your home should reflect its overall design theme. There is certainly a variety of styles and designs from which to choose, including wide trim with flutes and carved corner blocks that work well with a Victorian or Federal-inspired decor, or simpler casings that are more at home in a Country-style home. For most rooms, you will use the same style trimwork around doors that you selected for the windows, but feel free to change the style and look from room to room.

TYPES OF CASINGS

There are two basic types of window casings. Tapered casing is thinner on the edge closest to the window or door and thicker on the outside edge. Stock Colonial and clamshell casings are tapered casings. When you form corners with tapered casings, you must miter the joints.

Symmetrical casing is the same thickness on both edges and has a uniform pattern across its face. It rests on top of a plinth block or window stool and joins corner blocks or headers with square-cut butt joints. These offer a richly decorative look, and are easier to install because you don't have to miter the joints.

Casing Reveals

The edge of a doorjamb is flush with the surface of the adjoining wall, and there is usually a gap between the jamb and the nearby drywall. Casing bridges that gap. Typically, the door side of the casing covers most but not all of the jamb, leaving a narrow edge—typically ¼ inch—called a reveal. This adds definition to the molding and avoids an unsightly seam where the edge of one board lines up directly over another.

When working on a new jamb, establish the reveal width and stick with it to maintain a uniform appearance. When replacing existing trim, you may need to clean up the edge of an old jamb with a scraper and a sander even if you duplicate the old reveal. If you install plinths or corner blocks, which are slightly wider than the casing, experiment with their exact placement to maintain the reveal.

PREHUNG DOORS

A prehung door can make installation simple and quick. It eliminates the need to fit the door to the opening, to cut mortises for the hinges and lockset, and to fit the door stops. All the really fussy and time-consuming work is already done for you.

Lumberyards and home centers carry prehungs in a variety of door styles. In addition, you can choose between pine jambs that can be painted or stained or hardwood jambs, with red oak being the most common choice. Interior doors can be flush—with a flat veneered surface—solid wood panels, or molded fiberboard panels. You can also custom order just about any combination of door and jamb and have it prehung for you .

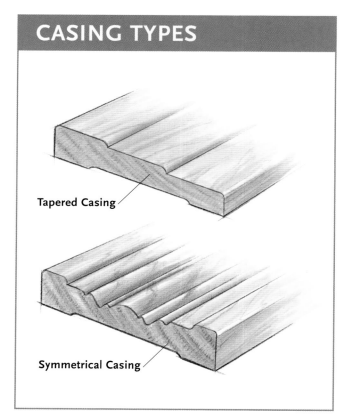

CASING TYPES

Tapered Casing

Symmetrical Casing

A typical reveal between a doorjamb and casing, above, creates a handsome transition at cased openings.

Door casings can be built up with molding, including an outer strip of backband molding, showing multiple reveals, opposite.

Door and Window Casing

INSTALLING A PREHUNG DOOR

project

When ordering a prehung door, specify the direction you wish the door to open. If you open the door toward you and the doorknob is on the right side, it is a right-handed door; if the knob is on the left when it opens toward you, it is a left-handed door.

The width of a standard prehung doorjamb used with typical 2x4 wall framing is 4⁹⁄₁₆ inches, which allows the doorjamb to just barely protrude beyond the drywall surface. This compensates for small irregularities.

TOOLS & MATERIALS

▪ Hammer ▪ Nail set ▪ Spirit level
▪ Saw ▪ Utility knife ▪ Shims ▪ Finishing nails ▪ Prehung door

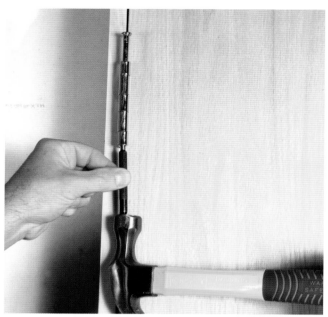

1 To remove the door from the frame, first knock out the hinge pins. Use a nail set or punch to loosen the hinge pins on your prehung door. Lift the pins from the hinges, and gently pull the door free from the jamb assembly.

4 Use a long, straight 2x4 and 4-ft. level (left) to check that the jack stud on the hinge side of the door is plumb—if it is not, you will need to place shims between the jamb and stud. Use 8d or 10d finishing nails to fasten the hinge jamb to the jack stud (right). Place two nails near the top of the jamb; then check that the edge of the jamb is plumb before nailing the rest of the jamb.

5 Use a flat bar to pry the jamb out, and slide tapered shims behind the jamb. Be sure to use two shims, one driven from each side, to keep the jamb square. Use shims at the top, middle, and bottom, and drive the nails just under the shims. If the jack stud is not plumb, use a flat pry bar to pry the jamb away from the stud; plumb the jamb; and install shims and nails every 16 in.

2 Stand the jamb assembly in the door opening with both side jambs resting on the floor. Use a 24-in. level to check that the head jamb is level in the opening (top). If necessary, place shims beneath one of the side jambs to bring the head level (bottom). Measure the height of the shim; then mark the bottom of the opposite jamb to remove that same amount.

3 Cut the bottom of the high side jamb along your layout mark. A small Japanese Ryoba saw, as shown, is an excellent tool for the job, but you can use any fine-cutting saw that is handy. Place the frame in the opening again to make sure the head is level.

6 Once the hinge jamb is nailed, re-hang the door, and use it as a guide for adjusting the latch jamb. Place shims between the jamb and jack stud to maintain a uniform gap between the door edge and jamb. Again, drive nails just under the shims. Test to see that the door opens and closes smoothly, and that the gap between door and jamb is uniform.

7 Use a sharp utility knife to score the shims at the point where they protrude beyond the wall surface. After scoring each shim, you should be able to snap it off easily.

INSTALLING JAMBS

As a general rule, the newer the house, the more likely it is to have room openings finished only in drywall rather than cased out with trimwork. Creating drywall-only openings is the least expensive way to build, but it can create an unfinished look. Trimming out these openings is often the first step in an overall effort to build architectural detail into your home.

Dealing with Flared Corner Bead

In drywall openings, a metal corner bead is applied to the corners to form a straight, neat edge. As a result, these corners tend to flare out, and they are thicker than the rest of the wall—a potential problem when applying casing.

If the corner flare is extreme enough to make it difficult to install casing, start your job with some demolition. Beginning at the bottom of the wall, use a flat pry bar to expose the corner bead and pry it away from the wall. Most beads are installed with ¼-inch drywall nails and will come away easily. Work your way up each corner and across the top of the opening; then pry off the drywall strip that lines the inside of the opening to expose the jack studs and header. If the drywall extends into the opening, use a drywall saw to trim it flush to the inside surfaces of the studs and header.

Making a Custom Jamb

Begin your casing project by installing the jamb. Once it's correctly aligned with the walls, adding the casing will be fairly easy. You can certainly purchase standard jambs from a lumberyard, and doing so can save you time, if they happen to fit your walls. Often, however, you need to custom-cut jambs to suit your wall thickness. This is not difficult, using 1x6 pine stock.

Pages 46–47 show the basic carpentry steps involved in making a custom jamb; pages 48–49 show how to measure for a custom installation.

BEFORE

AFTER

Basic passageways are transformed with a surrounding of trim that ties into baseboards and chair rails.

Jamb Width. Normal modern construction, with 3½-inch-wide studs and ½-inch drywall, produces a wall that is 4½ inches thick. A jamb should be 1/16 inch wider to allow for variations, so a standard jamb is 4⁹/₁₆ inches wide. However, if the corner bead flares out, and if the wall bows a bit, you will need a wider jamb.

Using a combination square or a ruler, check several points on all three interior surfaces of the opening, noting each measurement. If the numbers vary by more than ⅛ inch, you'll need to adjust the width of the jamb pieces to account for the thicker parts of the opening. Another option that's worth a try is to use a hammer and a block of scrap wood to compress the wall. Just slide the block along the wider parts of the opening, hitting it firmly with the hammer. If that doesn't work, try removing some of the corner bead on one or both sides of the opening.

Jamb Lengths. The opening may be out of square, but the jamb and casing should be square for a neat appearance. Start by making a level reference line, as shown on page 48, and measure off this to determine the lengths of the side jambs. It's important that the tops of the two side jambs be level with each other, even if the head of the opening is not level.

The side jambs will be cut with ⅜-inch-deep rabbets, into which will fit the header jamb, which is not rabbeted. So the side jambs run the full height of the opening, while the head jamb generally is ¾ inch shorter than the opening's width (⅜ plus ⅜ equals ¾). To determine the length of the header jamb, find the narrowest point in the opening, then subtract 1 inch. This allows ¾ inch for the combined thicknesses of the wood left in the rabbeted joints, plus ¼ inch for shimming.

Assembling the Jamb. Pages 46–47 show how to build the jamb on a work table or floor. You can cut the rabbets in the tops of the side jambs using a router with a rabbet bit or with a circular saw and a chisel. Keep the parts square as you work, and join the pieces together using nails and glue.

Attaching the Jamb. Attach a brace to the jamb assembly, as shown below, so it stays stable while you work. Set the three jamb pieces in the opening, and check all the angles and edges. The corners should be square, the sides plumb, and the header level. The edges of the jamb should be flush with the wall surface at all points. Take the time to get everything perfect; otherwise, installing the casing will be difficult, and you will end up with unattractive gaps between casing and wall.

To hold the assembly in place at first, you'll need to set a few pairs of overlapped shims. Then you can start checking the margins against the opening and use a level to check for plumb. Continue by inserting pairs of shims at the midpoints of the jamb pieces, and then halfway between the midpoints and the tops and bottoms of the jamb stock. This is a process of gradual adjustment in which you need to be checking constantly with a level, adjusting the shims, and checking again for plumb and level.

To finish the installation, drive and set nails through the jambs just below the shims. Use a sharp utility knife to trim the protruding sections of the shims flush with the edges of the jamb.

Adding Casing

Cut and install the casing of your choice as shown on pages 52–63. On those pages you will see how to install simple colonial or clamshell casings with mitered corners, Victorian casing with corner blocks and plinth blocks, as well as traditional, Victorian, and Arts and Crafts style casings.

BRACING THE JAMB

ONCE THE GLUE HAS SET ON THE RABBETED JOINTS OF THE JAMB, YOU CAN MAINTAIN THE BOND AND PREVENT RACKING BY FASTENING A TEMPORARY BRACE ACROSS THE LEGS. LEAVE THE BRACE LONG ON BOTH SIDES TO HELP POSITION AND HOLD THE JAMB ASSEMBLY IN THE OPENING. WHEN YOU'RE FINISHED WITH THE SHIMMING AND NAILING, SIMPLY REMOVE THE SCREWS AND BRACE.

ASSEMBLING A JAMB

Custom-building a jamb to fit an odd-size opening is not particularly difficult, but it does take some time and attention to detail. If you have a standard-size opening, it may be worth the extra cost to buy a prefabricated jamb set.

If your walls are a standard 4½ inches thick and straight, you can just buy 4⁹⁄₁₆ inch jamb stock. However, things are often not perfect. See pages 48–49 for tips on measuring the jamb's width and lengths.

You can build with inexpensive common-grade lumber (as shown on these pages), which has some knots and other imperfections. For a cleaner look and less wood prep, consider paying more for jamb stock, which is free of knots and very straight, or other clear lumber.

The jamb will be highly visible every time people pass through the doorway or wall opening. Use a sander, plane, or jointer to remove any imperfections before you begin.

TOOLS & MATERIALS

▌Combination square ▌Router or circular saw ▌Clamps ▌Chisel ▌Drill ▌Hammer or nailer ▌Wood glue ▌Nails ▌Jamb stock

JAMB ASSEMBLY

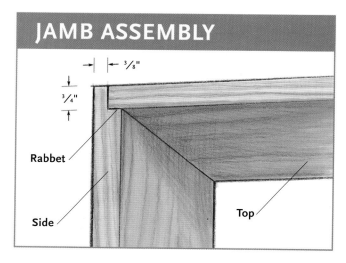

³⁄₈"

³⁄₄"

Rabbet

Side

Top

1 Cut the three jamb pieces to length. The head jamb is ¾ in. longer than the inside of the finished opening's inside width because it rests in ³⁄₈-in.-deep rabbets. The side jambs are ¾ in. longer than the opening's inside height. On the side pieces, mark the joint outline with a square for a ¾-in. jamb leg.

4 Use the saw to remove all the wood, or clean up the thin strips between kerfs using a sharp chisel. First hold the chisel flat and at a right angle to the cut, as shown, and remove most of the material. Then turn the chisel to scrape alongside the cut. Finally, you may need to hold the chisel upright to remove small ridges.

2 Set the blade depth on a circular saw to reach halfway (³⁄₈ in.). Test on a scrap piece to be sure you have the correct depth.

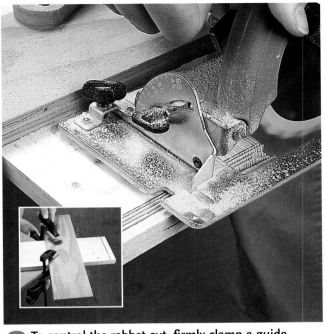

3 To control the rabbet cut, firmly clamp a guide board and the jamb to a stable bench (inset). Make the innermost cut with the saw along the guide. Then make multiple passes to kerf the remaining wood. Keep the saw's base firmly on the board, so all cuts are square to the board.

5 When the rabbet is cleaned up and ready for assembly, mark a nailing line on the outside of the joint. It should be ³⁄₈ in. down so that the nails enter the center of the head jamb's thickness.

6 Place the pieces on a flat surface, and check that they are square. You may want to set the pieces around a square block for support. Add glue to the mating surfaces of the jamb parts just prior to assembling them (inset). Recheck for square; hold the pieces firmly together; and drive nails to attach.

INSTALLING A JAMB ON A DRYWALLED OPENING

project

An existing drywalled opening is likely less than perfectly square, straight, and uniform in thickness. If you only take a few measurements and install the jamb according to those measurements, there is a good chance that the casing will end up with unattractive gaps. Follow the jamb installation steps on these pages to ensure that the casing will lie flat against the wall and against the jamb at all points.

TOOLS & MATERIALS

▐ Measuring tape and level ▐ Combination square ▐ Hammer, finishing nails, and nail set ▐ Scrap block ▐ Jamb stock and shims ▐ Utility knife

1 Draw a level reference line that spans the opening. Measure from the line down to the floor on each side; then measure up from the line to the top of the opening on each side. Add the measurements for each side. Take the shorter of the two measurements, and subtract ¼ in. for shimming; this is your side jamb length.

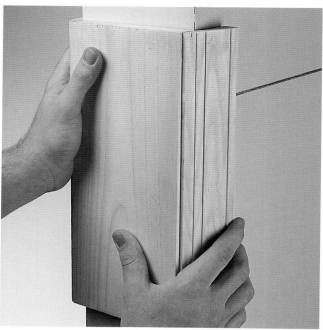

4 Check your measurements with a jamb template. Rip a short length of 1×6 to the width you think will match the opening depth. Attach two pieces of casing to the ripped 1×6. It should slide smoothly along the opening. If it's too tight in some spots, try with a wider template. It's OK if the wall is slightly narrow in some spots.

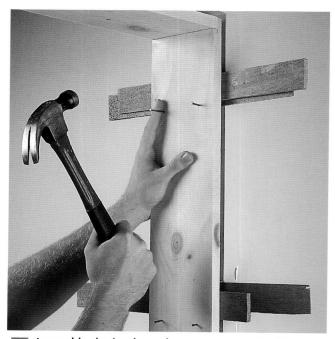

5 Assemble the jamb as shown on pages 46–47, and tack a temporary brace at the bottom to keep the assembly firm. Slip the assembly in place. You can tack nails below shims to hold them up, but the tight fit from overlapping generally makes this unnecessary.

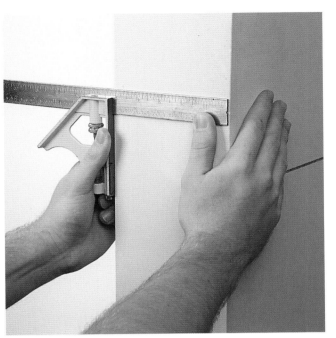

2 You also need to determine the thickness of the walls (which is the width of the jambs). Check it at several points to be sure that your jamb stock will fully cover the interior faces of the opening.

3 If you find only small bulges in the wall edges, try to reduce them by hammering firmly on a wood block, or strip off the corner bead and use shims to make the opening plumb.

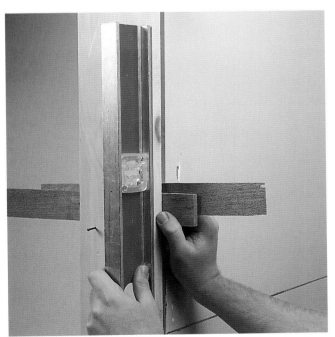

6 Insert pairs of shims at the midpoints of the jamb pieces and then halfway between the midpoints and the tops and bottoms of the jamb stock. As you check for plumb, adjust the shims by hand to start, and then tap on the thick ends with a hammer. Continually check for plumb and level as you make shim adjustments.

7 Drive and set nails through the jambs and either through or just below the shims. Then you can use a sharp utility knife to trim the protruding sections of the shims flush with the edges of the jamb.

ROUTING A MOLDING PROFILE

THE GREAT SELECTION of router bits provides you a means of creating your own molding profiles to personalize a trim installation. Most profile bits feature a ball-bearing pilot at the bottom of the bit, which you can use to guide the cutter along an edge. One of the advantages of cutting your own molding is that you can generate slightly different profiles with the same bit by varying the depth of the cut.

Mount the bit in the router following all manufacturer's recommendations and cautions. Adjust the appropriate depth of cut for the bit and material thickness. Clamp a small piece of scrap lumber to your worktable, and test the cut before moving on to valuable material. When you are satisfied with the profile, clamp your stock to the table and make the cut. Remember to move the router from left to right as you face the edge of the board.

If you need to cut a profile on a lot of material, you should consider using a router table for the job. Once you have set up and adjusted the router in a table, you can push the material past the cutter instead of needing to clamp each board individually. Even though your bit may have a ball-bearing pilot, always install the router table fence and align it with the face of the pilot. By using accessory hold-down jigs on the table, you can eliminate any danger of kickback as well as

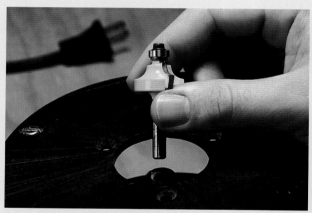

1 Select a profiling bit with a roller guide that rides along the edge of the board.

2 Set the router on the edge of the board to see the depth of the bit. Make a test cut on scrap.

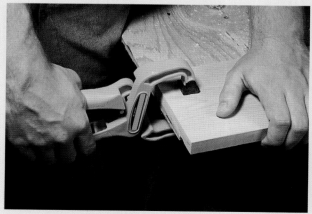

4 To work safely, clamp the board securely to a bench, and be sure the clamps are out of the router's path.

5 Always make your cut pushing against the rotation of the bit, and use multiple passes to avoid chatter marks.

maintain even pressure on the stock. This will avoid burn marks and irregularities in the profile.

Narrow moldings present a different problem. Because it is difficult to use a router on narrow stock, play it safe and always rout the profile on the edge of a wide board, and then transfer the work to a circular saw or table saw to rip the molded piece off of the wide stock to the desired dimensions.

TOOLS & MATERIALS
▌ Router and bit ▌ Clamps ▌ 1-by lumber

The best approach to selecting a casing style, above, is to use the same design throughout the house.

Traditional-style casing, below, is a simple but distinctive treatment for doors and windows.

3 Adjust the depth of cut. Some have a collar on the housing; others have a calibrated knob.

Use hold-down accessories when routing profiles on a router table.

DOOR CASINGS

Some casing styles feature mitered corners; other styles use butt joints; and there are certain treatments that layer a mitered molding over butt-jointed flat stock. All styles, however, have one element in common: a reveal. Instead of fastening the casing flush with the door side of the jamb, hold it back to allow a small, uniform margin of jamb to be exposed on its edge. The setback is known as the reveal, and this treatment applies to window casing and door casing alike. The actual dimension of the reveal you use is up to you, but ⅛ to 5/32 inch is typical. If the reveal is too large, you reduce the amount of jamb available for nailing the casing, and if it is too small, even the smallest discrepancy becomes visible. Whatever measurement you decide to use, it is important that you make it the standard for the entire job so that you maintain a uniform look throughout. Use a combination square as a gauge, and place light pencil marks at the corners, center, and ends of your jambs to indicate the amount of setback.

Evaluate the Condition of the Door

Begin by making sure that the head and side jambs are level and plumb. When you check the side jambs, use a long straightedge with the level to span the entire jamb length. Then use a framing square to check the head and side jambs. If you find that the corners are not square, use a sliding bevel gauge to determine the actual angle. Transfer the angle to a piece of scrap lumber or cardboard; then use an angle gauge to measure the angle. Use one-half of that angle for your miter saw setting to cut the corner joint.

smart tip

MARK ONCE

AS A GENERAL RULE, YOU ARE BETTER OFF DIRECTLY MARKING THE SIZE OF A TRIM PIECE RATHER THAN MEASURING WITH A TAPE MEASURE. WHEN YOU MEASURE AND MARK A PIECE FOR LENGTH, THERE IS AN INEVITABLE DEGREE OF VARIATION IN THE WAY THE DIMENSION IS TRANSFERRED TO THE WORK PIECE. BY MARKING THE SIZE OF A PIECE DIRECTLY IN ITS ULTIMATE LOCATION, YOU REDUCE THE OPPORTUNITY FOR ERRORS.

project

INSTALLING SIMPLE COLONIAL CASING

Along with clamshell or "ranch" molding, one-piece colonial casing is one of the most common and simplest treatments for door and window casing. The techniques for either type are essentially the same.

In a mitered casing installation, the desired result is a continuous and seamless border of molding around the door opening. As with all casings, it is important that the jamb be flush with (or slightly proud of) the wall surface. If not, fix the jamb before installing casing.

TOOLS & MATERIALS

■ Hammer ■ Combination square ■ Power miter saw ■ Nail set ■ Ranch or clamshell casing ■ Finishing nails ■ Wood glue

3 Miter cut the side pieces, leaving them a few inches long. Invert a piece so the miter point rests on the floor and the outside edge of the casing rests against the point of the head casing. If you will later install carpeting or flooring, rest the piece on a spacer (top). Mark the length of the casing, and make the square cut (bottom).

1 Mark the reveal by sliding the blade on the combination square (inset). Cut a miter on one end of the casing. Temporarily tack the piece so that the cut end is aligned with the layout line. On the uncut side, align the short side of the miter with one reveal mark; transfer the opposite mark to the casing, and make the cut.

2 Use 4d finishing nails to tack the head casing to the head jamb of the door, and 6d or 8d finishing nails to attach it to the wall framing. Leave the nailheads protruding at this point in case you need to remove the part for adjustment.

4 Apply a small bead of glue to both miter surfaces (inset), and tack the casing in place. Drive 4d finishing nails into the edge of the jamb and 6d or 8d finishing nails into the framing under the wall surface. Drive a 4d finishing nail through the edge of the casing to lock the miter joint together.

5 If you are having trouble getting the joints nice and tight, see "Closing Gaps," page 54 for tightening tips. Attach the casing with a pair of nails—one 4d and one 6d or 8d—every 16 in. Use a nail set to recess the nailheads about $1/8$ in. below the wood surface.

MAKE YOUR OWN

FACTORY-MADE COLONIAL CASING, as shown on the previous two pages, is designed to mimic the more elaborate forms of a traditionally installed built-up casing. However, using readily available stock, you can create a larger and more detailed casing that conveys a more nuanced sense of style than is available with an off-the-shelf profile. The process is not difficult; it uses 1x4 and 1x2 boards, and stock panel or base cap molding.

At the lumberyard, experiment with different combinations of lumber until you are satisfied.

While you can certainly leave the edges of the boards square, or ease them gently with sandpaper, the casing will be more interesting if you add a molded profile to the inside edge. In order to do this, install an ogee or cove bit in the router, and use it to cut the profile along one edge of each 1x4 board.

INSTALLING BUILT-UP COLONIAL CASING

project

Build your own Colonial casing for a custom look. Start with a jamb that is flush with the wall surface, and mark its edge for a reveal. Use a router to create an edge profile in a piece of casing stock or clear lumber. Cut this into a header and two side casing pieces, and install as you would standard Colonial casing. Cut and attach backband molding around the perimeter, and add panel molding to the face.

TOOLS & MATERIALS

▪ Hammer ▪ Nail set ▪ Router and bit
▪ Plate joiner and wafers (optional)
▪ Nail gun and nails (optional) ▪ Power miter saw ▪ Clamps ▪ 1x4 boards ▪ Backband molding ▪ Panel molding ▪ 4d and 6d finishing nails ▪ Wood glue

smart tip

CLOSING GAPS

When dealing with wide casing, it is pretty common to require a bit of adjustment to get the miters to close tightly. If the door-jamb protrudes beyond the wall surface even $\frac{1}{16}$ in. you may have difficulty closing the miter joint. In this case, you can place shims behind the outer edges of the casing to create a tight joint. Score the shims with a sharp knife, and snap off the protruding portion. The backband will cover the gap between the casing and wall.

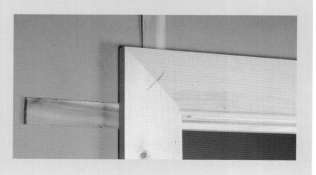

3 Tack the head casing to the head jamb with 4d finishing nails; then spread glue on the miter surfaces, in both slots, and on the joining plate. Insert the plate in one side of the joint, and assemble the joint. Attach the pieces with 4d finishing nails driven into the jamb and 6d or 8d finishing nails driven into the framing.

1 A router with an edge-profiling bit makes quick work of molding the inside edges of 1×4 stock for your custom casing. Experiment on scrap pieces until you achieve the edge profile that pleases you. Clamp the 1×4 blank to the worktable before beginning the cut. Alternatively, mount the router in a router table.

2 Cut appropriate miters for the corner joints. (See pages 52–53.) To reinforce the joint using a plate joiner (also called a biscuit joiner), mark the center of each joining plate slot on the face of the casing; then clamp a piece to the worktable and cut the slot. Hold the plate jointer firmly on the table as you make the cut.

4 Purchase backband molding that fits snugly around your basic casing and rests against the wall. (See "Scribing a Backband to the Wall," page 57.) Cut backband strips to size with 45-deg. bevels for the corner joints. Use 6d finishing nails or a nail gun to fasten the strips to the outside edges of the casing.

5 Miter-cut panel molding to fit tightly inside the backband border. Nail the molding to the casing using 4d finishing nails.

INSTALLING TRADITIONAL-STYLE CASING

In the 1920s through the 1940s, many homes were trimmed in a "traditional" style, which predates the use of the ranch and colonial casings used today. Doors and windows featured wide flat casings with a simple backband. The flat casing stock is joined at the head with a simple butt joint. This eliminates the need for fussing with a miter joint on wide stock—a situation that can get tricky if the wall surfaces are not absolutely flat.

TOOLS & MATERIALS

▮ Hammer ▮ Nail set ▮ Plate joiner and wafers ▮ Nail gun and nails (optional) ▮ Power miter saw ▮ 1-by casing stock ▮ Backband molding ▮ 4d and 6d finishing nails ▮ Wood glue

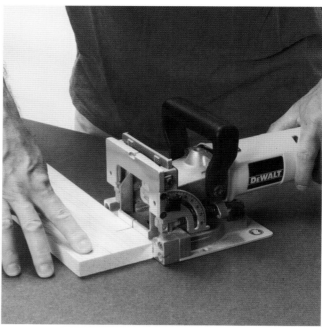

1 With this style, first cut and tack the side pieces in place alongside the reveal lines; then hold the header in place to mark for cutting. Lay them on a flat surface, positioned against each other. Mark the locations of joining plate slots on the bottom edge of the head casing; then use the plate joiner to cut the slots.

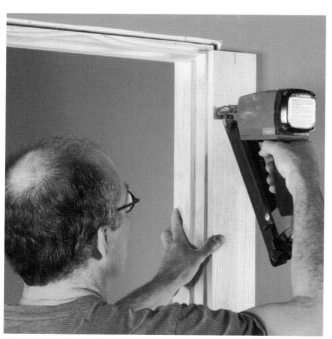

3 Use 4d or 6d finishing nails to fasten the side casing to the edge of the doorjamb. Wait until the head casing is in place to nail the outer edge.

4 Spread glue in the plate slots and on the joining plates; then assemble the head/side casing joints. Working quickly (because the glue dries fast), adjust the position of the header until it is perfectly aligned on both sides. Nail the head casing to the head jamb; then nail the outer edge of the casing.

2 Cut plate slots in the top ends of side casings. To avoid kickback when cutting into end grain, clamp the stock to the table, and use two hands to control the plate joiner.

5 Cut the backband strips to size with appropriately beveled ends. Use 6d finishing nails to fasten the bands to the outer edge of the casing.

SCRIBING A BACK-BAND TO THE WALL

IF YOU NOTICE that there are gaps between the wall and backband, it's a simple matter to scribe it to fit. Scribing involves marking the stock to match the wall profile and then removing material from the areas adjacent to the high points so that the molding can sit tight to the wall along its entire length.

Begin by applying a strip of masking tape to the outer surface of the backband. The tape will allow you to better see the scribed pencil lines. Next, hold the molding against the wall, in position, and set your scribers to a width that matches the widest gap between the wall and molding. Hold the two wings of the scriber parallel with the floor as you trace the wall profile onto the taped surface of the molding.

Remove the backband to a work surface, and use a sharp block plane to remove material until the pencil line is left exposed. Test the fit of the piece, and make any necessary adjustments.

If you remove stock from the top edges of a side backband, the top band will also need to be adjusted so that it does not protrude beyond the sides. If the top piece is already installed, it is a simple matter to plane the face to the required depth.

1. Apply masking tape to the outside edge of backband; hold the band against the wall; and use scribers to mark the required adjustment.

2. Use a sharp block plane to trim the backband to fit the wall profile. Plane just up to the scribed line. Test the fit, and adjust if necessary.

INSTALLING NEO-CLASSICAL CASING

"Neo-Classical" casing includes a range of options that are appropriate for a variety of design traditions. The basic casing structure is intended to suggest the structure of a column, with base, shaft, and capital replicated in the elements of the door trim.

There are three basic parts: at the bottom, a plinth block suggests the base of a column; the casing itself is a straight piece that is not miter-cut; the head casing, also called a frieze or an entablature, is typically assembled out of several pieces for a rich appearance.

Within this style, there are many variations and combinations you can try. Side casings can be plain flat stock, or the edges can be rounded or shaped into a cove or ogee profile. You can use fluted material for the side casing to mimic a pilaster or column, or any custom-made profile.

TOOLS & MATERIALS

▌Hammer ▌Nail set ▌Block plane
▌Nail gun and nails (optional) ▌Miter saw
▌Table saw ▌Square ▌1-by casing stock
▌Plinth blocks ▌Lattice ▌Crown or bed molding ▌Finishing nails ▌Wood glue

ALTERNATIVE HEAD ASSEMBLY

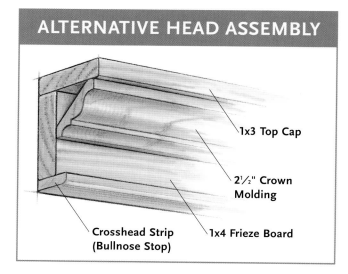

1x3 Top Cap

2½" Crown Molding

1x4 Frieze Board

Crosshead Strip (Bullnose Stop)

1 To determine the plinth's width, add twice the amount of the reveal to the width of the casing. It should be at least ½ in. taller than the adjoining baseboard. Mark guidelines on the top edge and face of plinth block stock to indicate the limits of the chamfer; then use a sharp block plane to cut the chamfer.

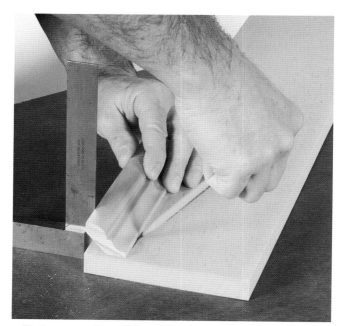

4 See page 61 and the illustration at left for standard ways to build a head assembly. Cut the head casing's frieze board to span across the side casing pieces. Hold the crown molding against a square, as shown, and mark the frieze board for the "drop" of the crown molding.

2 Hold the plinth block flush to the inside face of the doorjamb, and nail it to the jamb edge and wall framing.

3 Cut casing to length; set it on top of the plinth; hold it against the reveal line; and nail it to the edge of the doorjamb with 4d or 6d finishing nails. Use 8d finishing nails to fasten the outer edge to the wall framing.

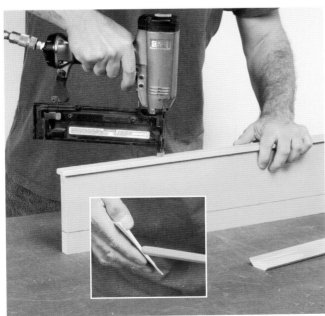

5 You can shape a bullnose profile on the ends of the crosshead strip with sandpaper (inset). If you use simple lattice instead of a bullnose molding, simply ease the sharp edges. Apply a small bead of glue to the bottom edge of the head casing, and then nail the crosshead strip to it. The strip should project an even distance beyond the face and both ends.

6 Cut the crown molding with miters at each end so that the short part is as long as the frieze board. Use brads to fasten the crown molding to the frieze board. Make sure its bottom edge is aligned with the previously scribed line.

Continued on next page.

Door and Window Casing

Continued from previous page.

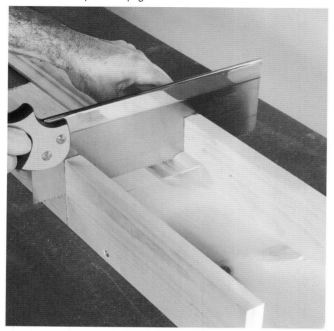

7 Cut short mitered returns on crown molding stock using a simple crosscutting jig and handsaw. Or better yet, use a power miter saw. (See "Making Mitered Returns," page 274.)

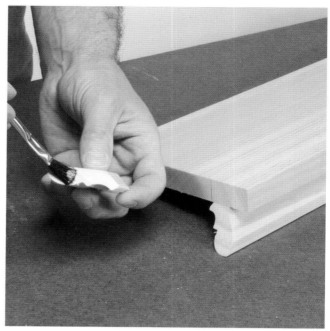

8 Apply glue to the mitered return joint, and carefully place the small pieces on the head assembly. Drill pilot holes; then drive small brads to hold the parts in place while the glue sets. These pieces crack easily, and they are difficult to get just right. If yours doesn't look perfect, remove it and cut a new piece.

9 The top cap is typically made of lattice molding. It should overhang the crown molding by an equal amount—typically, ¼ in.—on both sides and the front. Install a top cap over the top of the casing and crown molding. Use brads to fasten the part in place.

10 Nail the head assembly to the head jamb and wall framing. Because this molding tends to be thicker than others, you will probably want to use 6d nails to attach to the jamb and 8d nails to attach it to the framing.

NEO-CLASSICAL CASING ASSEMBLY

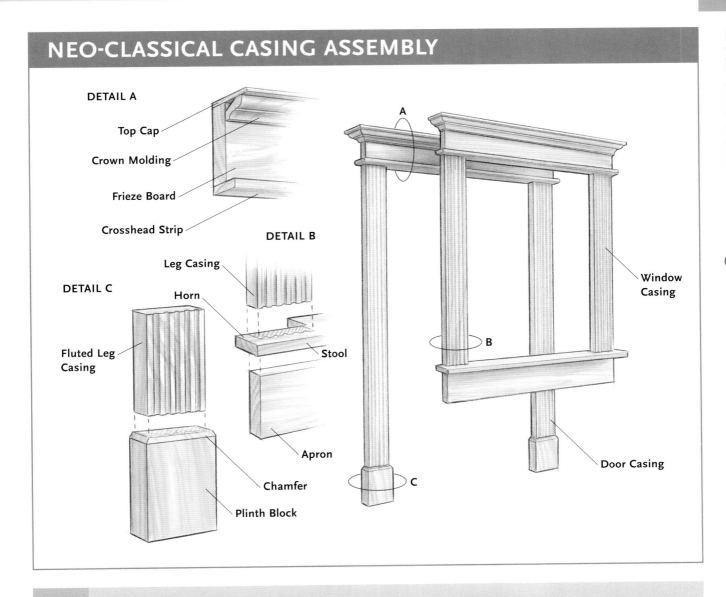

DETAIL A

Top Cap

Crown Molding

Frieze Board

Crosshead Strip

DETAIL B

Leg Casing

DETAIL C

Horn

Fluted Leg
Casing

Stool

Apron

Chamfer

Plinth Block

A

B

C

Window
Casing

Door Casing

USING SPECIALTY MOLDING

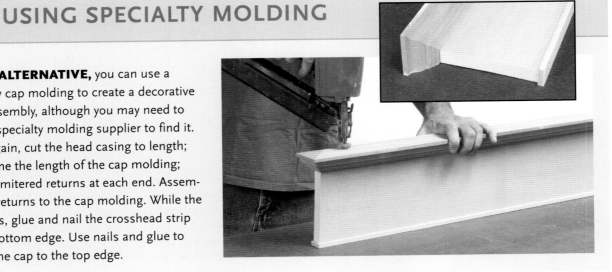

AS AN ALTERNATIVE, you can use a specialty cap molding to create a decorative head assembly, although you may need to go to a specialty molding supplier to find it. Once again, cut the head casing to length; determine the length of the cap molding; and cut mitered returns at each end. Assemble the returns to the cap molding. While the glue sets, glue and nail the crosshead strip to the bottom edge. Use nails and glue to fasten the cap to the top edge.

INSTALLING VICTORIAN CASING

project

Victorian trim employs symmetrical casing, as well as plinth blocks at the bottom and rosette blocks at the top corners. "Bellyband" casing, which displays a combination of bead, cove, and ogee profiles, is usually used, but fluted casing is also possible. Home centers offer scaled-down versions that are about 3 inches wide. However, true Victorian casing is usually 5½ inches wide—and for that you will probably have to look to a specialty millwork supplier or make your own fluted casing.

TOOLS & MATERIALS

■ Hammer ■ Nail set ■ Nail gun and nails (optional) ■ Power miter saw ■ Casing stock ■ Plinth blocks ■ Rosette blocks ■ Finishing nails

1 Cut, chamfer, and install the plinth blocks. (See pages 58–59.) The plinth should be as wide as the rosette blocks so that the reveal is the same at the top and bottom. Cut one end of a length of casing square, and rest that end on top of a plinth. Mark the top end flush with the inside edge of the head jamb. Cut, and tack in place.

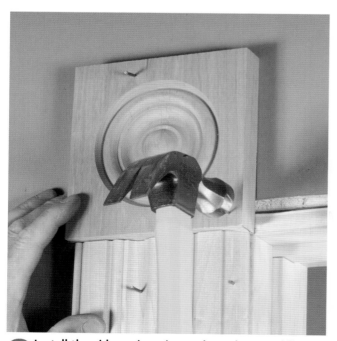

2 Install the side casing pieces along the reveal lines. Tack the rosette blocks in place, resting on top of the side casings. Leave the nailheads exposed to make adjustment easier.

3 Measure the distance between the blocks, and cut the head casing to length. Slide it in place between the blocks, and nail it to the jamb and wall framing. If necessary, you can pull the nails holding the rosettes and adjust their position to eliminate any gaps at the casing joints.

INSTALLING ARTS AND CRAFTS CASING

project

Arts and Crafts style celebrates simple, strong lines and a lack of elaborate ornamentation, but at the same time, the style allows quite a bit of latitude in the particular trim details that are used. Door and window casings are often fashioned from flat, wide stock that is joined with butt joints. You could use a small cornice and crosshead strip on the head casing, and a gently molded, tapered profile for side casing is also appropriate. Finish with a warm brown stain and a clear sealer.

TOOLS & MATERIALS

▌Hammer ▌Nail set ▌Nail gun and nails (optional) ▌Power miter saw ▌Angle gauge ▌1-by casing stock ▌Finishing nails ▌Masking or painter's tape

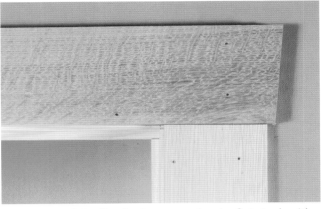

An Arts and Crafts design uses simple, flat stock with the head casing overhanging the side casing.

smart tip

THE RIGHT WOOD

ARTS AND CRAFTS STYLE FAVORS QUARTER-SAWN WHITE OAK AND MAHOGANY LUMBER. TRADITIONALLY, $^{11}\!/_{16}$-INCH-THICK STOCK IS USED FOR THE HEAD CASING AND ¾-INCH STOCK IS USED FOR THE SIDE CASING.

1 Draw reveal lines on the jamb. Rip head and side casing stock to a width of 4½ in. Measure, cut, and tack the side pieces in place. Use an angle gauge to mark 5-deg. angles on the end of the head casing. Use a miter saw to make the cuts. The short point of the angle should overhang each side casing by ⅜ in.

2 Mark the locations of joining plate centers onto the head casing, transferring them from the previously marked side casing slots. Tape protects the wood, which will receive a clear finish. Cut the matching plate slots. Apply glue to the slots and plates, and fasten the casing to the jamb and wall.

WINDOW TRIM

Some aspects of window trim are identical to those on door trim. However, there are differences. Windows have no plinth blocks. Window stools, aprons, and extension jambs are particular to window trim. And the option of picture-frame casing applies only to windows, not doors.

Before you trim a window, take a few minutes for preparation work. Most windows are installed with shims between the jambs and rough framing to help maintain the position of the unit. Check to make sure they are firmly lodged in place, with nails driven either through the shim or in very close proximity. Make sure no shims protrude beyond the wall surface; cut off any that do. Many installers stuff fiberglass insulation in the space between the window and framing. This practice is fine as long as the insulation is not overly compressed, which causes it to become ineffective. As an alternative, purchase a can of non-expansion foam insulation and use it to fill the spaces around the window. If you use the foam, first pry out any fiberglass insulation so that the foam can completely fill the cavity void.

Window casings can follow a traditional style or be totally unique.

project

ADDING JAMB EXTENSIONS

Because exterior walls may be framed at different thicknesses and receive different interior wall treatments, the finished depth of a wall can vary considerably from house to house. Rather than offering windows with slightly different jamb widths, most window companies offer interlocking jamb extensions. You can also make your own by ripping stock to width using a table saw. Maintain one factory edge on each jamb to minimize edge preparation, and mount that edge facing into the room.

TOOLS & MATERIALS

- Hammer ▪ Nail set ▪ Measuring tape
- Square ▪ Drill-driver ▪ Power miter saw
- Table saw ▪ 1-by stock ▪ Trim screws
- Spray foam

smart tip

OVERSIZE JAMBS

IF THE JAMBS PROTRUDE JUST A BIT TOO FAR PAST THE WALL (⅛ INCH OR LESS), YOU CAN USE A SHARP BLOCK PLANE TO TRIM THEM BACK. BUT IF THE JAMBS EXTEND FARTHER INTO THE ROOM, IT'S BETTER TO MOUNT THE CASING AND INSTALL A FILLER STRIP BETWEEN THE BACK OF THE CASING AND THE WALL TO FILL THE GAPS.

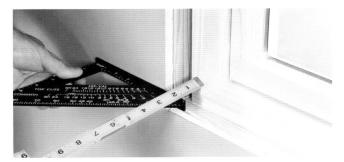

1 Measure the depth of required jamb extensions (top). Ideally, the jambs should be about $\frac{1}{16}$ in. proud of the wall. Measure at several places, and use the largest dimension. If jamb extensions are wider than $1\frac{1}{4}$ in., assemble them into a frame before attaching them to the window. Drill and countersink pilot holes, and screw the parts together (bottom).

2 If there is no insulation around a window, use non-expanding foam to fill any gaps before installing the jamb extensions. When the foam sets, you can easily cut off any excess.

3 Place the jamb-extension assembly into the window opening, and align the inside surfaces with the factory window jambs. If the jamb extensions stand too proud of the wall, plane or sand them down; skim-coat the wall to straighten it; or slip shims behind the casing when you install it.

4 Use trim screws to fasten the jamb-extension assembly to the factory window jambs. If you center the screws in the edge of the jambs, the holes will be covered by the casing.

STOOL AND APRON

Traditional window trim includes a wide, horizontal shelf-like member at the bottom of the window, often incorrectly called a window sill; the correct term is window stool. (Sill refers to the downward-sloped exterior piece, on the same level as the stool, which is designed to shed water and snow.) Stools are generally cut from ⁵/₄ stock. You can sometimes purchase dedicated stool stock from a mill-work supplier; this material will usually have a molded profile along its front edge and sometimes an angled rabbet that is designed to sit over the sloped window sill. You can make your own stool, either with or without a molded edge, from ⁵/₄ lumber.

The stool extends past the window jambs onto the wall surface—these extensions are known as horns. Horns support the side casings and extend about ¾ inch beyond the casing on both end and face. The gap between the wall and the bottom of the stool is covered by a trim piece called an apron.

Window casing is essentially the same as door casing, and can use any of the styles shown on pages 52–63.

INSTALLING A STOOL AND APRON

project

Install jamb extensions if needed. Older windows require extensions only on the top and sides because the stool could rest directly on the interior portion of the sill. On newer windows, you may need extensions all around, even when a stool will be used. On these windows, the bottom extension provides support for the stool and eliminates the need for separate blocking.

TOOLS & MATERIALS

▪ Basic carpentry tools ▪ Saber saw ▪ Router and bits ▪ Power miter saw ▪ Table saw ▪ Nailing gun and nails (optional) ▪ ⁵/₄ stool stock ▪ Casing and apron stock ▪ Rosette blocks ▪ Finishing nails ▪ Wood glue

WINDOW CASING ASSEMBLY

Head Casing

Rosette

Leg Casing

DETAIL A

Stool

Horn

Apron

A

Stool (Sill)

Apron

3 Use a combination square to measure the distance between the jamb edge and the window sash; this is the depth of the notch for the horns on the window stool.

1 Lay out reveal lines on the jambs. Align a piece of casing with the reveal line, and mark its outside edge on the wall. Place another mark ¾ in. away to indicate the end of the window stool. Repeat on the opposite side of the window. Measure the distance between the marks to get the stool length, and cut the stool.

2 Hold stool stock in place against the window, and use a square and sharp pencil to mark the inside dimensions of the window jambs onto the stool surface.

4 Hold the body of the combination square against the edge of window stool stock; then run a pencil along the end of the blade to lay out the cutout for the stool horns. Also mark for the square line. Hold the stool stock against the window again to make sure you have the notch correctly marked.

5 Place a piece of casing stock along the horn cutout line, and lightly mark along its front face. Add ¾ in. to this dimension to determine the overall width of the window stool.

Continued on next page.

Door and Window Casing

Continued from previous page.

6 Rip cut the stool to the desired width. Use a saber saw or hand-saw to cut the notches at both ends of the window stool.

7 Place the stool in the opening to mark for any additional notches. You may need to cut a rabbet in the bottom of the stool, alongside the window. The horns should fit snugly against the wall and there should be a uniform gap between the sash and the stool of about $\frac{1}{32}$ in.

8 This detail of the notch and rabbet on the edge of the window stool accommodates the jamb and a stop.

12 Apply the desired casing to the sides and head jamb, resting the casing firmly on the stool. Follow the methods discussed for door trim. For a Victorian-style casing, make a square cut on each side casing blank, and rest the cut on the stool to mark its length. It should be flush with the underside of the head jamb.

13 Place a rosette head block in place so that it overhangs the side casing evenly on each side. The inside corner of the block should be flush to the inside corner of the window jambs.

9 To avoid any binding, use cardboard to test the gap between stool and sash. If necessary, trim the leading edge of the stool. You may need to use a block plane to adjust the fit of the stool against the sash.

10 Shape the front edge and ends of a window stool with a router. It is most common to use a roundover, chamfer, or ogee bit. Or create a mitered return to carry the profile back to the wall surface. For a simpler treatment, just sand the edges of the stool.

11 Use 8d finishing nails to fasten the stool to the window jamb or sill (top). If necessary, place shims beneath the stool to keep it level. Drill pilot holes through the edge of the horns before driving 8d or 10d finishing nails to fasten the stool to the wall framing (bottom).

14 Cut head casing stock to length—it should fit snugly between the rosette blocks. Nail it to the head jamb and window header.

15 Cut mitered returns on the ends of apron molding stock. Apply glue to both surfaces before assembling (top). If necessary, use a sharp block plane to trim the top edge of the apron so that it fits tight to the stool. Attach the apron (bottom). You can also drive nails through the stool into the top edge of the apron.

TROUBLESHOOTING CASING PROBLEMS

TRIMWORK CAN BE CHALLENGING when everything goes according to plan, but especially so when problems arise. Unfortunately, it is relatively rare that all parts of an installation proceed without running into something unexpected, so it's good to be prepared for those situations.

Most problems with casing arise from a limited universe of causes. And although it can be tempting to lay blame on the shoulders of an errant drywall installer or previous carpenter, a problem with trim can be the result of a relatively innocent combination of small discrepancies, or oversights, that are not considered critical at that prior stage of the job. For exam-

ple, a framing carpenter might reasonably assume that a small hump in wall framing would be absorbed and nullified by the drywall sheathing. Or a drywall finisher could be more concerned with creating a smooth taped joint than with the later effects of the resultant swelling in the wall surface. Of course, there is always a case when some door or window installer loses their concentration, and as a result, the jamb does not line up properly with a wall surface. Regardless of the cause, it is important to remember that trim is the place where all problems start to surface and become visible, so learn to accept those conditions as a natural part of the process.

FIXING BULGING DRYWALL

TOOLS & MATERIALS

▌ Surform or abrasive tool
▌ Casing stock

1 Hold a piece of casing in position, and make a light pencil mark along the outside edge over the high spot. Work inside the line.

2 Use a Surform or similar abrasive tool to grind down the drywall surface until it is flush to the jamb.

FIXING OPEN MITER JOINTS

TOOLS & MATERIALS

▌ Hammer ▌ Nail set
▌ Block plane ▌ Caulking gun ▌ Casing stock
▌ Caulk ▌ Shims
▌ Finishing nails

1 A protruding jamb can cause an open miter joint. Plane a back-bevel on each half of the miter.

2 If you still see a gap after installing the casing, you'll need to shim the back of the casing.

Bulging Drywall

It is relatively common to encounter a situation where the drywall surface has a hump, or high spot, adjacent to a door opening. This can be the result of bowed framing lumber or too much joint compound. In either case, the easiest way to remedy the situation is to grind the drywall down so that it is flush to the edge of the jamb.

Smooth the surface. First hold a piece of casing in place, and mark the location of the outside edge so you do not damage an exposed wall surface. Then use a Surform tool or other abrasive tool to abrade the drywall surface until it is flush with the jamb. Test your progress frequently with a straightedge so that you do not remove too much material. If you inadvertently damage the adjacent drywall, either lightly sand the surface or apply a skim coat of new drywall compound to repair the damaged area.

Protruding Jambs

Where a doorjamb extends beyond a wall surface, you may need to place shims between the back side of the casing and wall. Some tapered casing can be nailed to the wall, but you may have to plane a bevel on the face of the miter. Or you may have to do both.

When your casing includes a backband, the strip can often cover the gap. If no backband is used and the gap is uniform in size, you can apply a filler strip behind the casing to fill the gap. If all else fails, you can caulk or apply a thin coat of drywall compound to the wall to bring the surface flush to the edge of the jamb.

USING FILLER STRIPS

TOOLS & MATERIALS

▪ Table saw ▪ Hammer ▪ Nail set ▪ Nail gun and nails (optional) ▪ Filler material ▪ Finishing nails

1 When a jamb protrudes beyond the wall surface, slide filler strips between the casing and wall until the edges are flush.

2 Drive nails through both the casing and filler strips. A pneumatic nail gun eliminates the need to drill pilot holes.

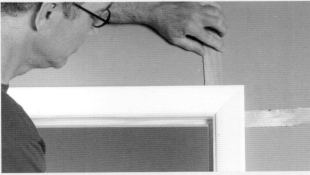

3 Carefully place shims behind the upper portion of each casing leg to help close the miter joint. Cut away the excess shims.

4 Use a good grade of latex painter's caulk to fill the gap between the back side of the casing and the wall surface.

base, chair rail, and wainscoting

3

THE WALLS OF YOUR HOME provide the opportunity to install a variety of trim, including baseboards, chair rails, plate rails, and wainscoting. Many wall treatments have their origins in practical uses—for example, chair rails were first installed to keep the backs of chairs from damaging wall finishes. Today, chair rails are installed more for their decorative qualities. Other elements, such as wainscoting, make a definite design statement. Many projects require specialized cutting techniques; find information on these in "Tools and Techniques," page 247.

BASE TRIM

Base trim includes a variety of board and molding applications to the bottom of a wall. The trim serves a practical purpose in that it covers the inevitable gap between the wall surface and floor, but it also serves a design function in that it provides a strong visual line around the base of a room and acts as the foundation for the rest of the trim. Of course, the decision as to what type of base-trim treatment you will use is tied into the trim motif of the room as a whole. Certain base treatments are more appropriate with some trim styles than others, but a few different options provide an adequate selection for most situations. If your trim package is based on stock molding profiles, there is simple, one-piece baseboard stock available. But if you are committed to a style that features wider, more complex moldings, the base trim should be of taller, heavier stock—usually a three-piece assembly. Keep in mind that specialty millwork suppliers can offer a wide variety of base profiles that you will otherwise not find. So, to expand your options or just to be inspired, it is worth exploring these resources.

One-Piece Baseboard

Most lumberyards and home centers offer one-piece baseboard moldings in two different styles to match their stock casings—colonial and ranch (also called "clamshell"). The height of these moldings can run from 3 to 5½ inches, and most are about ½ inch thick. Select a profile and size that is compatible with the rest of the trim details in the room.

If the floor is to be carpeted, the simple baseboard is all you will require. But for a tile or hardwood floor, you should also plan to install a flexible shoe molding to cover inevitable gaps between the different materials.

Built-up Base Trim

Most traditional trim styles feature a three-piece base-trim treatment consisting of a flat or molded base, a decorative cap molding, and flexible shoe molding. Some elaborate styles add additional layers or embellishments to the mix, but once you understand the basic principles and techniques for the installation, you can add or subtract elements to suit your taste.

Base-Trim Height. The height of the base trim should be in proportion to the trim in the rest of the room, but it should relate to the size and height of the room, as well. A room with 8-foot-high ceilings can accept a base-trim treatment that is 5 inches high, but a room with 9- or 10-foot ceilings needs a more substantial base—perhaps one that is 8 or 9 inches high. If you are in doubt as to the appropriate height of the molding, cut some scrap stock to various dimensions, and place it on the floor in the room to better judge the proportions.

Covering Mistakes. Even though the central portion of a built-up base-trim assembly is relatively rigid, the layered construction provides a means for accommodating irregularities in both the wall and floor surfaces. Both the cap molding and shoe molding are flexible enough to conform to slight dips and humps so that most gaps can be eliminated.

Detail of one-piece baseboard with stock Colonial door casing.

Detail of three-piece base trim with traditional casing.

Base, Chair Rail, and Wainscoting

Evaluate Room Conditions

In most situations, base trim can be laid with its bottom edge parallel with the existing floor. But in those situations where a floor is dramatically out of level—say by more than ½ inch in a 12-foot span—you should make an effort to install the base level. The alternative would leave you feeling as though you were walking into a fun house when you enter the room. So start by checking along each wall to see whether the floor is level.

Check for Level. Select a long, straight 2x4, just shy of the length of the wall, and lay it on edge in front of the wall. Place a spirit level on the top edge. If necessary, place a shim under one end of the board to bring the bubble to the center of the vial; then measure the height of the shim required. If the difference is considerable, make a notation on the wall of the amount of correction required so that you can make the adjustment during fitting and installation of the base molding.

Clean Up Drywall. On newly drywalled walls, it is common to find a buildup of drywall compound around the base of the wall. Make a careful examination of the wall condition, and use a putty knife to scrape any lumps from either the wall or floor surface. Inside corners are a particularly troublesome spot in this regard, as it is difficult to finish the bottom of a corner joint without the compound trailing off into the room. Excess compound can prevent the base trim from extending fully into the corner, so scrape or sand those areas to leave a clean, plumb surface.

A multipiece base-trim treatment can be a strong design element in a room, yet it is easy to install.

ROOM CONDITIONS

Use a long, straight 2x4 with a 4-ft. level to check that the floor in the room is level. As long as any difference is less than ¼ in. across the length of a room, you really do not need to make any adjustment. If the problem is severe, scribe the bottom edge of the base trim to absorb the difference.

It's common to find a buildup of excess drywall compound around the base of a wall or on the adjacent floor. Check the perimeter of the room, and use a putty knife to scrape off any offending pieces that might interfere with the base trim.

Base, Chair Rail, and Wainscoting

SUGGESTED CUTTING SEQUENCES

RECTANGULAR ROOM

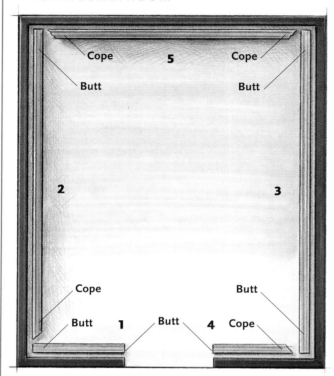

ROOM WITH SCARF JOINTS

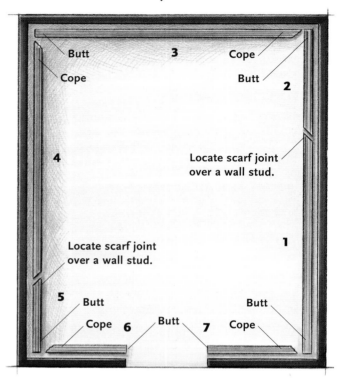

L-SHAPED ROOM

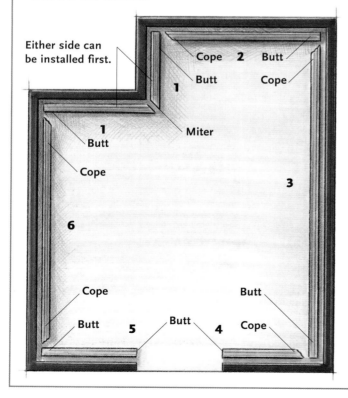

DOUBLE L-SHAPED ROOM

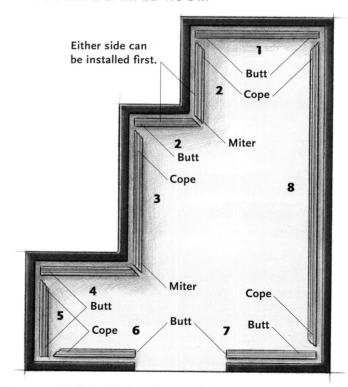

ROOM WITH BAY WINDOW

3 Miter

2

4

1

Miter

Miter

5

Butt

Butt

Cope

Cope

8

6

Butt

Butt

Cope 9 Butt 7 Cope

ROOM WITH ALCOVE

Either side can
be installed first.

Either
side can be
installed
first.

1
Butt

Cope

2

5

2

5

Butt

Butt

Miter

Cope

Cope

4

6

Cope

Butt

Butt

Cope

Butt 3 Butt 7 Cope

Plan the Installation. To make your job proceed as efficiently as possible, you should plan the order of installation of the base trim pieces. The inside corners of each base molding element need to be coped to provide tight joints, and you should minimize those situations that demand coped joints on both ends of a single piece of stock. To that end, make a simple map of each room with the order of installation noted and with the type of cut required—butt, miter, scarf, and cope. By planning ahead, your installation will go smoothly and you will end up with the neatest job.

If your room is to receive wall-to-wall carpet, it is customary to raise the base treatment up from the subfloor about ½ inch to allow the carpet installer to tuck the ends under the trim. In these situations, a shoe molding is not required, as the nap of the carpet covers any gaps caused by small dips in the floor. Cut blocks of ½-inch-thick stock (small pieces of colonial or ranch base work well) to use as temporary spacers under the base trim. Simply place them around the room, and rest the trim on them when nailing to the wall.

Base trim needs to be nailed to the wall framing. A wide one-piece baseboard is fastened with a nail driven into each wall stud and similarly spaced nails driven into the bottom plate of the wall. While typical framing dictates that there is a stud every 16 inches along a wall, this is sometimes not the case. It can save you considerable time and frustration by locating the wall studs before starting the installation. Use an electronic stud finder to scan each wall at base-trim height, and make a light pencil mark on the wall or floor to indicate stud centers. If you are working with finished wall or floor surfaces, you can place a piece of masking tape on either surface to receive the pencil marks.

To avoid unnecessary marks on a finished wall surface, place a strip of masking tape on the wall just above the baseboard height to mark stud locations. Use an electronic stud finder to locate framing members.

Baseboard Installation

One-piece baseboard, shown here, is the default approach. In most situations it is best to begin with the longest closed wall in a room. (See "Suggested Cutting Sequences," pages 76–77 .)

Locate the studs. If nailheads are not visible, use a stud sensor, rap on the wall, or drill exploratory holes just above the baseplate, where they will be covered by the new baseboard. Lightly mark the wall or floor with stud locations.

The first piece of baseboard can be cut square, so it is the easiest to fit. Measure the length of the wall, at baseboard height, and add $\frac{1}{16}$ inch. (See "Cutting Baseboard to Length," below.) Position the baseboard, and drive a nail into each stud and one near each stud into the wall plate. A pneumatic nail gun automatically sets the nails. If you

Coped inside corners help ensure that changes in humidity or building movement will not cause the trimwork to separate and show gaps at the corner.

smart tip

BASE TRIM BEFORE FINISH FLOORING

A FINISHED HARDWOOD OR TILE FLOOR CAN BE INSTALLED EITHER BEFORE OR AFTER THE BASE TRIM. IF THE BASE TRIM WILL PRECEDE THE FLOOR, USE SMALL BLOCKS OF THE FINISHED FLOOR MATERIAL AS SPACERS UNDER THE TRIM PIECES. PLACE AN ADDITIONAL LAYER OF CARDBOARD ON TOP OF EACH OF THESE SPACERS TO PROVIDE A SMALL MARGIN SO THAT THE FLOORING CAN EASILY SLIP UNDER THE WALL TRIM. THE BASE SHOE WILL HIDE ANY GAPS BETWEEN THE TRIMWORK AND THE FLOOR.

nail by hand, set the nails as you finish nailing each piece. If you wait until the entire room is finished to set the nails, you could cause gaps to open in some coped joints by driving one of the pieces further toward the wall surface.

Inside Corner Joints

At inside corners, use coped joints (See "Coped Joints," page 272.) Cut a piece of stock to about 2 inches longer than needed. Use a miter saw to cut an open 45-degree bevel cut on the end that will receive the coped joint. Use a coping saw to cut along the exposed profile, keeping the saw blade angled to provide a back-cut or clearance angle that is slightly greater than 90 degrees.

Test the fit of the coped joint. (If the molding is to fit against another inside wall, you will need to slightly angle the piece.) Use a combination of knife, rasp, and file to adjust the coped profile until you have a tight fit. Then cut the baseboard to fit.

CUTTING BASEBOARD TO LENGTH

WHENEVER YOU CUT a piece of baseboard, it is a good practice to add an extra $\frac{1}{16}$ inch to the length to ensure a tight fit and to allow you some room to adjust the joint. When fitting a piece of base between two surfaces, an extra $\frac{1}{16}$ inch allows you to spring the molding into position, pushing the end joint closed. And

when fitting an outside corner joint, the extra length gives you the opportunity to work toward a tight fit—something that does not always come automatically, especially in corners that are not perfectly square. Remember that some fitting and recutting is an expected part of trim installation.

INSTALLING AN INSIDE CORNER

To install molding in an inside corner, you will have to create a coped joint where the profile of one piece of trimwork fits over the face of a piece it meets in the corner. This creates a tight joint that is unlikely to separate. To cut a coped joint, use a coping saw to follow the profile of the molding. You may have to make a few tests cuts to master the technique. (For more on cutting coped joints, see "Cutting a Coped Joint," page 154, and "Coping Chair Rail Molding," page 272.)

TOOLS & MATERIALS

▌Hammer ▌Nail set ▌Nail gun and nails (optional) ▌Power miter saw ▌Coping saw ▌Files or rasps ▌Baseboard molding ▌Finishing nails ▌Shim stock

1 At inside corners, cut a square end on the first piece of baseboard, and run it into the drywall corner. Because only the top portion of the molding will be visible, it does not need to be tight along its entire height. Note the use of a piece of finished flooring and cardboard as a spacer beneath the baseboard.

2 Cope the end of the second piece for an inside corner joint. Test the fit. An open joint can be the result of one of a number of factors, including a wall that is not perfectly flat or straight, a piece of debris behind the molding, or a less than perfect coping job. Use a knife, rasp, file, or sandpaper to make the necessary adjustments.

3 Here is a completed inside corner joint on one-piece baseboard. It is not unusual for a joint to require some modification to close tightly.

Base, Chair Rail, and Wainscoting

Outside Corner Joints

At an outside corner, first determine the angle of the corner. It's not uncommon for a corner to be out of square.

On two pieces of scrap 1x6 stock, each about 18 inches long, make a 45-degree bevel cut on the end. Test-fit them at the corner. If the joint is open at the outside, slightly increase the angle of the cut; if it is open at the wall, try a slightly reduced angle. After just a few joints you will learn the amount of adjustment required to make a joint fit. Note that it is important that both pieces of a miter joint have an identical angle. Resist the temptation to cut one piece at a steeper angle than the other beause the result would be one piece of molding protruding farther at the corner—and then the only remedy would be to sand off the excess, leaving end grain visible at the joint. Another way to test the angle is shown below.

FIGURING CORNER ANGLES

WHILE TESTING AN OUTSIDE CORNER with test blocks is an efficient method of determining a workable miter angle, there is also a direct approach involving elementary geometry. Fit a sliding bevel gauge around the outside corner, and position it so the legs are snug to the wall surface. Use the gauge to trace the angle onto a piece of scrap lumber or stiff cardboard. Next, place the point of a compass at the apex of the angle, and scribe an equal distance along each leg of the angle. Reposition the point of the compass at each of these marks and, using the same distance setting, scribe two new intersecting arcs. Draw a line from the apex of the angle through the intersecting point to indicate ½ of the original angle. You can then use an angle gauge to measure the resulting angle, and set your miter saw accordingly.

TOOLS & MATERIALS
▎ Sliding bevel gauge ▎ Compass ▎ Straightedge
▎ Angle gauge ▎ Stiff cardboard

1 Transfer the angle (left). Place a compass at the apex of the angle, and scribe an arc along each leg (right).

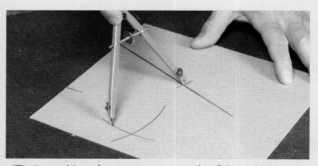

2 Reposition the compass at each of these intersecting marks, and scribe two new intersecting arcs.

3 Draw a line connecting the intersection of the new arcs with the apex of the original angle.

4 Use an angle gauge to measure the resulting angle. Use that setting on the miter saw to cut the joint.

INSTALLING AN OUTSIDE CORNER JOINT

project

Once you have determined the precise cutting angle, hold a piece of molding against the wall, and mark the floor (or on masking tape) to indicate the outside surface of the molding; repeat on the other wall. The intersection of the resulting "X" indicates the outside edge of both bevel cuts. Cut the pieces to the previously determined angle. Note: for multipiece installations, record the angle of the outside corner so that you can reuse it.

TOOLS & MATERIALS

▮ Hammer ▮ Nail set ▮ Nail gun and nails (optional) ▮ Power miter saw ▮ Baseboard molding ▮ 4d finishing nails ▮ Glue ▮ Masking or painter's tape ▮ Shim stock

1 Test the angle of outside corners with 1x6s cut at a 45-deg. bevel (top). If the joint is not tight, modify the cuts until you achieve a perfect fit. Place masking tape strips on the floor around the corner; then mark along the outside face of the baseboard. Hold stock for each side of the joint in place; use these lines to mark the long point of each miter (bottom).

2 Cut the two pieces, and test fit them at the corner. If needed, adjust the angle of the bevels on both pieces to produce a tight joint. Attach with nails driven into each stud and into the bottom plate near each stud. If you are hand nailing, drill pilot holes whenever you are near the edge of a piece, and set the nails.

3 Apply glue to the surfaces of the miter joint, and place the second piece in position. Make sure the joint comes together tightly before nailing it to the wall. Use 3d finishing nails or brads to pin the joint together.

Dealing with Out-of-Level Floors

Small gaps between floor and baseboard are covered by shoe molding, but if the floor is very wavy you may need to scribe-cut the molding to fit. Cut the baseboard to length. Shim the piece so its top edge is level. Open a scriber to the largest shim thickness, and run it along the floor to mark a contour line along the face of the baseboard. Use a plane or jig saw to remove stock up to the scribed line.

If the floor is dramatically out of level, you should scribe the baseboard to absorb the discrepancy. Note: if the scribe cut runs to the end of a piece, an adjacent piece will also need to be adjusted so the top edges will align.

NAILING BASE TRIM

- Stud Wall
- Drywall
- 1¼" Base Cap
- 6d Finishing Nail
- 8d Finishing Nail
- 5½" Baseboard
- ¾" Shoe
- 4d Finishing Nail into Baseboard

project

INSTALLING THREE-PIECE BASE TRIM

At its simplest, three-piece trim uses a flat baseboard with added cap and shoe molding. The height of the baseboard and the cap molding profile are yours to decide. You can shape the edge of the baseboard to a rounded or chamfered profile, or leave it square.

Start with ¾-inch flat stock. If the stock is square, inside joints can be simply butt-jointed. If you shape a rounded or chamfered edge on the stock, use the router to mill all the material at one time. Use coped joints at inside corners.

TOOLS & MATERIALS

▮ Hammer ▮ Nail set ▮ Nail gun and nails (optional) ▮ Power miter saw ▮ Coping saw ▮ Baseboard ▮ Cap and shoe molding ▮ Finishing nails ▮ Glue ▮ Shim stock

3 At an outside corner, use the technique shown on page 81 to mark the floor for the outside edges and cut the shoe molding. For the cap, just measure to the wall corner and use this for the shorter dimension. Apply glue to the surfaces of miter joints before nailing the molding to the wall. If you must hand-drive nails near the end of a piece, drill pilot holes first.

1 For square stock, use butt joints for inside corner joints. Fit the first piece, and nail it in place. Cut the second piece a few inches long, and test the fit before cutting to length (inset). Once the flat baseboard molding is installed, you can move on to the cap molding. Nail the cap to the wall studs, angling the nails to draw the cap down tightly to the baseboard.

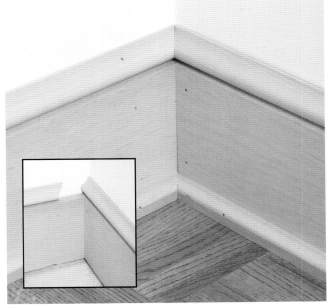

2 Both cap molding and shoe molding require coped joints at an inside corner. Square-cut the first piece; then cut a coped joint on the second piece. Test each joint, and make necessary adjustments with knife, rasp, or sandpaper until you achieve a tight fit (inset).

4 When a shoe molding ends at a plinth block, hold the shoe molding against the block, and place a pencil mark on the end to indicate the exposed portion of the molding.

5 Cut the shoe with an open miter that leaves the layout line in place. Nail the shoe molding to the baseboard using 4d finishing nails. Make sure you don't nail the molding to the flooring. This detail of three-piece base trim shows an intersection with a Victorian casing and a plinth block. Three-piece base trim complements a number of trimwork styles.

ELECTRICAL RECEPTACLES IN BASEBOARD

A tall baseboard or low receptacle may mean you have to cut a hole for the receptacle. You may like the look of a receptacle in the middle of the molding. Consult with an electrician or your building department; they may have special regulations for installing electrical boxes onto wood. Be sure the wiring is to code and does not overload any circuits, and use approved cables and electrical boxes. All outlets should be at a uniform height above the floor. Shut off power to the circuit.

TOOLS & MATERIALS

▌Drywall saw ▌Power drill and bit ▌Saber saw ▌Screwdriver ▌Electrical box for template ▌Base trim material ▌Pan-head screws

1 Cut baseboard stock to length, and lay it on the floor in front of the wall. Transfer the position of each electrical cable to the baseboard, indicating the center of each electrical outlet (top). Center each outlet box vertically on the baseboard stock, and trace around the box to mark the cutout required (bottom). Remember to leave stock to support the "ears" that hold the box in place.

2 Drill holes at corners, and use a saber saw to make cutouts for electrical boxes. Keep the saw kerf just to the outside of the layout lines to provide a margin of adjustment (top). Mount the boxes to the baseboard with small pan-head screws (bottom). Feed electrical cable into each box, and clamp in a code-approved manner.

3 Cut holes for the electrical boxes in the wall. Push the boxes into the cut holes in the wall, and attach the baseboard and other trim pieces if applicable. Restore power, and test.

CORNER AND PLINTH BLOCKS

IF YOU FIND THE PROSPECT of cutting all those coped and mitered joints less than appealing, there is an alternative approach to base trim. You can install corner blocks at either inside or outside corners and simply let the base trim end squarely against the blocks. Some millwork houses manufacture blocks designed for just this purpose, most often as part of a trim package with matching base molding; these tend to have decoratively molded tops. However, you can certainly fabricate your own blocks if you cannot find some that you like. Blocks that are designed for outside corners should have an L-shaped cross section to wrap around both wall surfaces, while those for inside corners can be square. In all cases, the thickness of a corner block should exceed that of the base trim so that it provides a neat, finished look at the joint.

Cutting Jig for Plinth and Corner Blocks. When door trim includes plinth blocks at the base of the casing, the base trim simply is cut to butt tightly to the block. Sometimes a plinth block can be installed so that its edges are not perfectly plumb. In this case you need to scribe the end of the base trim to fit the angle of the block. A simple jig can be used to mark the angle. Cut a slot in a piece of scrap stock wide and

tall enough to slip over the baseboard molding. Hold the length of baseboard in position so that its long end runs past the plinth block. Slide the marking jig over the base, and hold it tight to the side of the plinth. Then run your pencil along the outer edge of the jig to mark the angle on the baseboard. The same technique can be also be used to mark the intersection of a corner block and baseboard trim.

OUTSIDE CORNER BLOCK

INSIDE CORNER BLOCK

A plumb commercial plinth block fits tightly against colonial-style casing.

Use a marking jig to scribe the length of baseboard at a plinth or corner block.

WORKING AROUND WALL REGISTERS

WALL REGISTERS can present a challenge when installing baseboard trim. If you are installing a simple baseboard and the register cover is flat against the wall, cut the baseboard at a 45-degree open bevel, so the long side rests against the wall and tucks behind the cover. Cut the base shoe at a 45-degree bevel as well, and install so the long point of the bevel aligns with the short point of the baseboard bevel.

Protruding Registers. If your register cover is the type that protrudes from the wall, you can simply make a square cut at the ends of the base and shoe molding and let them die neatly against the sides of the register.

The most elegant option when dealing with a register cover is to carry the base trim around the sides and top of the plate, as shown in the examples below.

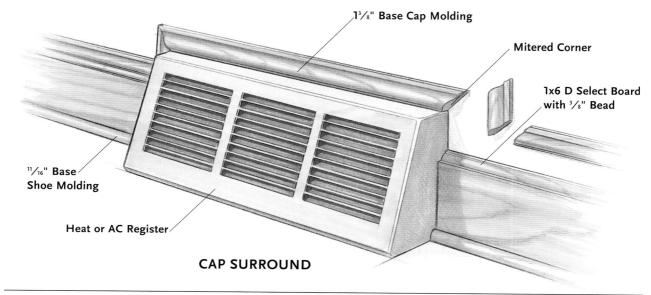

1³/₈" Base Cap Molding

Mitered Corner

1x6 D Select Board with ³/₈" Bead

¹¹/₁₆" Base Shoe Molding

Heat or AC Register

CAP SURROUND

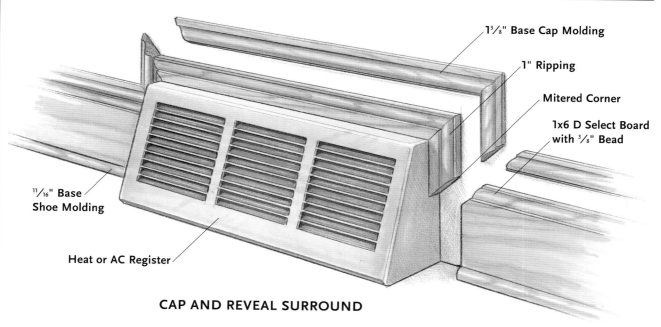

1³/₈" Base Cap Molding

1" Ripping

Mitered Corner

1x6 D Select Board with ³/₈" Bead

¹¹/₁₆" Base Shoe Molding

Heat or AC Register

CAP AND REVEAL SURROUND

INSTALLING BASE TRIM AT STAIRWELLS

project

The intersection of base trim with the top and bottom ends of a stair stringer presents a number of options, depending on the stair construction and type of base trim.

The most common approach involves trimming the end of the baseboard at the top of the stair so that the stringer angle is continued to the top of the base. At the bottom, you can butt the baseboard into the plumb cut at the end of the stringer.

TOOLS & MATERIALS

▮ Sliding bevel gauge ▮ Hammer
▮ Nail set ▮ Nail gun and nails (optional)
▮ Power miter saw ▮ Straightedge
▮ Baseboard material ▮ Finishing nails
▮ Shim stock

1 At the bottom end of a stair, you can make a square cut on the end of the baseboard stock and butt it into the plumb cut of the stair stringer (top). Determine the angle between the base and stringer using a sliding bevel gauge. Cut and install cap molding to make a smooth transition (bottom).

2 At the top of a stair, hold baseboard stock against the plumb cut of the stringer, and mark the angle of the stringer onto the baseboard (inset). Trim the baseboard to the line. Use a sliding bevel gauge to determine the angle between the stringer and top edge of the baseboard; then bisect the angle to determine the miter cuts. (See "Figuring Corner Angles," page 80.) Install cap molding to the top edges of the stringer and baseboard.

3 For an alternative approach, use a plinth block to make the transition between the base trim assembly and the stair stringer. Make sure that the plinth block is tall enough to provide a clean terminus for both the base and the cap molding.

CHAIR, PICTURE, AND PLATE RAILS

Chair rails, picture rails, and plate rails are all horizontal applications to a wall surface. Chair and plate rails are often installed as part of a wainscoting, but can be used on their own to provide a strong trim component to a room.

Chair Rail

Chair-rail molding can consist of a single piece of stock or a combination of profiles mounted at a height of 30 to 36 inches above the floor. Originally, chair rail was designed to protect wall surfaces. Today, it is used as a decorative element to create a strong horizontal line around a room, dividing the wall height into distinct areas.

There are moldings that are sold specifically as chair-rail stock, but you can use a wide variety of other moldings, including a flat piece of 1x3.

Picture Rail

A picture rail consists of a particular molding with a rounded top profile that projects away from the wall surface. You can use special hooks and wire to hang paintings, prints, or photographs from the rail. And depending on the height of the rail, it can also serve to delineate a frieze at the top portion of a wall surface or to suggest a small crown molding when mounted near the ceiling.

Picture rail molding can be used for hanging pictures, or it can help delineate a frieze at the top of the wall.

INSTALLING A CHAIR RAIL

project

Some chair rails feature a projecting cap that provides a flat surface on top. Whatever the configuration, it is important to consider the intersection of a chair rail with vertical trim elements, such as door and window casings. If the casing protrudes farther into the room than the rail, you can simply let the rail butt into the side of the casing. But if the rail protrudes beyond the casing, fashion it into a finished return to give a finished appearance.

TOOLS & MATERIALS

▌Spirit level ▌Hammer ▌Nail set ▌Nail gun and nails (optional) ▌Miter saw ▌Files and rasps ▌Chair rail stock ▌Finishing nails ▌Wood glue ▌Masking or painter's tape

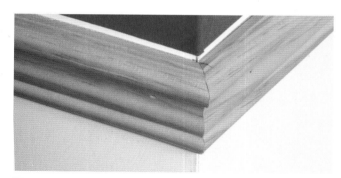

3 Cut the miter angles on both halves of an outside corner joint to test the fit before nailing the first piece to the wall. Glue and nail the second piece in place (top). Make a square cut on the end of a one-piece chair rail to allow it to butt into the edge of a door or window casing (bottom).

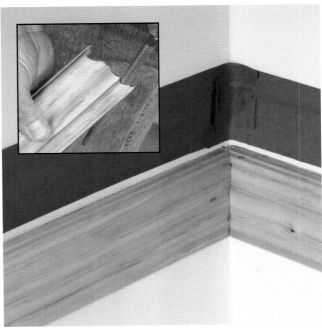

1 Mark a level line around the room to indicate the top edge of the chair rail. Apply masking tape to the wall just above the line, and mark for wall studs. Use a stud sensor, or drive exploratory holes where they will be covered. For an outside corner, hold the first piece in place, and mark the inside of the miter cut (inset).

2 For an inside corner joint, run the first piece square into the corner; then cut a coped joint on the second piece (inset). This detail shows a completed inside corner joint on a one-piece chair rail. (See "Coping Chair-Rail Molding," page 242.) Repeat the process for a built-up assembly.

4 When a chair rail includes a cap, create an elegant termination point by notching the cap around the casing. Hold the cap stock against the casing to mark the depth of the notch.

5 Cut the cap stock to notch tightly around a door or window casing; then shape a rounded or chamfered transition on the end of the piece.

Plate Rail

A plate rail is similar to a chair rail, but is mounted higher on the wall—normally 60 to 72 inches from the floor. Consisting of a narrow shelf with a shallow groove parallel with its front edge, the plate rail is frequently used as a cap for an Arts and Crafts-style wainscoting. Decorative plates or other types of artwork can be propped against the wall with their lower edge engaged in the groove. You could omit the groove and use the shelf to display small collectibles. A plate rail can be used in conjunction with other styles of wainscoting, or simply as a trim element on its own.

A plate rail is made of three components, as shown below. A horizontal rail attaches against the wall, and supports the back edge of the shelf. An apron or crown molding supports the shelf's front edge. If the installation is part of a wainscoting treatment, the top rail of the wainscoting forms the support rail for the shelf.

MILLING AND INSTALLING A PLATE RAIL

project

A plate rail's shelf is usually 3¼ to 4½ inches wide with a simple edge treatment. For the apron, choose a molding that provides graceful support for the front edge of the shelf. As an alternative, install small individual brackets between the shelf and rail to provide support for the shelf. In that case, you have the option to provide a molded strip, between the brackets, to add another decorative element and cover the joint between shelf and rail.

TOOLS & MATERIALS

▮ Router and edge guide ▮ Core-box bit ▮ Hammer ▮ Nail set ▮ Nail gun and nails (optional) ▮ Power miter saw ▮ 1-by stock ▮ Apron stock ▮ Wood glue ▮ Finishing nails

PLATE-RAIL CONSTRUCTION

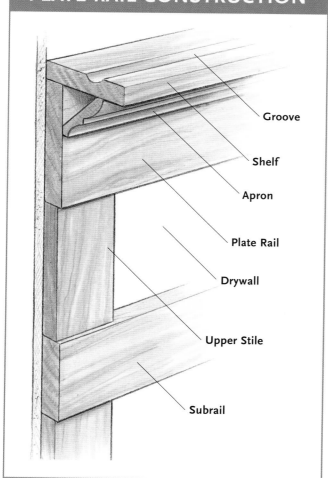

Groove

Shelf

Apron

Plate Rail

Drywall

Upper Stile

Subrail

3 For the shelf, include an overhang at an exposed end or where the shelf must return onto a casing. Cut the appropriate miters on shelf stock, and apply glue to the joint surfaces. Use small nails to pin the parts together while the glue sets. You can also use small joining plates. (See "Making Mitered Returns," page 274.)

Base, Chair Rail, and Wainscoting

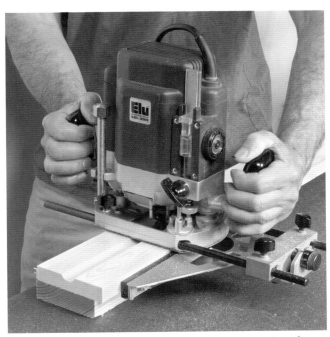

1 For an independent plate rail, begin by ripping the shelf and rail stock to width. In the top, mill the groove, about $3/8$ in. deep, using a router with a $1/2$- or $5/8$-in.-diameter core-box bit and edge guide. Test the depth of cut on scrap material before approaching the actual shelf stock.

2 Use a level to lay out guide lines on the wall to indicate the top of the rail. Find studs, and mark the wall where the lines will be covered. Nail the rail to the wall using 8d finishing nails. If the rail is formed from flat stock, butt joints are fine at all inside corners. If the rail has a profile, you need to cut coped joints.

4 If the shelf has a square-edge profile, use a butt joint at the inside corners. But if you decide to add a decorative edge to the shelf, you can cut an inside miter joint at the corner. Run a bead of glue along the top edge of the rail; then place the shelf in position. Use 8d finishing nails to fasten the shelf to the top rail.

5 Finally, cut the apron trim, and mount it to the rail/shelf assembly. Use coped joints at inside corners and mitered returns at any exposed ends. Then nail the trim to both the rail and shelf. If your plate rail has exposed ends, construct mitered returns on the ends of the apron molding.

WAINSCOTING

Wainscoting involves applying either vertical boards (shown on pages 92–96) or frame-and-panel assemblies (pages 98–103) to the lower part of a wall, and capping the installation with an integral chair rail. Wainscoting can be compatible with almost any style decor. A simple country- or rustic-style treatment would consist of tongue-and-groove boards with a beaded or V-groove molded profile.

A room in the Arts and Crafts theme would typically feature plain-edge frame stock surrounding flat panels, often in quarter-sawn white oak, cherry, or mahogany, but this style is regularly executed in paint-grade materials as well. For a more layered decor—such as Georgian, Federal, or Greek Revival—panel molding can be added to either a flat-panel or raised-panel design.

The height of wainscoting varies from 30 to 36 inches, or extends to 60 inches in Arts and Crafts-style rooms. Avoid dividing the wall height in half; it just looks awkward.

Tongue-and-Groove Bead-Board Wainscoting

A simple and common type of wainscoting consists of an application of tongue-and-groove boards to the lower portion of a wall. This is a popular treatment in kitchens, bathrooms, and other informal rooms.

Tongue-and-groove wainscoting features an applied base trim and chair-rail cap to complete the installation. Here, you can personalize your installation. Feel free to modify the basic design shown on these pages.

CORNER CONSTRUCTION

3⅛"   3⅛"

½" Plywood

4d Finishing Nail

Chamfered Edge

INSTALLING BEAD-BOARD WAINSCOTING

project

Fir bead-board is a popular choice. It is manufactured in thicknesses ranging from ⅜ to ¾ inch, as well as widths of 3 or 5 inches. Bead-board stock is available as random length milled stock and also in prepackaged kits. In addition, you can also find the same pattern milled into various hardwood species. You also could use knotty pine or cedar.

TOOLS & MATERIALS

▪ Hammer ▪ Nail set ▪ Nail gun and nails (optional) ▪ Power drill with screwdriver tip ▪ Power miter saw ▪ Table saw ▪ Circular saw ▪ Spirit level ▪ Block plane ▪ Drywall saw ▪ ½-inch CD plywood ▪ Tongue-and-groove bead-board wainscoting ▪ Finishing nails ▪ Wood glue ▪ Utility screws

3 Cut a number of boards about ¼ inch short of the full wainscot height. Beginning at an inside corner, hold the first board in place. Always work with the tongue of the board exposed and the grooved edge facing the corner. Use a level to check that it is plumb; then drive finishing nails through the face of the board.

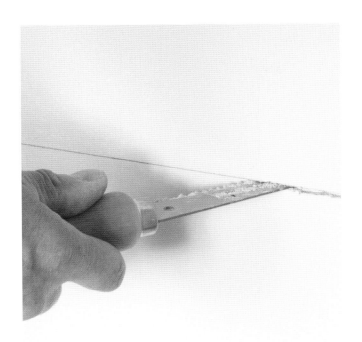

1 Vertical wainscoting must be nailed at frequent intervals, so either install plywood, as we show, or blocking between studs. Mark a level line at the height of the bottom of the wainscoting cap; then use a drywall saw and utility knife to cut the drywall. Remove the drywall from that line to the floor.

2 Install ½-in. CD plywood panels in place of the drywall. Nail or screw the plywood to the wall studs and soleplate. (If you wish to save material, you could install three or four nailing strips instead of full panels, but the time saved and additional backing provided make the full-panel system a good approach.)

4 For the rest of the boards, drive nails at an angle through the base of the tongue, so they will be covered by the next piece. Use a cutoff piece of wainscoting stock as a block to coax boards together. You can use a hammer to tap on the waste block without damaging the delicate tongue.

5 As you approach an inside corner, measure between both the top and bottom of the next-to-last board and the corner. Transfer these measurements to the last board, and use a circular saw or saber saw to cut it to width. The last board does not have to fit snugly; the gap will be covered by the first piece on the next wall.

Continued on next page. **93**

Continued from previous page.

6 Engage the groove of the last board on a run with the tongue of the previous board, and push it into place. You may need to use a flat pry bar to pry it snug against the previous board. Drive nails through the face of the board in the corner, where they will be covered by the first piece of the adjoining wall.

7 Place the first board on the adjacent wall into position, and use a level to check that it is plumb. If it is, nail it in place.

10 The second half of an outside corner requires that you remove the groove plus an amount equal to the thickness of the stock to create an equal reveal on each side of the corner.

11 Use a level to check that the first board at an outside corner is plumb. Allow the outer edge of the board to protrude just beyond the backer so you can fashion a tight corner joint. Face-nail the first corner board.

8 If an inside corner is not plumb, hold the first board plumb, and use scribers to mark the face for the adjustment. Keep both wings of the scriber parallel with the floor as you slide it. Use a sharp block plane to remove the required stock; then test the fit of the board. Once you are satisfied with the joint, face-nail the strip.

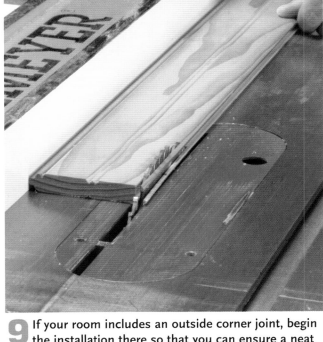

9 If your room includes an outside corner joint, begin the installation there so that you can ensure a neat and balanced joint at this more visible point. Create a tight butt joint by first ripping the groove off of the first board. Use sandpaper or a sharp plane to remove saw marks. (See "Corner Construction," page 92.)

12 Hold the second corner board in place, and plumb it. If needed, plane off the required stock so that it does not project beyond the corner. Apply glue to the joint, and drive nails through the second board into the first. Also drive nails into the plywood. Set the nail heads, and fill with wood filler.

13 Use a sharp plane to shape a bevel on the outside corner of wainscoting panel stock.

BASEBOARD AND CHAIR RAIL OVER WAINSCOTING

project

Installing a one-piece baseboard and a chair rail over wainscoting uses many of the same techniques as for installing those pieces onto a wall. (See pages 74–83 and 88–91.) The chair rail is topped with a piece of cap molding that covers the top of the wainscoting pieces as well as the chair rail. Cover the top cap with several coats of a clear finish, such as varnish or urethane, or paint, as it will collect dust and will need to be wiped down often to be kept clean.

TOOLS & MATERIALS

■ Basic carpentry tools ■ Power miter saw ■ One-piece baseboard stock ■ Chair-rail stock ■ Cap-molding stock ■ Finishing nails ■ Wood glue ■ Shim stock

1 Nail one-piece baseboard to the wainscoting panel stock (top). Remember to use appropriate spacers for carpeting, hardwood, or tile flooring. Cut miters for the outside corners of apron molding. Test-fit the joints to check for proper fit; then apply a bead of glue; and nail the molding in place (bottom).

2 It's common for drywall surfaces to flare out at the corners. Cut the stock to length with appropriate end joints; then use a scriber to mark the required adjustment on the face of the cap. Remove the waste material. Nail the chair-rail cap to the top edge of wainscoting panels and apron molding; then pin the miter joint together with a 4d finishing nail or brad (inset).

3 Mark the end of the apron molding to indicate the depth of the casing. Then cut a mitered return piece that meets the face of the casing. Nail the apron to the wainscot paneling (inset). Cut a notch in the chair-rail cap stock to fit tightly to the casing. Ease the edges of the cap, or shape a rounded end; then nail it to the top edges of apron and wainscot paneling.

DEALING WITH ELECTRICAL BOXES

AS YOU PROCEED across the wall, it is inevitable that you will encounter electrical outlets. Make sure that the electrical circuits are turned off; then remove the cover plates and outlets. When you approach an outlet box, take careful measurements from the edge of the last strip before the box to determine its position. Mark the location of your cutout on the board and, if necessary, drill clearance holes in each corner so that you can insert a saber saw blade.

Use the saw to make the required cutout. For ease of installation, allow about 1/16 inch extra space around the box on all sides. Test the fit of the board, and make any necessary adjustments. If the electrical box straddles two boards, mark and cut the second part of the cutout, and mount the second board. Remember to provide clearance for the outlet mounting screws. Depending on the thickness of your wainscoting and local electrical codes, you might need to install extension sleeves to the electrical boxes before reinstalling the outlets.

TOOLS & MATERIALS

▪ Folding stick ruler ▪ Power drill and bit ▪ Saber saw
▪ Pencil ▪ Combination square ▪ Tongue-and-groove
bead-board wainscoting ▪ Box extension

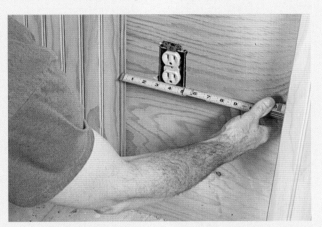

1 Measure the distance between an outlet box and the nearest full board. Transfer the measurements to a piece of wainscoting stock. Allow an additional 1/8 in. for adjustments.

2 Transfer the height of the bottom and top of an electrical box directly to the wainscoting stock. Use a saber saw to make the necessary cutout. Make sure that you leave clearance for the outlet mounting screws.

3 To protect against the risk of fire—and to meet electrical code—install an extension to the existing electrical box. Slide it into position, and make the necessary electrical connections.

Flat-Panel Wainscoting

Although it may look intimidating, installing frame-and-flat-panel wainscoting is a reasonable do-it-yourself project. And it can be customized in a variety of ways to conform to many different interior design schemes.

The simplest approach is an unadorned, paint-grade wainscoting. But you can also opt for a clear or stained finish using pine or hardwood. Base and cap molding can be simple one-piece moldings or complex assemblies. You can also install a molding around the perimeter of each panel to completely alter the feel of the wainscoting.

This basic system can be constructed entirely on site or prefabricated in sections in your home workshop, and it is suitable for new construction or a renovation project for an existing room. For a painted finish, your best choices are solid poplar for the frame, birch plywood for the backer and panel stock, and pine for the moldings.

Lay Out the Project. Determine the panel layout for the room. Use graph paper to make a simple scaled drawing of each wall with windows, doors, outlets, switches, and heat registers all included. Draw the chair rail; then determine the width of the cap and baseboard. It is perfectly fine to hold the wainscoting frame up from the floor and apply blocking at the bottom of the wall to support the base trim. Using this technique will allow you to save on material for extra-wide rail stock that would be buried behind the baseboard. Sketch in the top and bottom rails next. Make sure that your base trim overlays the bottom

rail enough to provide adequate support for all trim pieces.

Doors and Windows. In some situations, you can modify the casing details to provide additional depth, and so the wainscoting trim simply dies into the casing. This could be as simple as adding a backband to the edge of a casing or a panel molding to the face. But other times it will be necessary to provide a more intentional terminus for the wainscoting at a casing. One of the more elegant ways to solve this problem is to construct a small pilaster at the casing that extends far enough into the room to accept the wainscoting trim.

Panel Dimensions. Experiment with the placement of frame stiles to achieve a pleasing division of space across the wall. The width of your panels does not need to be identical on each wall; however, the general proportions of the panels should be close.

TYPICAL FRAME-AND-PANEL CORNER JOINTS

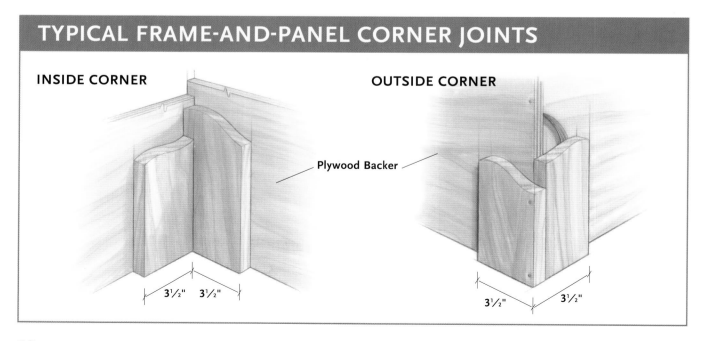

INSIDE CORNER

OUTSIDE CORNER

Plywood Backer

3½" 3½"

3½" 3½"

FLAT-PANEL WAINSCOT CONSTRUCTION

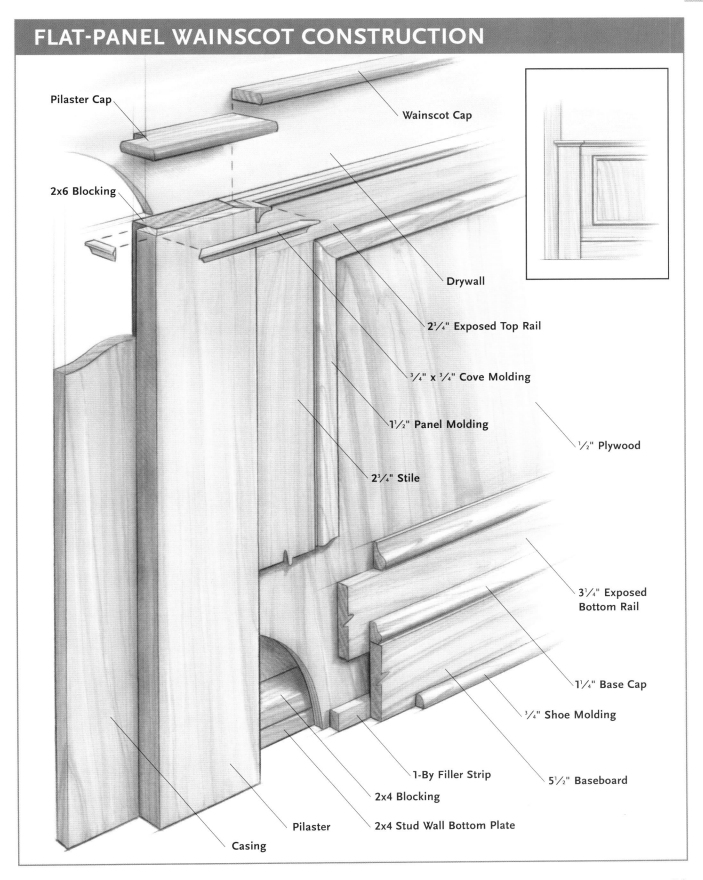

Pilaster Cap

2x6 Blocking

Wainscot Cap

Drywall

2³⁄₄" Exposed Top Rail

³⁄₄" x ³⁄₄" Cove Molding

1¹⁄₂" Panel Molding

2³⁄₄" Stile

¹⁄₂" Plywood

3¹⁄₄" Exposed Bottom Rail

1¹⁄₄" Base Cap

³⁄₄" Shoe Molding

5¹⁄₂" Baseboard

1-By Filler Strip

2x4 Blocking

2x4 Stud Wall Bottom Plate

Pilaster

Casing

INSTALLING FLAT-PANEL WAINSCOTING

project

Prepare to attach the panels. If you are working in a newly constructed room, apply ½-inch-thick plywood to the studs up to the height of the top rail to serve as both the panel faces and frame backer; then apply drywall to the rest of the wall. If the room is finished, remove the drywall up to the rail height, and install the plywood in its place. Or carefully note the exact locations of all studs.

TOOLS & MATERIALS

▪ Hammer ▪ Nail set ▪ Nail gun and nails (optional) ▪ Spirit level ▪ Saber saw ▪ Power miter saw ▪ Plate joiner ▪ Power drill and bits ▪ Clamps ▪ Square ▪ 1-by stock ▪ ½-inch birch plywood ▪ Wood glue ▪ Finishing nails ▪ Joining plates

1 Cut panels to fit; make sure that seams fall where they will be covered. If you must deal with electrical receptacles, consult with an electrician or your building department. (See page 84.) Mark the outline of the boxes on the plywood panels before installing the panels. Allow ¹⁄₁₆ in. on each side for ease of adjustment.

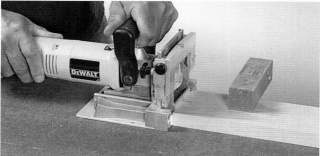

4 Use the plate joiner to cut slots in the top and bottom rails. Firmly press both the joiner and rail stock to the table top to accurately register the slots (top). Clamp a stile to the worktable before using the plate joiner to cut slots in the end-grain (bottom). This technique keeps hands far from the spinning blade.

5 Cut blocks to support the bottom rails at the proper height. Use a 4-ft. level to check for level. If necessary, place shims below one or more of the blocks to adjust the position of the rail.

2 Drill clearance holes for the saw blade; then use a saber saw to make the cutout for electrical outlet boxes. Cut holes in the wall if/as needed. Thread the electrical cable through the holes; attach the panels to studs up to rail height; and finish installing the boxes and securing the electrical cables and receptacles.

3 Attach panels to the wall, using 8d nails and/or construction adhesive. Cut rails to length, using miter joints at outside corners. Clamp a bottom and top rail together to mark the locations of the frame stiles. Place a mark to indicate the center of each stile to use when cutting slots for joining plates.

6 Nail the bottom rail to the plywood panel. Place two nails every 16 in. along the length of the rail. Cut the stiles to equal lengths. For consistent stile widths at inside corners, the first stile to be installed will need to be ³/₄ in. wider than a normal stile. At an outside corner, the first stile installed will need to be ³/₄ in. narrower.

7 Spread glue on a joining plate as well as in the matching slots. Place the plate into the slot in the rail before installing the first stile.

Continued on next page. **101**

Continued from previous page.

8 At an inside corner, install the first stile. Check for plumb. Spread a bit of glue in the mating plate slots and on the joining plate, and attach the stile to the bottom rail. Use a level to check that the stile is plumb, and apply pressure to the rail/stile joint to keep it closed while you drive nails to lock the stile in place.

9 When you have installed all the stiles on one wall, test that the top rail will fit onto the joining plates. Apply glue to the slots in the top rail and stiles; insert joining plates into the slots in the stiles; and position the rail. Push down to close the joints while you nail the rail to the backer panel.

12 Rip narrow strips to act as backers to support the bottom edge of base trim. Nail the strips to the plywood panel at floor level.

13 Place baseboard in position, and nail it to both the bottom rail and backer strip. After all baseboards are installed, run the cap molding around the room.

10 If the joints between the top rail and stiles are reluctant to close, you can use a clamp to pull the rail into position before nailing it to the plywood backer.

11 Proceed around the room, installing the panel frames on one wall at a time. To maintain uniform stile exposure on each side of a corner, rip the first stile ³/₄ in. narrower than normal. Place the second stile in position, and nail the corner joint together.

14 Cut cove apron molding to size with appropriate end joints; then nail it to the top rail. Keep the top of the molding flush with the top edge of the rail. Rip stock to width for the cap so that it overhangs about ³/₄ in. You may choose to shape the front edge with a router. At inside corners, use a butt or miter joint. Glue and nail the cap.

15 Installing inside moldings is not difficult, but it is labor intensive. Each piece must be measured or scribed individually, and you must take the time to make accurate miter cuts. To add molding to wainscoting panels, first cut the molding to length with 45-deg. miters at each end. Test fit all four pieces; then nail.

Modular Construction of Wainscoting Panels

If you have a home workshop or can set aside a space as a temporary shop, you can also prefabricate wainscoting panels in wall-length units. Then you can bring these panels to the site and install them in sections. In addition to minimizing installation time, this system has two other notable advantages. First, you can clamp the frame parts to pull the joints tight and ensure no gaps. And second, you can fasten the plywood panel backer to the frame by screwing it through the back side, eliminating the need to fill nailholes in the face of the frame. Of course, you still will need to apply the cap, apron, and base molding after the panels are installed. If you find the calculations for a complicated room too difficult, you can combine prefabricated panels for the simple walls with some that are built on site for the more complex areas.

Begin by taking careful measurements of your room. Create a detailed drawing for each wall which includes all window and door openings, outlets, and registers. You will need to plan the order of installation for each wall section because it is necessary to account for the thickness of the adjacent frames when calculating panel size. When laying out panel size and stile locations, remember that joints in the plywood panels will need to fall behind stiles. Depending on the amount of space available for your work space, you can fabricate a continuous panel assembly for an entire wall or two or three subassemblies that can be joined on site.

The basic layout for prefab panels is the same as for site-built panels. As a general rule, it is wise to design the panels to be slightly long to allow for some adjustment and scribing in corners that are not perfectly plumb—in most cases, an extra ½ inch per unit is sufficient.

Combine wainscoting and plate rail, left.

Plan where panels meet casing, above.

You can use the same layout described above for constructing the frames; this includes the use of a backer strip at the bottom edge to carry the base trim. Simply size the plywood panels to extend below the bottom rail the appropriate amount.

Build the wainscoting frames first. Apply glue to the joining plate slots and on each joining plate; then assemble the rails to the stiles. Use bar clamps, positioned at each stile, to draw the joints tight, and leave the clamps in place until the glue sets—at least one hour. For an alternative construction technique, you can use pocket screws. (See page 264.) Use the jig to drill two pilot holes at the ends of each stile; then temporarily clamp the stiles to the rails while you drive the screws to assemble the frames.

Cut the plywood panels to size. Lay one of the assembled panels face side down on a worktable or cleared floor surface, and position a plywood panel over it. Drill and countersink pilot holes; then fasten the panel to the frame with 1-inch flat-head screws. Repeat this process for each panel assembly.

Follow your installation plan, installing one wall of paneling at a time. Check each panel to make sure that it is level; place shims beneath the bottom edge of the assembly to hold it in place while you fasten it to the wall. Screw the panels to the wall with long screws driven into the studs. Bore and countersink pilot holes for all screws so that the heads sit slightly below the rail surface. If you place the screws at the top and bottom edges of the panel, the apron and base molding will cover the screw heads.

Heating registers and receptacles, above left, can be made to blend in with the trimwork package.

Plate rails, above, can be used to display items.

Create layouts, below, for custom looks.

wall frames

4

WALL FRAMES offer a unique opportunity to customize the trimwork in any room. However, they tend to work best in the formal more public rooms, such as living and dining rooms. Wall frames are a series of large picture frames that provide an elegant raised pattern along a bare stretch of wall. Once you have the trimwork in place, you can paint the interior of the frames to create a three-dimensional illusion of layers of depths and densities—a truly sophisticated design look. If you combine wall frames with a distinctive chair-rail and base-trim assemblies, you'll be designing your own unique trimwork treatment.

DESIGN BASICS

Wall framing dates to the mid-1700s, the Georgian period, when plaster began to replace wooden wall panels in the decoration of homes.

Pioneered in the 1750s by British architect John Adam, wall frames provided elegant accents for large expanses of flat plaster and helped popularize contrasting color schemes, enhancing a room's sense of space. Over the next hundred years, wall frames became standard in European interiors. Heavy wooden paneling did not return to vogue until the Victorian era.

Wall-frame trimwork divides walls into large, aesthetically pleasing units. It makes a stronger statement than you can make with paint or wallpaper alone. You can design and install a wall-frame treatment just below a chair rail or both above and below it. The frames above the rail maintain the same width and the same spacing from other elements on the wall as those below. A well-designed wall-frame treatment follows these basic design principles.

Scale and Proportion. In a well-proportioned design, the base molding is taller than the chair rail, and the chair rail looks more substantial than the door and window casings. The molding used in the wall frames is the smallest element on the wall. But all of these elements should be scaled to the size of the room.

Balance. In a symmetrical arrangement, if a wall can hold only three wall frames, you can make the middle one wider. If a wall can hold five frames, make the middle and two end frames narrower. You can even use both approaches in the same room when doors and windows dictate fewer or more frames.

Rhythm. Repetition of an element, such as a wall frame, gives a design a feeling of rhythm and draws the eye along. You can also create rhythm by progressing from small to large elements and by contrasting differing frame sizes.

Emphasis. Wall frames lend dramatic emphasis to the lower wall and serve as a pedestal for the middle portion of the wall. If you choose not to use wall frames below the chair rail, using different wallpapers above and below can have a similar but less effective impact.

Harmony. Architecturally speaking, harmony is a pleasing balance between diversity and unity. Diversity comes from the intersections of various horizontal and vertical moldings on the wall, and the repetition of the wall frames shows a unity of design.

This wall-frame treatment, opposite, exhibits the principles of scale and proportion, balance, rhythm, emphasis, and harmony.

Three-dimensional wall frames, a picture rail, and an elaborate cornice accentuate the drama of this sitting room, above.

Wall Frames

Intervals

An interval is the area within an individual wall frame, defined by the frame's outside dimensions. Unlike margins, opposite, for which dimensions must be constant (except for special areas like bays with windows), interval width and height can vary as needed to accommodate placement of doors, passageways, windows, fireplaces, and other elements.

Arriving at the right wall-frame size and shape is largely a matter of intuition. Basic design concepts presented in this chapter will help guide you in the process, but by just holding the margins constant and allowing the dimensions of the intervals to expand and contract (within reason) in response to wall runs, you can maintain an overall sense of proportion, balance, and continuity.

The paint scheme in this newly remodeled room emphasizes the uniformity of the vertical and horizontal margins, below.

The wall frames in this bay, opposite, line up with the window casings, and the vertical margins are wider than those in the rest of the room.

Margins

Margins are the spaces above, below, and in between wall frames. A margin of 2¾ to 3 inches usually looks best. You can make all the margins identical in a design, or you might want to vary the margins above and below the frames a little. Try making both the top and bottom margins wider, or make just the top margin narrower. As a general rule, the difference should be ½ inch or less, and no margin should ever be less than 2½ inches.

You can break from uniform margins near windows or in narrow wall sections on one or both sides of a door. You can also reduce horizontal margins under a window. When a space is too narrow to insert a wall frame, just leave it empty.

Under a window, make the wall-frame width line up with the outside edges of the window casing. For a bay window, this usually means that the vertical margins between the frames under the windows will differ greatly from those on the rest of the wall.

If you follow the Golden Rectangle principle (page 112), you may need to adjust the margins in order to make the rectangles fit.

DESIGN GOLD

The underlying principle for selecting intervals in a wall-frame treatment is known as the Golden Rectangle, a concept conceived by the architects of ancient Greece. According to this concept, the eye finds the shape of a rectangle more pleasing than that of a square. The principle further holds that the ideal dimensions for a rectangle occur in a ratio of approximately 3 : 2. (See "Golden Rectangle," right.) You can rely on this time-tested principle for interval shapes and dimensions.

When determining dimensions for a series of wall frames, consider the overall look you want to achieve. Do you have standard 8-foot-high walls or custom 9- or 10-footers? Is the room a cavernous great room or a more intimate sitting room? The impact of the look will be determined by the height and orientation of the wall frames and the subsequent rhythm they generate.

Horizontal versus Vertical Orientation

Wall-frame treatments 36 inches or less in height are generally designed using horizontal frames, that is, with their longer sides horizontal. This orientation results in a restrained, moderated look. (In small rooms, narrow, vertical frames may work well.) Install the top edge of the chair rail at 32 or 36 inches for this treatment. You can incorporate a subrail in the design if you place the chair rail at 36 inches but not at 32 inches. At the latter, shorter height, the four elements (chair rail, subrail, wall frames, base molding) would be too crowded for a pleasing appearance.

Wall frames in a vertical orientation are generally more suitable for designs in which the chair rail is at a height of 60 inches. This height is most appropriate for 9-foot or taller walls and may be overwhelming on 8-foot or shorter walls. The tall and narrow shape gives the frames more presence: at these heights, they are especially effective in larger rooms. The main benefits of this orientation are a heightened sense of rhythm and texture as well as an increased emphasis of the frame's vertical properties. Use a tall, substantial base molding to help the design look rooted.

GOLDEN RECTANGLE

ONE TIME-HONORED architectural design principle holds that the ideal size for a rectangle is one in which one side is a little over 1.5 times larger than an adjacent side. (The actual aspect ratio is 1 : 0.635, or 1.575 : 1.) The drawings below illustrate the basis for the principle and a practical application.

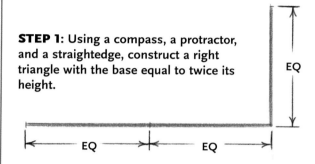

STEP 1: Using a compass, a protractor, and a straightedge, construct a right triangle with the base equal to twice its height.

STEP 2: Strike an arc equal to the height across the hypotenuse.

STEP 3: Strike an arc across the baseline, creating the long side of the Golden Rectangle.

$BC : AB = AB : AC$

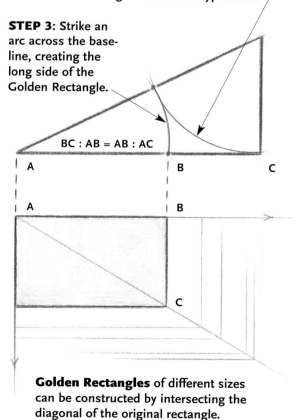

Golden Rectangles of different sizes can be constructed by intersecting the diagonal of the original rectangle.

Horizontal and vertical orientation of wall frames greatly affects the rhythm of the treatment. The wider the wall-frame intervals are, the more time it takes the eye to make the transition from one interval to the next as its field of vision travels across the wall. Therefore, horizontal wall frames impart the feeling of a slower, more passive pace, whereas vertical frames give the impression of a faster, more active pace. The idea of rhythm and pace can be further enhanced by the color scheme you choose when you paint: brighter colors for vertical treatments; more subdued colors for horizontal frames.

Three rectangles, above, a bit more than 1½ times as long as they are tall, follow the Golden rectangle rule, creating a unique sense of serenity and order.

Tall wall frames make a grand statement in the dining room at left, and the vertical orientation and bright color treatment impart a feeling of energy.

Wall Frames

WALL-FRAME LAYOUTS

Measure each wall run in the room, making allowances for doorways, windows, and other openings. Estimate how many ideally sized wall-frame intervals will fit into each run. With your estimate in hand, fill out the worksheet at right for each wall.

Determining Vertical Dimensions

In a room with either an 8- or 9-foot ceiling, the recommended chair-rail height is 32, 36, or 60 inches. Avoid heights between 36 and 60 inches, or the room will appear cut in half horizontally.

To determine the vertical dimension of a wall frame, put your own dimensions into the following steps:

- Width of chair rail $3\frac{1}{2}$"
- Width of margin between bottom
  of chair rail and top of subrail   3"
- Width of subrail   1"
- Width of upper horizontal margin   3"
- Width of lower horizontal margin   3"
- Height of base molding $6\frac{7}{8}$"
- Height of chair rail minus sum
  of vertical dimensions ($36" - 20\frac{3}{8}"$) = $15\frac{5}{8}$"

The result is a wall-frame height of $15\frac{5}{8}$ inches.

Dealing with Outlets and Switches

If a vertical side of a wall frame falls on an electrical outlet, either move the outlet or install an outlet box extension and a spacer frame into which you can butt the side of the wall frame. (See the photo opposite top.)

Turn off the power to the outlet at the circuit breaker; then remove the outlet cover and the outlet's two mounting screws. Pull the outlet out of its box. Slip it through a ¾-inch box extension, and line up the mounting holes among the outlet, box extension, and box. Using mounting screws ¾ inch longer than the original ones, fasten the outlet through the extension.

To make the frame, rip an 18-inch piece of one-by stock down to a width of ¾ inch. From that, assemble a four-sided frame with mitered corners, just long and wide enough to accommodate the box extension. The exterior dimensions of the frame will be slightly larger than those of the outlet cover. Ease the outside edges of the frame with sandpaper. Apply dots of panel adhesive to the back

WALL FRAMES WORKSHEET

USE THE INFORMATION given in this worksheet to determine the width of your wall-frame intervals. First, estimate how many intervals would fit each run of wall yet be equivalent to each other. For example, if you had a 12 × 18-foot room, you might make an estimate based on 36-inch-wide intervals. The 12-foot wall would have four, and the 18-foot wall would have six. (Of course, the actual intervals will end up being smaller, just over 32 inches, because you'll have to account for 3-inch margins. This is merely to arrive at an estimated number of intervals with which to work.) Then make the following calculations for each wall:

Length of wall run   **(L of WR)**
Width of vertical margins   **(W of VM)**
Number of intervals   **(# of I)**
Number of vertical margins   **(# of VM)**
(proposed number of intervals plus one)

1. (W of VM × # of VM)

2. (L of WR - Step 1)

3. (Step 2 ÷ # of I)

4. Total from Step 3 = average interval width

Continue modifying estimates for each wall run until you are able to determine the closest possible sets of interval widths for all the walls in a room.

smart tip

DEPENDING ON THE ROOM, WIDTHS OF WALL FRAMES USUALLY VARY FROM WALL TO WALL. THIS IS OKAY AS LONG AS YOU KEEP VARIATIONS AS SMALL AS POSSIBLE WHILE TRYING TO MAINTAIN DIMENSIONS CLOSE TO THE IDEAL 1:0.635 RATIO OF THE GOLDEN RECTANGLE. OF COURSE, DOORS AND WINDOWS WILL DICTATE EXCEPTIONS TO THIS RULE.

of the frame, and slip the frame over the extended outlet. The outlet's "ears" may extend just a bit past the extension, so you may have to cut shallow grooves in the inside top and bottom of the frame to clear them. Replace the outlet cover.

Then, when it comes time for installation, you'll hold the wall frame in position, mark where it intersects the outlet, cut that section out, and install the frame as usual. Switches present an obstacle only if the chair rail is at 60 inches. In this case, consider moving the switch. Call an electrician if you're not familiar with moving switch boxes and other electrical work.

Electrical outlets may interrupt wall frames. In these cases, install an electrical box extension, make a wooden box to enclose the extension, and allow the side segments to butt the frame.

THE DYNAMICS OF HEIGHT

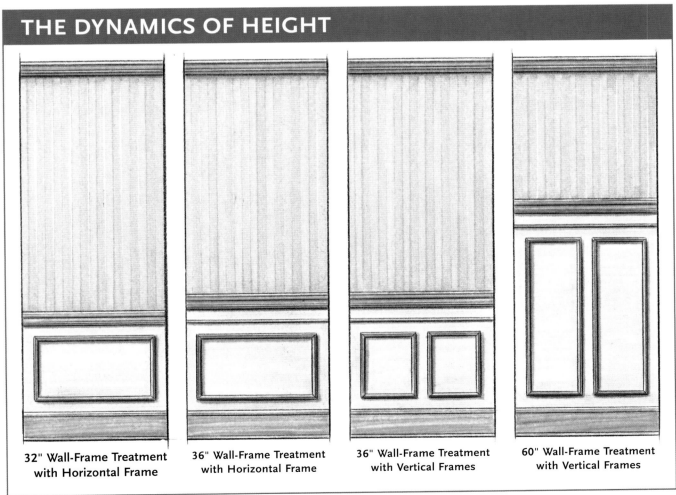

32" Wall-Frame Treatment with Horizontal Frame

36" Wall-Frame Treatment with Horizontal Frame

36" Wall-Frame Treatment with Vertical Frames

60" Wall-Frame Treatment with Vertical Frames

REPEATING WALL FRAMES

As you think about the design of your wall-frame treatment, you might want to make use of a motif (a repeated design) of different frame sizes. A motif in which a wide wall frame is flanked by narrow ones establishes a rhythm of narrow-wide-narrow—an example of bilateral symmetry.

Each section of a wall-frame motif (narrow-wide-narrow) is called a unit. Typically, a short run of wall will contain a single unit, and a longer run of wall might contain two. You'd need an unusually long wall to accommodate three or more units.

The total number of narrow intervals must always exceed the total number of wide intervals by one. In addition, when you use more than one unit on a wall, a narrow interval must always serve as a narrow flank between the unit just ended and the unit just beginning. Therefore, two units of a motif will look like this: narrow-wide-narrow-wide-narrow.

Motifs enhance the dynamics of a wall. To determine the width of both narrow and wide intervals in such a design, see "Motifs Worksheet," right.

MOTIFS WORKSHEET

Length of wall run	**(L of WR)**
Estimated number of units	**(# of U)**
Number of vertical margins	**(# of VM)**
(1 unit: 4 margins, 2 units: 6 margins)	
Number of intervals	**(# of WI, # of NI)**
(wide, narrow)	
Width of vertical margins	**(W of VM)**

1. **(# of VM) × (W of VM)**

2. **(L of WR) – Step 1**

3. **2(# of NI) + 3(# of WI)**

4. **Step 2 ÷ Step 3**

5. **Width of narrow intervals = 2 × Step 4**

6. **Width of wide intervals = 3 × Step 4**

DRAMA FOR YOUR WALLS

WALL FRAMES create an illusion of depth and density because 1) they are three-dimensional and 2) they divide the wall area into smaller, denser segments. The three-dimensional quality of wall frames is fundamentally different from that of the alternative treatment: raised panels. Despite the name, raised panels actually produce a concave-like, or receding, effect whereas wall frames are more convex, protruding outward. In terms of sculpture, concave units create negative space while convex units create positive space. Raised panels, therefore, deliver a uniform sense of volume, mass, and density, while wall frames create a higher level of tension and dramatic interest.

CONCAVE

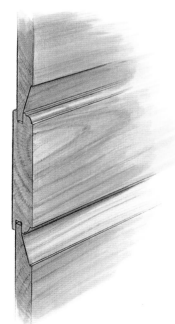

CONVEX

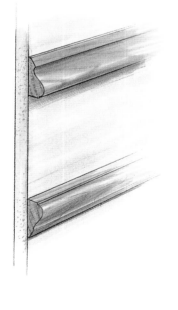

A single motif unit, which comprises a wide interval flanked by narrow intervals, is seen clearly on this wall.

ASSEMBLING AND INSTALLING WALL FRAMES

The most frequently used molding for making wall frames is base cap molding, also called panel molding. Its dimensions are usually $1\frac{1}{16} \times 1\frac{3}{8}$ inches. From online molding sources (which often spell it "moulding") you will find a good variety of base cap molding profiles and sizes, as well as a variety of materials. You may opt for either wood or a synthetic material.

Try to make each wall frame using the same molding stock from the same source (and the same bundle if possible). Otherwise, the molding profiles might not line up exactly.

Use the tips on pages 112–116 to plan the installation. If you will also incorporate wall-spanning vertical pieces, it usually makes sense to do those first, so you can use them to help align the frames. Draw lines on the walls, and stand back to make sure the layout pleases you.

Do not install wall frames piece by piece on the wall. It's quicker and more accurate to assemble wall frames on a table using a jig prior to installation. A jig is simple to make: attach the square corner of a small piece of plywood onto a plywood sheet that is at least 2 × 2 feet. Leave enough room to lay the wall frame pieces on top of the lower piece while you press them against the edges of the smaller plywood piece. Once attached, the frames will be just stable enough to carry and attach to the wall. (See "Installing Wall Frames," pages 118–119.)

The vertical pieces probably will not fall over a stud. Simply power-drive nails into the drywall or plaster.

Wall Frames

INSTALLING WALL FRAMES

project

A power nailer is highly recommended for this job. Nailing small pieces together using hand-driven nails or brads is possible, but it will be tedious, and the pieces will bounce around as you work. Working with a power nailer, you can hold the pieces perfectly aligned with one hand and drive the nail with the other hand. Take the time to carefully plan and map your layout, following the principles on pages 108–116.

TOOLS & MATERIALS

▌ Power drill with screwdriver bit and ¾-inch drywall screws ▌ Pneumatic nailer or hammer and nails ▌ Miter saw ▌ Measuring tape, pencil, and level ▌ Scrap plywood ▌ Caulking gun and panel adhesive ▌ Base cap molding for wall frames

1 Install any chair rails or other long vertical pieces. Using your plan, lay out the positions of the frames on the wall. Where possible, measure off existing pieces or walls, rather than using a level. Put a block the same width as the top margin against a chair rail or baseboard, and scribe a guide line on the wall.

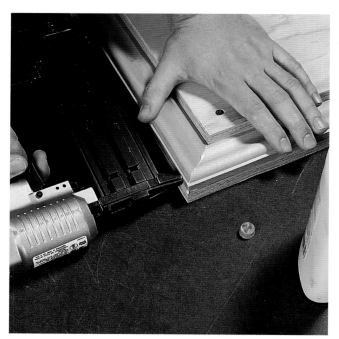

4 Cut two pieces of molding with 45-deg. angles on each end. Press them into place on the jig, and carefully examine the joint. If needed, slightly adjust the angle on your miter saw in order to achieve perfection. Apply glue to the mitered ends, and fasten them using an air nailer or hammer and brads. Keep your fingers clear.

5 Assemble a frame, and check for square. Using the spacer block from Step 1, align the wall frame with the corner marks, and check to make sure it fits. Apply small dots of panel adhesive along the back of the molding, and fasten it in place using 6d nails. Where possible, drive nails into studs.

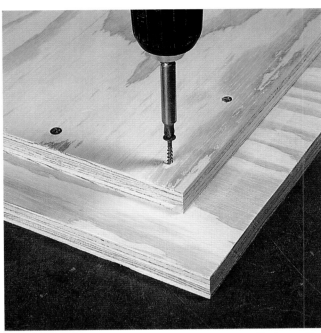

2 Measure and mark the top corners of each wall frame along the guide line. You may choose to mark the wall with all the lines. Or measure down to the baseboard; subtract the width of the desired margin; and cut all the verticals to that dimension.

3 Build a wall-frame jig by attaching a small piece of plywood (with two adjacent factory edges) to a 2 x 2-ft. plywood sheet. On the two sides of the lower piece, leave a space that is as wide as the molding.

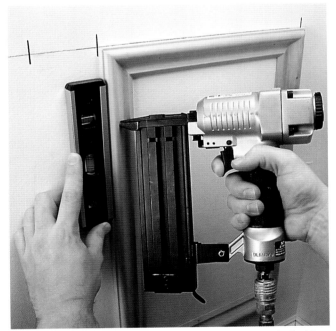

6 With the top edge fastened, plumb the vertical sides of the frame using a level, or measure to see that the frame is parallel with a nearby wall or other molding. Attach using 6d finishing nails. An air gun works best. If you don't have one, and hand-nailing causes too much bouncing, drill pilot holes and drive trimhead screws.

7 Double-check that the bottom of the frame is level, and then fasten it. Fill all holes, and caulk all around the frame.

CASE STUDY: DINING ROOM WITH BAY WINDOW

The floor plan on the opposite page shows the room at right, with a bay window and two doors. Here's how to prepare an area like this for a wall-frame treatment:

Measure the lengths of all wall runs. On the walls with windows, measure only the distance between the outside edges of the side casings of each window. Use the worksheet on page 114 for calculating the widths of wall frames to arrive at a suggested width for the frames on each run of wall surface.

Wall frames and cornices transform this large dining area from a cavernous space (inset) to a warm, inviting room, even without furniture.

Frame Widths

On any given wall, try to make all frames the same width. An exception occurs on a wall with one or more windows. Remember: a wall frame under a window should align with the outside edges of the window's casings.

Make the widths of the wall frames on all the walls as similar as possible. To do this, you may need to adjust the number of frames on each wall.

In this example, you have only three runs of wall, **A, E,** and **H,** on which you can make the frame widths similar to within 3 inches. The lengths of all of the other runs are so short that each can accommodate only a single wall frame.

BEFORE

AFTER

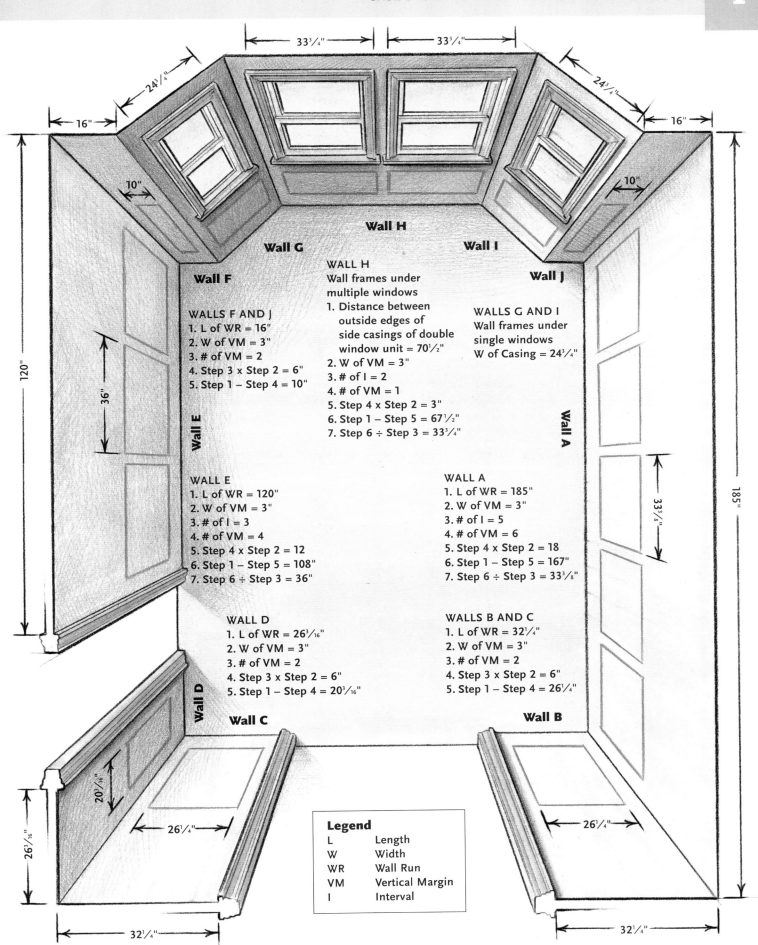

33³/₄" 33³/₄"

24³/₄" 24³/₄"

16" 16"

10" 10"

Wall H

Wall G Wall I

Wall F Wall J

WALL H
Wall frames under
multiple windows
1. Distance between
   outside edges of
   side casings of double
   window unit = 70¹/₂"
2. W of VM = 3"
3. # of I = 2
4. # of VM = 1
5. Step 4 x Step 2 = 3"
6. Step 1 – Step 5 = 67¹/₂"
7. Step 6 ÷ Step 3 = 33³/₄"

WALLS F AND J
1. L of WR = 16"
2. W of VM = 3"
3. # of VM = 2
4. Step 3 x Step 2 = 6"
5. Step 1 – Step 4 = 10"

WALLS G AND I
Wall frames under
single windows
W of Casing = 24³/₄"

120"

36"

Wall E

Wall A

185"

33³/₈"

WALL E
1. L of WR = 120"
2. W of VM = 3"
3. # of I = 3
4. # of VM = 4
5. Step 4 x Step 2 = 12
6. Step 1 – Step 5 = 108"
7. Step 6 ÷ Step 3 = 36"

WALL A
1. L of WR = 185"
2. W of VM = 3"
3. # of I = 5
4. # of VM = 6
5. Step 4 x Step 2 = 18
6. Step 1 – Step 5 = 167"
7. Step 6 ÷ Step 3 = 33³/₈"

WALL D
1. L of WR = 26³/₁₆"
2. W of VM = 3"
3. # of VM = 2
4. Step 3 x Step 2 = 6"
5. Step 1 – Step 4 = 20³/₁₆"

WALLS B AND C
1. L of WR = 32¹/₄"
2. W of VM = 3"
3. # of VM = 2
4. Step 3 x Step 2 = 6"
5. Step 1 – Step 4 = 26¹/₄"

Wall D

Wall C Wall B

20³/₁₆"

26³/₁₆"

26¹/₄" 26¹/₄"

32¹/₄" 32¹/₄"

Legend
L	Length
W	Width
WR	Wall Run
VM	Vertical Margin
I	Interval

STAIRCASE WALL-FRAME ANGLES

Wall frames above a stringer are parallelograms, which have the following characteristics:

• Opposite angles are always equal.
• One pair of opposing angles is always acute, or less than 90 degrees; the other pair is always obtuse, or more than 90 degrees.
• All four angles always add up to 360 degrees.

The first step in building staircase wall frames is to find their acute angle. You can determine the angle by cutting an identical one and measuring it.

Using a protractor. To use a protractor, place a straight board lengthwise on the staircase stringer, and strike a line on the wall along the board's upper edge, parallel with the stringer. Draw a plumb line on the wall intersecting the line you just struck; this is angle **A** below. Place the center of a protractor on the intersection of the plumb line and the line you struck, making the plumb line the baseline for the protractor. (The sloped line will point toward the right.) Determine the acute angle between the sloped line and the plumb line.

To find the obtuse angle, see "Calculating Wall-Frame Angles," below and "Measuring the Angle," opposite.

CALCULATING WALL-FRAME ANGLES

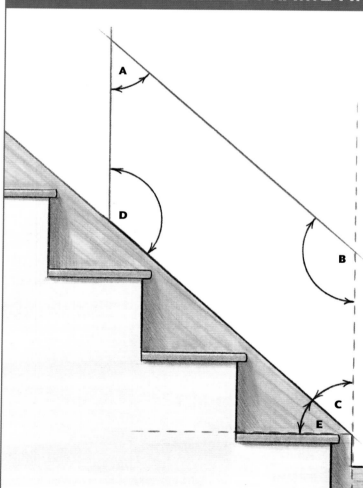

REMEMBER: the sum of the angles of a parallelogram equals 360°, and the opposite angles are equivalent.

Once you know one of the wall-frame acute angles (text above), you can determine the obtuse angles in two steps, as follows:

1. Subtract the sum of the acute angles from 360°.

360 - (Sum of acute angles) = (Sum of obtuse angles)

360 - (A + C) = (B + D)

2. Divide the result from Step 1 by 2 to get the obtuse angle

(Step 1) ÷ 2 = (Obtuse angle)

(B + D) ÷ 2 = B (or D)

To determine the stringer angle (E), subtract from 90° the wall-frame acute angle (A) you measured previously (text above).

90 - (A) = (E)

MEASURING THE ANGLE

Once you've found the acute angle using a protractor, as discussed on the page opposite, you also need to find the obtuse angle. To do this, you can again use the protractor. But because the stringer protrudes from the wall, it's usually easier to use a level and a sliding T-bevel, as shown in these steps.

Once you know the measurements of the two acute angles and the two obtuse angles, divide each by 2 to determine the angles you'll cut into the sides of the miter joint.

TOOLS & MATERIALS

▪ Pry bar ▪ Spirit level and pencil ▪ Sliding T-bevel ▪ Table saw or power miter saw ▪ Scrap one-by lumber

1 Remove all trim from the stringer skirtboard so that you have a flat area from which to work. Scrape away any excess blobs of paint, and make sure the section of stringer you will use for measuring is representative of the whole stringer. Then using a 2-ft. level and pencil, draw a plumb line down to the top of the skirtboard.

2 Align the handle of a sliding T-bevel with the plumb line, and adjust the blade to sit flat on the skirtboard. Make sure the blade rests firmly on wood, and not on a paint blob or other obstruction that could distort the angle. Lock the blade to capture the angle, and use it to mark a scrap piece of one-by lumber.

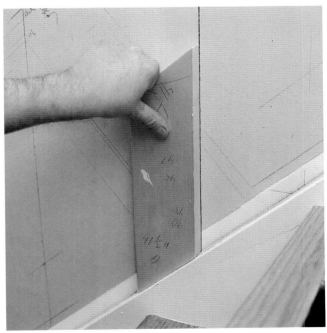

3 Cut the marked one-by using a table saw or power miter saw, and lay it on the skirtboard as shown. If the long edge aligns with the plumb line, the angle is accurate. Measure it using any method you prefer.

SIZING STAIRCASE WALL FRAMES

Before you can lay out the wall frames, determine the overall width of the wall-frame treatment in the stairway, represented by line **AE** in the drawing below. The easiest way to do this is to measure the horizontal distance across the stairway wall from a plumb line at the beginning of the stairs to a plumb line at the end.

Determining Overall Width for Wall Frames

Measure the overall width of a wall-frame treatment in one or two "giant steps." (See the drawing below.) Mark plumb lines where the stringer meets the baseboard at the top and bottom landings. From the top, mark a level line as far out as you can safely reach. Then mark Distance #1 by dropping a plumb line to a stair. Repeat the above procedure to determine Distance #2, and so on, until you reach the end of the stringer. Add your total distances.

OVERALL WALL-FRAME WIDTH

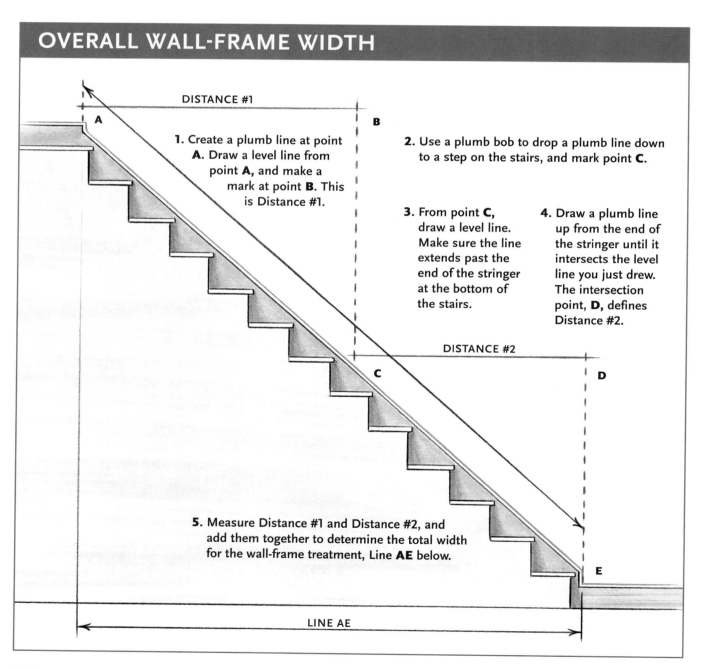

DISTANCE #1

A

B

1. Create a plumb line at point **A**. Draw a level line from point **A**, and make a mark at point **B**. This is Distance #1.

2. Use a plumb bob to drop a plumb line down to a step on the stairs, and mark point **C**.

3. From point **C**, draw a level line. Make sure the line extends past the end of the stringer at the bottom of the stairs.

4. Draw a plumb line up from the end of the stringer until it intersects the level line you just drew. The intersection point, **D**, defines Distance #2.

DISTANCE #2

C

D

5. Measure Distance #1 and Distance #2, and add them together to determine the total width for the wall-frame treatment, Line **AE** below.

E

LINE AE

Determining Individual Widths

Once you know the overall width available for wall frames in the stairway, you must calculate the individual wall-frame widths. The process requires three steps.

1. Decide whether you want vertical or horizontal frames, and approximate the number of wall frames you'll need. (See the photos on page 130 and the drawing below.) Try to match existing wall frames if you have any. If not, use a configuration that will work in nearby parts of the house.

2. Determine the individual horizontal wall-frame widths, following the instructions in the drawing below. If you're trying to match other wall frames, adjust your frame total, if necessary, and repeat the calculations until you end up with a width close to that of the existing frames.

3. Using the horizontal width you just determined, calculate the diagonal width of the wall frames. This is the dimension you need in order to lay out the frames along the length of the stringer.

WALL-FRAME SIZES

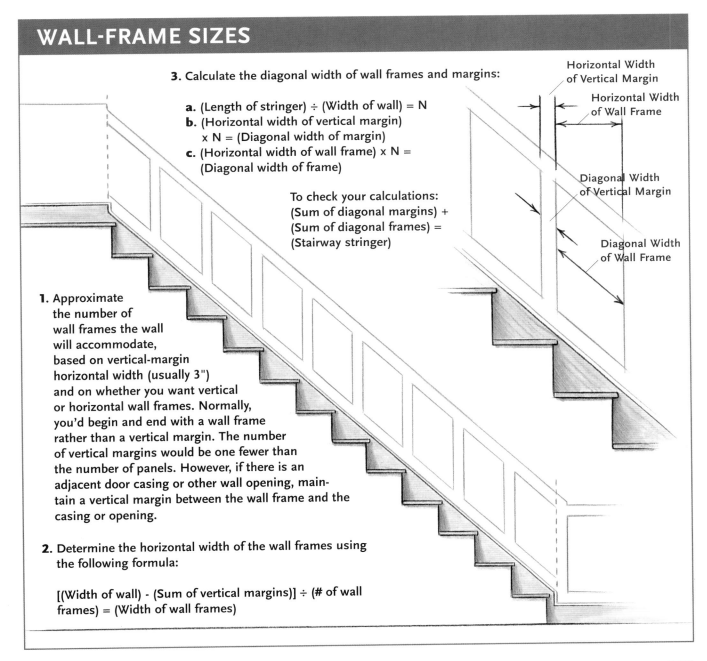

3. Calculate the diagonal width of wall frames and margins:

a. (Length of stringer) ÷ (Width of wall) = N
b. (Horizontal width of vertical margin)
x N = (Diagonal width of margin)
c. (Horizontal width of wall frame) x N =
(Diagonal width of frame)

To check your calculations:
(Sum of diagonal margins) +
(Sum of diagonal frames) =
(Stairway stringer)

Horizontal Width
of Vertical Margin

Horizontal Width
of Wall Frame

Diagonal Width
of Vertical Margin

Diagonal Width
of Wall Frame

1. Approximate the number of wall frames the wall will accommodate, based on vertical-margin horizontal width (usually 3") and on whether you want vertical or horizontal wall frames. Normally, you'd begin and end with a wall frame rather than a vertical margin. The number of vertical margins would be one fewer than the number of panels. However, if there is an adjacent door casing or other wall opening, maintain a vertical margin between the wall frame and the casing or opening.

2. Determine the horizontal width of the wall frames using the following formula:

[(Width of wall) - (Sum of vertical margins)] ÷ (# of wall frames) = (Width of wall frames)

CHAIR-RAIL LOCATION

Situation 1. The base is the same height as the staircase stringer. (See the top illustration at right.) Make the transition of the base cap on the plumb line of the transition between the base trim and stringer.

Join the two lengths of chair rail so that the bottom of the joint falls on the same plumb line as that of the stringer. When you also have a subrail, make its joints align with the chair rail's.

To find the angle between the stairway and landing chair rails, add 90 degrees to the wall-frame acute angle you found earlier. For example, if the acute angle is 48 degrees: **90° + 48° = 138°**. Divide this angle in half to determine the miter cut: **138° ÷ 2 = 69°**

Situation 2. The door casing of an adjacent passageway is close to the beginning of the stringer. Here, you'll have the chair rail run directly into the side of the casing that is closer to the stairs and that runs parallel with the plumb cut of the stringer. (See the drawing at right.) The angle you cut into the end of this chair rail is the same as the wall-frame acute angle.

Situation 3. You plan to install the same wall-frame treatment on both landings, and the stringer is higher than the base. In this case, you have two options:

Option 1. Miter the stairway chair rail directly into the chair rails on the upper and lower landings. The difference in height between the base and the stringer will make the stairway wall frames shorter than the frames on the landings. (See photo on page 128.)

Option 2. Raise the chair rail over the stringers by inserting a transitional 90-degree strip piece between the landing and stairway chair rails, as in the drawing at right. This lets you make the height of the wall frames over the stringer the same as those at both landings. Miter the bottom of the transitional piece into the chair rail with a 45-degree cut. The intersection of the chair rail over the stringer with the top of the transitional piece forms the same angle as the wall-frame obtuse angles. To determine the dimensions of the transitional piece of chair rail, do your layout on paper or directly on the wall where the trim will go.

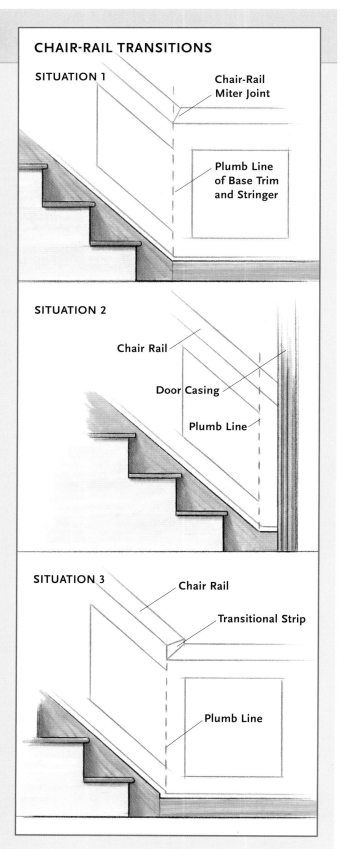

CHAIR-RAIL TRANSITIONS

SITUATION 1

Chair-Rail Miter Joint

Plumb Line of Base Trim and Stringer

SITUATION 2

Chair Rail

Door Casing

Plumb Line

SITUATION 3

Chair Rail

Transitional Strip

Plumb Line

ALTERNATIVE TO CHALK LINES

After you've determined the angle measurements and wall-frame dimensions (pages 122 to 125), find the exact point where the chair rails (and perhaps subrails and base cap moldings) meet. It's usually best to align their joints with that of the stringer and base trim. Exceptions may be dictated by differing heights of components on the landings. You may use chalk lines, as shown opposite. However, where walls are wavy, it may be difficult to snap chalk lines, so a straightedge and T-square can be more accurate.

TOOLS & MATERIALS

■ Power miter saw ■ 48-inch T-square and pencil ■ Spirit level ■ Scrap one-by lumber

1 Use a level to draw a plumb line on the wall. Then make a layout board: cut a piece of one-by with the wall-frame acute angle on one end. Adjust the angle cut until the one-by matches the plumb line. Cut it to chair rail height, and mark other layout heights—such as for subrails—on it.

2 With the straightedge angles precisely adjusted, you can use the layout board to strike plumb lines anywhere on the stairs and to make other layout marks for the wall-frame design.

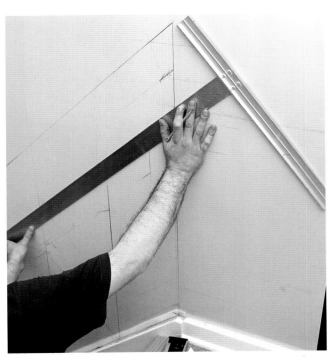

3 Use a 48-in. T-square or a 4-foot level to connect layout marks, and strike long horizontal guidelines exactly parallel with the stairway. Draw all the lines; then stand back and examine the result. Mistakes are easy to make, and it is best to correct them now.

Wall Frames

Laying Out Stairway Chair Rails

To pinpoint the location of the chair rail and its transitions, estimate the height of the chair rails and decide how wide you want the horizontal margins. (The top horizontal margin should match the vertical margins; the bottom margin can be smaller.)

After estimating the height of the chair rail over the stringer and the lower landing, drop plumb lines that will be taller than these estimated heights. One example of this process is shown in "Laying Out a Chair-Rail Transitional Piece," opposite.

Using Spacer Boards to Locate Chair Rails. With all the plumb lines marked on the wall, rip two boards about 18 inches long to serve as margin spacer boards. (See the illustrations on page 131 for similar boards.) One spacer board should equal the planned width of the vertical margins and the top horizontal margin, assuming that the vertical and top margins are the same. Use the other spacer board to lay out the bottoms of the wall frames. Rip the board to a width equal to the planned width of the lower margin plus the width of the base cap molding. (See the drawing opposite for how to use the spacer boards for chair-rail layout.)

Laying Out Landing Chair Rails

Moving to the landing, mark the height of the top and the bottom of the chair rail by measuring up from the floor. Follow the instructions in the illustration opposite for determining the transitional strip piece between the landing chair rail and the stairway chair rail, if it's necessary in your case.

Door casings are sometimes a little too far for the chair rail to butt them; in these cases, the molding has to make a short jog.

The smooth chair-rail transition is possible because the stairway wall frames are smaller than those on the landing.

LAYING OUT A CHAIR-RAIL TRANSITIONAL PIECE

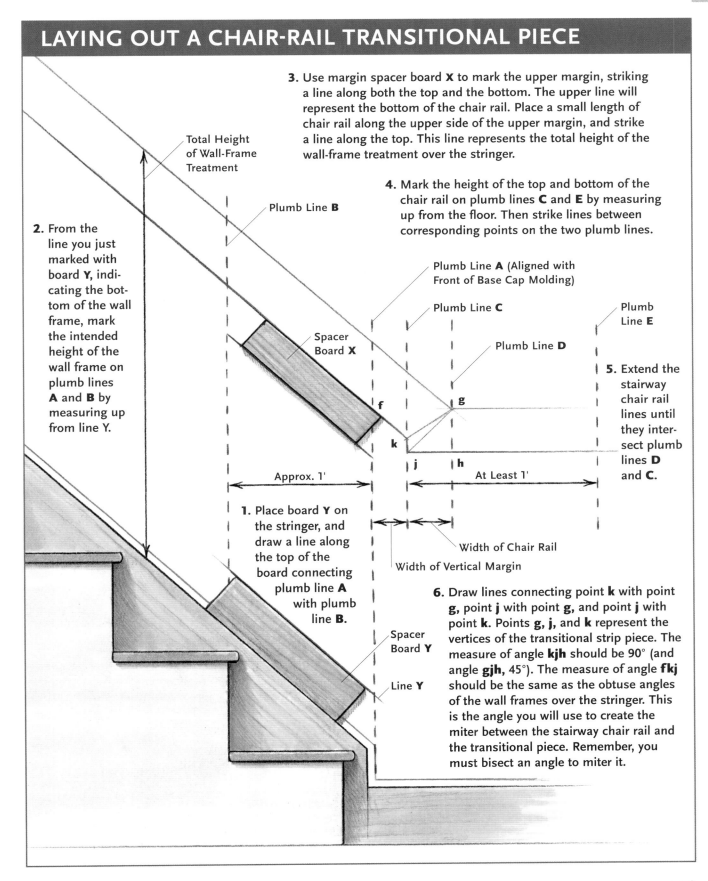

3. Use margin spacer board **X** to mark the upper margin, striking a line along both the top and the bottom. The upper line will represent the bottom of the chair rail. Place a small length of chair rail along the upper side of the upper margin, and strike a line along the top. This line represents the total height of the wall-frame treatment over the stringer.

4. Mark the height of the top and bottom of the chair rail on plumb lines **C** and **E** by measuring up from the floor. Then strike lines between corresponding points on the two plumb lines.

Total Height of Wall-Frame Treatment

Plumb Line **B**

Plumb Line **A** (Aligned with Front of Base Cap Molding)

Plumb Line **C**

Plumb Line **E**

Plumb Line **D**

Spacer Board **X**

2. From the line you just marked with board **Y**, indicating the bottom of the wall frame, mark the intended height of the wall frame on plumb lines **A** and **B** by measuring up from line Y.

5. Extend the stairway chair rail lines until they intersect plumb lines **D** and **C**.

f

g

k

j   h

Approx. 1'

At Least 1'

Width of Chair Rail

Width of Vertical Margin

1. Place board **Y** on the stringer, and draw a line along the top of the board connecting plumb line **A** with plumb line **B**.

Spacer Board **Y**

Line **Y**

6. Draw lines connecting point **k** with point **g**, point **j** with point **g**, and point **j** with point **k**. Points **g, j,** and **k** represent the vertices of the transitional strip piece. The measure of angle **kjh** should be 90° (and angle **gjh,** 45°). The measure of angle **fkj** should be the same as the obtuse angles of the wall frames over the stringer. This is the angle you will use to create the miter between the stairway chair rail and the transitional piece. Remember, you must bisect an angle to miter it.

INSTALLING STAIRCASE FRAMES

You should have already removed the stringer's existing cap molding in your preparation and layout procedures. If you haven't, remove it now because you'll be replacing it with new base cap molding.

Lay out on the wall the transition of the chair rail at the lower landing, as described previously. Then lay out the transition at the upper landing. A number of different situations may exist at the top of the stairs. Deal with them by applying the general design principles of wall-frame treatments and trying to be as consistent as possible. Draw guidelines representing the top of the chair rail on the stairs and on the two landings. Make sure that the stairway's chair rail height is the same at both ends of the stringer. Install the chair rail. (See "Installing a Chair Rail," pages 88–89.)

Now mark the upper and the lower horizontal margins. To do this, place the upper-margin spacer board against the underside of the chair rail. Holding a pencil at the bottom of the spacer board, slide it the full length of the chair rail to strike a pencil guideline. Next, while sliding the lower-margin spacer board along the top of the stringer, run a pencil line to mark the top of the lower margin.

If you're installing a subrail, rip a spacer board to the desired width, and strike a line on the wall. This is the easiest and most accurate way to determine exactly where the subrail should fall. If the transition points for the subrail don't coincide precisely with those for the chair rail, adjust them as necessary. (See the bottom right photo on page 128.)

Next, lay out the vertical margins for the wall frames. The best way to do this is using spacer, or layout, boards. (See "Using Spacer Boards for Vertical Spacing Layout," opposite.)

The installation process for wall-frame treatments in staircases is the same whether the frames are horizontally oriented, left, or vertically oriented, right. You will have chosen the configuration that most closely matches the wall frames in the upper and lower landings or an adjoining room.

USING SPACER BOARDS FOR VERTICAL SPACING LAYOUT

HERE'S AN EASY WAY to simultaneously lay out both the vertical margins and the location of each diagonally shaped wall frame. Again, always start and end with a wall frame and not a margin. The only exception occurs when a stringer butts at one or both ends to a door casing. In this situation, you need to insert a vertical margin to separate the wall frame from the door casing.

To lay out the wall frames and mark the vertical spacing, you will use two template spacer boards.

First Spacer Board. Cut the wall-frame acute angle into both ends of a narrow board that has a length equal to the combined width of one wall frame and one vertical margin. You'll use this to double-check your calculations and simultaneously mark wall-frame widths and margin spacing. Place the spacer lengthwise on the stringer so that its lower end falls precisely on the plumb line marking the start of the first wall frame.

Draw a line along the upper edge of the spacer, and mark the point where the board ends. Move the board up the stringer, as shown, repeating the marking process until the upper end of the board reaches the point at which the last wall frame will fall at the top end of the stringer. This should be precisely where the stringer abuts the baseboard, so the spacer should overshoot the baseboard by the width of the vertical margin. (If the frame mark doesn't fall as shown, you'll need to remeasure or recalculate your spacing to determine why.)

Second Spacer Board. Cut the wall-frame acute angle into the end of another board ripped to the width of the vertical margins. Cut this board about 1 inch shorter than the distance between the chair rail and the stringer. Place the board vertically on the stringer at the lower side of each point you marked with the other spacer board. Holding a spirit level on the spacer board to be sure it is perfectly plumb, strike a line along each side of the board with a pencil, and repeat up the stairs as shown.

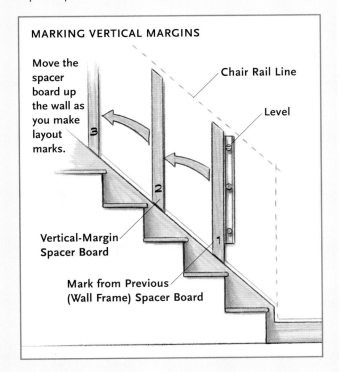

MARKING WALL FRAMES

Move the spacer board up the wall as you make layout marks.

Chair Rail Line

Plumb Line

Wall-Frame Spacer Board

MARKING VERTICAL MARGINS

Move the spacer board up the wall as you make layout marks.

Chair Rail Line

Level

Vertical-Margin Spacer Board

Mark from Previous (Wall Frame) Spacer Board

Wall Frames

Making the Cuts

Odd angles can be a source of confusion because most miter saws do not actually indicate the correct angle. Remember to subtract the angle you want from 90 degrees to find the setting on the saw.

For angles that fall between 45 and 90 degrees, you can just dial in the appropriate angle on the power miter saw and make the cut. To cut steeper angles less than 45 degrees (which will appear as larger than 45 degrees on most miter saw gauges), use a jig, as shown at right.

It's best to cut all vertical sides at one time and then all diagonals. The quickest way to do this is to total up the pieces you'll need (for example, 18 vertical sides and 18 diagonal sides), and crosscut them a few inches long. That way, they'll all be ready for final cutting. Cut and label the angle that is less than 45 degrees on the vertical pieces; then cut and label the angle on the other end of the molding pieces. Repeat the procedure for the diagonal pieces. Now you're ready to assemble the wall frames.

LABELING MOLDING CUTS

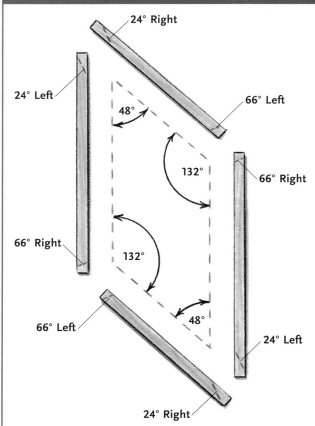

24° Right
24° Left
48°
66° Left
132°
66° Right
66° Right
132°
66° Left
48°
24° Left
24° Right

JIG FOR CUTTING ACUTE ANGLES

Angles more acute than 45 degrees cannot be cut with a miter saw. So build a jig as shown here. The jig attaches to your table saw's miter gauge and uses clamps to keep the molding in place during the cut. You'll have to reassemble the jig and move it to one side or another of the saw blade for a different cut, so make every cut you'll need before adjusting the jig. Calculating odd angles can produce mistakes, so cut and assemble a sample frame, and then test it for fit before cutting the rest.

TOOLS & MATERIALS

- Screwdriver (and/or drill), 1¼-inch screws
- Sliding T-bevel and pencil ▮ Hold-down clamps ▮ Plywood ▮ Scrap one-by lumber

3 Set a sliding T-bevel to the angle you want to cut, and transfer the angle to the saw side of the jig.

1 Cut a piece of plywood about 12 to 14 in. square. Cut a 1x2 to the length of one side, and screw it along one edge.

2 Adjust the table saw's miter gauge to cut at precisely 90 deg.; test-cut a scrap of wood to check for accuracy. Hold the jig, with the 1x2 facing up, against the gauge and flush with the saw blade. Screw the jig to the table saw's miter gauge. (The blade guard is removed for clarity.)

4 Screw a scrap piece of flat trim or one-by lumber to the jig, aligned with the angle guideline.

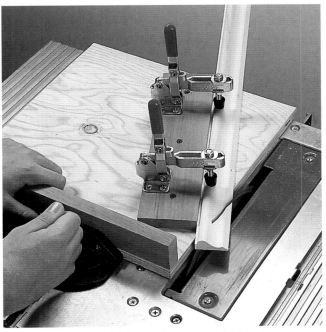

5 Buy special hold-down clamps made for this purpose, and screw them to the angled member of the jig. Position the trim piece so that it slightly overhangs the plywood, and clamp it firmly against the angled member. To cut precisely along a line, hold the piece by hand; start the cut; and then tighten the clamps.

Wall Frames

Assembling the Wall Frames

Carpenter's glue and a pneumatic brad nailer are a good means of assembly, although a pneumatic nailer is by no means required. Glue and nail each corner, first joining each of the vertical lengths to one of the diagonal lengths and then fastening the pairs of sides together. (See "How to Make Wall-Frame Assembly Jigs," below.) Allow the glue to set for about 15 minutes between procedures.

With the frames constructed and the glue set, use the spacer boards shown on page 131 to position the frames, sticking them to the wall with dots of panel adhesive. Then nail them in place with 6d nails.

Base Cap Molding. Now that you've installed the frames, the last procedure is to apply a base cap molding to the top of the stringer and the base trim on the landings. In most cases, the landing base trim ties directly into the front of the vertical edge of the stringer. In this situation, two possibilities may occur:

Base Trim without Cap. If the base trim on the lower landing is shorter than the stringer and does not have a cap or you don't want one, apply base cap molding to the stringer only. Bevel the end of the molding to match the acute angle of the wall frames, and end it at the plumb line of the stringer.

Base Trim with Cap. If the lower-landing base trim has a cap or you're installing one, apply the molding to the taller front vertical edge of the stringer and on up the stairway. (Note: The angle between the landing base cap and the cap on the front edge of the stringer is 90 degrees. The angle formed as the base cap molding makes the transition from the front vertical edge of the stringer onto the diagonal portion of the stringer is identical to the obtuse angle of the wall frame.)

HOW TO MAKE WALL-FRAME ASSEMBLY JIGS

THIS TYPE OF JIG helps you hold the glued, mitered ends of two pieces of molding firmly together while you fasten them. You'll need two such jigs: one for acute angles, as shown, and one for obtuse angles.

Cut two short, narrow wood strips so that they form the acute angle of the wall frames. Cut and join them as precisely as you would the actual moldings; otherwise any error will be carried to all the frames. To form the acute angle, cut the right half of the angle into the end of one strip and the left half of the angle into the other strip.

Position the two strips so that they form a point near the corner of a work surface, such as a sheet of plywood or particleboard that measures about 2 x 2 feet.

Back the point of the strips away from the corner, as shown. This gives you room to drive fasteners into the joints of the wall frames. Join the jig strips by screwing or nailing them to the work surface.

A jig like this, secured to a work surface, allows you to hold the frame pieces for a tight fit and secure nailing.

Fully assembled, installed, and painted, a wall-frame treatment in a staircase makes an elegant traditional statement.

PAINTING WALL FRAMES

The right paint job will enhance your wall-frame treatment. Paint the entire wall treatment with a single color of low-luster paint, or use a tone-on-tone approach to enhance its depth.

Single-Tone Scheme. Using a single color of semi-gloss or eggshell paint gives your walls a Neoclassical, sculpture-like look. Visually, the area inside the wall frames recedes, or seems farthest away, while the moldings seem closer to you, and the rest of the wall floats in between.

Tone-on-Tone Approach. With this approach you again use one color—but in three different shades. This strategy creates subtle differences in the perceived depth of the different elements. The darker the shade of paint on a section of wall, the more it recedes visually, while lighter shades appear to lift elements off the wall's surface. Normally, the deepest shade is used for the area inside the wall frames, a slightly lighter color for the surface outside the frames, and white paint with just a hint of the color for the moldings.

Painting the wall frames using a single-tone color scheme, left, creates a sublte 3-D effect. A multi-tone color scheme, bottom left, accentuates the three-dimensional nature of the treatment. Darker areas recede while lighter areas appear to come toward you.

This tone-on-tone color scheme, opposite, is more subdued than the one at left, but the 3-D illusion is just as successful.

crown and cornice molding

5

PEOPLE ARE OFTEN CONFUSED about the difference between a cornice and crown molding. A cornice is any trimwork that dresses up the junction between wall and ceiling. The most common cornice is *crown molding,* a single piece of trim that sits at an angle between wall and ceiling. Crown molding is available in an endless number of profiles. Most cornices include a crown molding, but many cornice designs feature a combination of molded and flat stock applied to the wall, the ceiling, or both to create an elegant transition between the two planes.

CORNICES AND CROWN MOLDING

The size of the cornice should be in proportion to the ceiling height in the room. On an 8-foot-high ceiling, a very wide molding would be overbearing, so keep the trim from extending more than 4 inches from the ceiling. Rooms with ceilings over 9 feet high need wider and more substantial moldings. In these cases, aim for a cornice that drops at least 5 inches from the ceiling surface.

For the novice, installing cornice trim is more involved than any other trim element. However, if you take the time to understand the basics of cutting the joints and installing these elements, there is no reason to shy away from this job.

Cornice Materials

Like other millwork items, cornice trim is available in a variety of materials.

MDF Cornices. MDF is stiff and straight, without defects, and it machines very easily. It is an excellent choice for paint-grade work since it features a very smooth surface with no discernable grain. It can be drilled, nailed, and glued much like wood, and it accepts both latex and oil–based paints. You can nail it by hand, as long as you first drill pilot holes, but a pneumatic nailer works much better.

Polyurethane Cornices. Resin moldings are available in an increasing number of profiles and sizes, and in rigid and flexible formulations. It is especially valuable for situations where you need to trim a curved wall surface— either concave or convex. Some manufacturers provide flexible resin moldings to match stock profiles that they offer in wood trim, so you can mix materials.

Polystyrene Cornices. This material is manufactured in a variety of simple and intricate profiles that can mimic vintage plaster moldings at a fraction of the cost of the real thing—if you could even find the real thing. Plastic moldings are extremely lightweight, and you can install them easily and quickly without the necessity of cutting fancy joints. Plastic molding is typically available with matching corner and connecting trim blocks that will allow you to limit your cutting to square butt joints. And any gaps can easily be filled with caulk or joint compound.

Wood Cornices. Of course, for stained or clear-finished trim, your most widely available choices are clear pine or red oak moldings. However, while caulk and filler can be used to correct many faults on a paint-grade job, stained molding must be perfect. The fit of each coped and mitered joint must be tight all along the profile, and gaps between a molding and the wall or ceiling must often be scribed rather than filled. The time required will be two or three times that for a paint-grade job.

smart tip

DECORATIVE CORNER BLOCKS

IF THE PROSPECT OF CUTTING ALL THOSE COPED AND MITERED JOINTS IS JUST TOO OVERWHELMING, THERE ARE FITTINGS AVAILABLE THAT ELIMINATE THE NEED FOR THOSE DEMANDING JOINTS. MUCH LIKE PLINTH AND CORNER BLOCKS FOR BASEBOARD, THERE ARE ALSO DECORATIVE BLOCKS THAT CAN BE USED FOR CORNICE TRIM. THESE ELEMENTS ARE AVAILABLE IN WOOD, RESIN, AND POLYSTYRENE, AND IT IS NOT EVEN NECESSARY THAT YOU USE THE SAME MATERIAL FOR THE BLOCKS AS FOR THE REST OF THE TRIM MEMBERS—AS LONG AS EVERYTHING WILL BE PAINTED. BLOCKS ARE AVAILABLE FOR INSIDE AND OUTSIDE CORNERS, AND ALSO AS CONNECTORS TO BE USED IN PLACE OF SCARF JOINTS.

Eliminate cutting by using decorative corner blocks for cornice applications. The pieces shown here are made of resin.

INSTALLING PLASTIC MOLDING

project

Polystyrene or resin moldings are available in a wide variety of styles, including many classic profiles that are made to resemble designs that can only be achieved with built-up wood moldings. If your local home center or lumberyard does not carry them, try online sources. Though they must be cut accurately, these moldings are lightweight and easy to handle. And they will likely cost less than wood or other materials.

TOOLS & MATERIALS

▮ Miter saw ▮ Pencil ▮ Hammer ▮ Nail set
▮ Sanding block ▮ Caulking gun ▮ Drywall
taping knife ▮ Paintbrush ▮ Crown molding
▮ Finishing nails ▮ Joint compound
▮ Construction adhesive ▮ Paint

1 With a section of molding held in place, mark guidelines along the top and bottom (top). In most cases, there is no need to install blocking behind the molding. At an inside corner, make miter cuts rather than coping the joint. After cutting and test-fitting the trim pieces, lay a bead of adhesive just inside your guidelines (bottom).

2 Press the molding into the adhesive, and attach it with finishing nails. Sink the nailheads just below the surface.

3 Use a small taping knife and some joint compound to fill any gaps in the corner and to cover all nailheads (inset). Allow to dry, and then sand smooth. At a contoured inside corner, caulk may work better. Allow to dry, and then apply a coat of primer. When the primer dries, follow with one or two finish coats.

Crown and Cornice Molding

ESTIMATING MATERIALS

Once you have decided on your cornice design, you'll need to measure the job and estimate the materials that you will require. Most types of molding stock are available in lengths from 8 feet to 16 feet in 2-foot increments. Fashioning clean, tight joints is the most difficult and time-consuming part of a cornice installation, so when possible, use a single piece of molding on each wall of a room. This speeds the installation process and lets you concentrate on the corner joints. Of course, there are times when a wall is longer than the available stock, or when it makes strategic sense to splice a length of molding. You should plan to fashion a scarf joint where the two pieces of molding meet. (See "Making Scarf Joints," page 271.)

Overestimate. When a single piece of molding will cover a wall, make sure you purchase stock that is at least 6 inches longer than the wall dimension to give yourself plenty of extra material for making the corner joints. If you must join two or more pieces of molding on a wall, plan on 2 feet of extra stock to make the joints. For each profile in a room, it's a good practice to purchase some extra stock, in case you make a mistake in cutting or need it for possible future repairs—a piece that will cover the longest wall in the room will provide good insurance.

Locating Studs and Ceiling Joists

In most situations, molding applications rely on using nails or screws to fasten the stock to the wall studs and top plates, and ceiling joists—the framing members that provide the basic structure of the building. You can usually expect to find wall studs spaced every 16 inches around a room, as well as at inside and outside corners. However, ceiling joists typically run in one direction only, and for those walls parallel with the joists, it is unlikely that they will fall just where you need them for fastening the ceiling trim. Even for those walls where joists are available, there are often situations where you need nailing where there is no joist, and then you will need to provide blocking. (See "Blocking," page 144.) So, in anticipation of the installation, spend some time locating these framing members, and also formulate a plan for fastening where they are missing or where a better means of attachment is prudent. Of course, if you intend to install a single bed molding as your cornice trim, it is small enough so that you can nail it exclusively to the wall plates, and these can be found at any spot along the room perimeter. A flat, band, or frieze molding can also be fastened solely to the wall framing and, once installed, can serve as a nailing base for subsequent layers of molding—at least on the wall side. A similar band can also be applied to the ceiling, fastening it to ceiling joists when possible and using hollow-wall fasteners when necessary. (See "Hollow-Wall Anchors," page 145.)

To locate the studs and joists, run an electronic stud finder over the walls and ceiling close to the corners where they meet. If you are working in an unfinished room, place a light pencil mark on the surfaces to indicate the centers of framing members. If the walls have been painted or are covered with wallpaper, run a strip of painter's blue masking tape down the walls and ceiling, just beyond the outer extremes of the cornice profile. You can then use a soft pencil or marker to indicate the stud and joist centers on the tape.

NAILING FLAT MOLDING

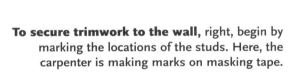

- 8d Finishing Nail
- Chair Rail Molding
- 6d Finishing Nail
- 3¼" Baseboard Molding
- ½" Drywall

2-By Top Plates

To secure trimwork to the wall, right, begin by marking the locations of the studs. Here, the carpenter is making marks on masking tape.

Continuous blocking, below, ensures a firm surface for fastening trimwork.

BLOCKING

CEILING MOLDING must be firmly fastened to withstand the stresses caused by changes in humidity and the inevitable settling and movement that occur in any home. For moldings that span the joint between walls and ceiling, this normally means nails are driven at both the top and bottom. The bottom edge of most profiles can be nailed to either the wall framing or a frieze board and, sometimes, the top edge can be nailed to the ceiling joists. However, when good nailing is absent, the best solution is to provide solid blocking that can accept the nails at the ceiling level. Many carpenters install blocking along all walls, so that they always have a place to fasten the molding

The Spring Angle. The angle at which cornice molding rests against the ceiling and the wall is called the spring angle. This is given with two numbers: the first indicates the angle to the ceiling, and the second number is the angle to the wall. The most common spring angles are 45/45 and 52/38. Learn your molding's spring angle before you cut the blocking.

Blocking Materials. Blocking is most commonly cut from 2x4 or 2x6. The 1½-inch thickness provides a good nailing surface to hold even heavy molding in place. Each cornice profile requires its own type and size of blocking. For the particular projects described in this book, blocking is always specified where it is necessary.

Sizing Blocking. To determine the size of the blocking for a single, sprung molding, draw a cross-section of your molding profile as it will be installed, and measure the distance from the wall to the back side of the molding at the ceiling line. Subtract ⅛ to ¼ inch from that dimension, and rip the backing stock to size at the appropriate spring angle for your molding. By sizing the blocking to leave a space behind the molding, you will allow yourself a bit of adjustment room to adjust the stock up and down to accommodate small variations in the wall and ceiling surfaces.

For more complex cornice designs, draw the cross-section of the entire profile; then you can determine the appropriate type of blocking. Sometimes an L-shaped assembly made from common pine or construction-grade plywood is appropriate, and other times two or three individual pieces are necessary.

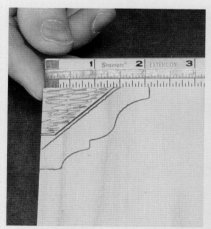

1 Determine the size of blocking by drawing a cross-section of the molding and measuring from the wall line to the back side of the molding at the ceiling line. Subtract ⅛ in. from that dimension, and rip blocking stock to width at the appropriate spring angle.

2 Adjust the table-saw bevel angle to match the spring angle of your molding; then rip blocking strips from 2x4 stock. Always use a push stick at the end of the cut so that your hands stay far from the blade. (Guard removed for clarity.)

3 Screw blocking strips to the top plate of the wall framing. Drill and countersink pilot holes for screws so that the heads do not protrude beyond the angled face of the strips.

HOLLOW-WALL ANCHORS

HOLLOW-WALL ANCHORS can provide a means of firmly fastening blocking to the ceiling when there are no conveniently located ceiling joists. For many years, toggle and molly bolts were considered the standard anchors for plaster or drywall surfaces. While molly and toggle bolts are considered to be the strongest type of anchors, they can be somewhat awkward to install and are hard to position accurately. Because cornice molding is not a structural or functional element, it is not critical that the blocking be able to support a great amount of weight.

An excellent alternative is to use a spiral anchor.

These anchors, commonly sold under a variety of names, are available in both metal and nylon, but the metal variety is considerably stronger and more reliable. To use a spiral anchor, drill a small pilot hole to indicate the desired location, and then use a hand screwdriver to turn the anchor into the drywall until the wide head is flat against the surface. You can then drive a screw through the blocking into the anchor. For an even stronger installation, you can also spread some construction adhesive on the upper surface of the blocking to bond with the drywall.

1 Hold a piece of blocking in place, and drill pilot holes through the blocking to mark the location of anchors in the ceiling.

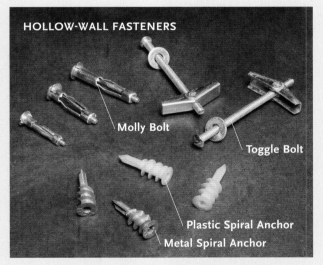

HOLLOW-WALL FASTENERS

Molly Bolt

Toggle Bolt

Plastic Spiral Anchor

Metal Spiral Anchor

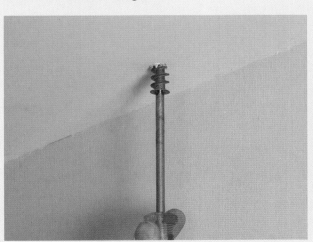

2 Install spiral anchors using a screwdriver. Turn the anchors until the head sits flush with the drywall surface.

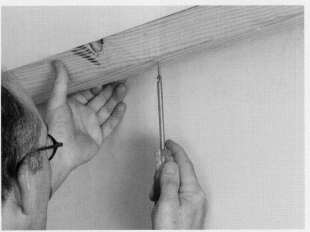

3 Drive screws through the blocking so that they engage the spiral anchors in the ceiling.

CUTTING SPRUNG MOLDINGS WITH A SIMPLE MITER SAW

MOLDINGS THAT SIT at an angle between the wall and ceiling must be cut with a compound miter, which includes both a bevel and miter. With a simple miter saw, you can accomplish these cuts by holding the molding in the saw at its appropriate spring angle; you need only set the miter angle because the bevel angle will then automatically set itself. To hold the molding in the right position, cut it upside down in the saw—the saw fence represents the wall, and the saw table represents the ceiling.

1 Create a positioning jig by cutting a straight strip as long as the miter saw table. Position the strip so that it supports the molding against the fence at the proper spring angle.

2 Screw the support strip to the saw table. Keep the screws outside the range of the saw blade (top). Make cuts at 45 deg. left and right to cut through the strip; remove the portion between the cuts (bottom).

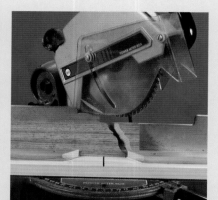

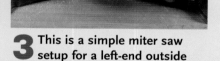

3 This is a simple miter saw setup for a left-end outside miter (right-hand side of the joint).

4 This is a simple miter saw setup for a right-end outside miter (left-hand side of the joint).

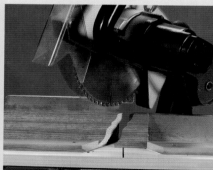

5 This is a simple miter saw setup for a left-end inside miter or coped joint (right-hand side of the joint).

6 This is a simple miter saw setup for a right-end inside miter or coped joint (left-hand side of the joint).

CUTTING SPRUNG MOLDINGS WITH A SLIDING COMPOUND MITER SAW

Crown and Cornice Molding

A SLIDING COMPOUND MITER saw can cut a compound miter while you hold the stock flat on the table. You'll need to set both a miter angle and a bevel angle. These adjustments are controlled independently, and many saws have detents (preset stops) for the most common angle combinations. Because the molding is laid flat instead of at an angle, the angle settings are different from those used for a simple miter saw. Refer to a chart (like the one on pages 148–149) to find the correct settings. If your saw tilts only to one side for bevel cuts, you must flip the molding around to obtain the correct angle combinations.

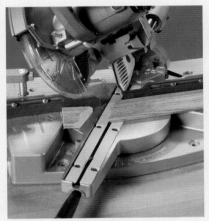

1 This is a sliding compound miter saw setup for a right-end outside miter (left-hand side of the joint). The bottom edge of the molding is held against the saw fence.

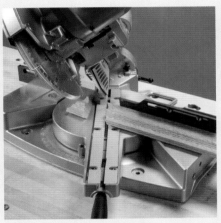

2 This is a sliding compound miter saw setup for a left-end outside miter (right-hand side of the joint). The top edge of the molding is held against the saw fence.

3 This is a sliding compound miter saw setup for a right-end inside miter or coped joint (left-hand side of the joint). The top edge of the molding is held against the saw fence.

4 This is a sliding compound miter saw setup for a left-end inside miter or coped joint (right-hand side of the joint). The bottom edge of the molding is held against the saw fence.

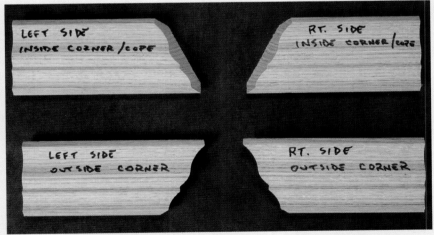

Molding samples illustrate the four basic miter cuts. It is a good idea to make samples like these and keep them for reference when adjusting the saw. It's easy to get confused as to the orientation of the molding, especially when using a sliding compound miter saw.

Crown and Cornice Molding

COMPOUND MITER SAW SETTINGS FOR CUTTING CROWN MOLDING

Corner Angle	52/38 Spring Angle		45/45 Spring Angle		Corner Angle	52/38 Spring Angle		45/45 Spring Angle	
	Miter Angle	Bevel Angle	Miter Angle	Bevel Angle		Miter Angle	Bevel Angle	Miter Angle	Bevel Angle
179°	0.31	0.39	0.35	0.35	134°	14.7	17.9	16.7	16
178°	0.62	0.79	0.71	0.71	133°	15	18.3	17.1	16.4
177°	0.92	1.18	1.06	1.06	132°	15.3	18.7	17.5	16.7
176°	1.23	1.58	1.06	1.06	131°	15.7	19.1	17.9	17.1
175°	1.54	1.97	1.41	1.41	130°	16	19.5	18.3	17.4
174°	1.85	2.36	2.12	2.12	129°	16.4	19.8	18.6	17.7
173°	2.15	2.75	2.48	2.47	128°	16.7	20.2	19	18.1
172°	2.5	3.2	2.8	2.8	127°	17.1	29.6	19.4	18.4
171°	2.8	3.5	3.2	3.2	126°	17.4	21	19.8	18.7
170°	3.1	3.9	3.5	3.5	125°	17.8	21.3	20.2	19.1
169°	3.4	4.3	3.9	3.9	124°	18.1	21.7	20.6	19.4
168°	3.7	4.7	4.3	4.2	123°	18.5	22.1	21	19.7
167°	4	5.1	4.6	4.6	122°	18.8	22.5	21.4	20.1
166°	4.3	5.6	5	4.9	121°	19.2	22.8	21.8	20.4
165°	4.6	5.9	5.3	5.3	120°	19.6	23.2	22.2	20.7
164°	5	6.3	5.7	5.7	119°	19.9	23.6	22.6	21
163°	5.3	6.7	6	6	118°	20.3	23.9	23	21.4
162°	5.8	7.1	6.4	6.4	117°	20.7	24.3	23.4	21.7
161°	5.9	7.5	6.6	6.7	116°	21	24.7	23.8	22
160°	6.2	7.9	7.1	7.1	115°	21.4	25.1	24.3	22.3
159°	6.5	8.3	7.5	7.4	114°	21.8	25.4	24.7	22.7
158°	6.8	8.7	7.8	7.8	113°	22.2	25.8	25.1	23
157°	7.1	9	8.2	8.1	112°	22.6	26.2	25.9	23.6
156°	7.5	9.4	8.6	8.5	111°	22.9	26.5	25.9	23.6
155°	7.8	9.8	8.9	8.8	110°	23.3	26.9	26.3	23.9
154°	8.1	10.2	9.3	9.2	109°	23.7	27.2	26.8	24.2
153°	8.4	10.6	9.6	9.5	108°	24.1	27.6	27.2	24.6
152°	8.7	11	10	9.9	107°	24.5	28	27.6	24.9
151°	9.1	11.4	10.4	10.2	106°	24.9	28.3	28.1	25.2
150°	9.4	11.8	10.7	10.6	105°	25.3	28.7	28.5	25.5
149°	9.7	12.2	11.1	10.9	104°	25.7	29	28.9	25.8
148°	10	12.5	11.5	11.2	103°	26.1	29.4	29.4	26.1
147°	10.3	12.9	11.8	11.6	102°	26.5	29.7	29.8	26.4
146°	10.7	13.3	12.2	11.9	101°	26.9	30.1	30.2	26.7
145°	11	12.7	12.6	12.3	100°	27.3	30.4	30.7	27
144°	11.3	14.1	12.9	12.6	99°	27.7	30.8	31.1	37.3
143°	11.6	14.5	13.3	12.9	98°	28.2	31.1	31.6	27.6
142°	12	14.9	13.7	13.3	97°	28.6	31.5	32	27.9
141°	12.3	15.3	14.1	13.7	96°	29	31.8	32.5	28.2
140°	12.6	15.6	14.4	14	95°	29.4	32.2	32.9	28.5
139°	13	16	14.8	14.3	94°	29.9	32.5	33.4	28.8
138°	13.3	16.4	15.2	14.7	93°	30.3	32.9	33.9	29.1
137°	13.6	16.8	15.4	15	92°	30.7	33.2	34.3	29.4
136°	14	17.2	15.9	15.4	91°	31.2	33.5	34.8	29.7
135°	14.3	17.6	16.3	15.7	90°	31.6	33.9	35.3	30

To set the miter angle, adjust the miter gauge on the saw. The bevel angle is set by adjusting the tilt of the saw blade.

Corner Angle	52/38 Spring Angle		45/45 Spring Angle		Corner Angle	52/38 Spring Angle		45/45 Spring Angle	
	Miter Angle	Bevel Angle	Miter Angle	Bevel Angle		Miter Angle	Bevel Angle	Miter Angle	Bevel Angle
89°	32.1	34.2	35.7	30.3	44°	56.7	46.9	60.3	41
88°	32.5	34.5	36.2	30.6	43°	57.4	47.2	60.9	41.1
87°	33	34.9	36.7	30.9	42°	58.1	47.4	61.5	41.3
86°	33.4	35.2	37.2	31.1	41°	58.7	47.6	62.1	41.5
85°	33.9	35.5	37.7	31.4	40°	59.4	47.8	62.8	41.6
84°	34.4	35.9	38.1	31.7	39°	60.1	48	63.4	41.8
83°	34.8	36.2	38.6	32	38°	60.8	48.2	64	42
82°	35.3	36.5	39.1	32.3	37°	61.5	48.4	64.7	42.1
81°	35.8	36.8	39.6	32.5	36°	62.2	48.5	65.3	42.3
80°	36.3	37.1	40.1	32.8	35°	62.9	48.7	66	42.4
79°	36.8	37.5	40.6	33.1	34°	63.6	48.9	66.6	42.5
78°	37.2	37.8	41.1	33.3	33°	64.3	49.1	67.3	42.7
77°	37.7	38.1	41.6	33.6	32°	65	49.2	67.9	42.8
76°	38.2	38.4	42.2	33.9	31°	65.8	49.4	68.6	43
75°	38.7	38.7	42.7	34.1	30°	66.5	49.6	69.2	43.1
74°	39.3	39	43.2	34.4	29°	67.2	49.7	69.9	43.2
73°	39.8	39.3	43.7	34.6	28°	68	49.9	70.6	43.3
72°	40.3	39.6	44.2	34.9	27°	68.7	50	71.2	43.4
71°	40.8	39.9	44.8	35.2	26°	69.4	50.2	71.9	43.5
70°	41.3	40.2	45.3	35.4	25°	70.2	50.3	72.6	43.7
69°	41.6	40.5	45.8	35.6	24°	71	50.4	73.3	43.8
68°	42.4	40.8	46.4	35.9	23°	71.7	50.6	73.9	43.9
67°	42.9	41.1	46.9	36.1	22°	72.5	50.7	74.6	44
66°	43.5	41.4	47.4	36.4	21°	73.2	50.8	75.3	44
65°	44	41.7	48	36.6	20°	74	50.9	76	44.1
64°	44.6	41.9	48.5	36.8	19°	74.8	51	76.7	44.2
63°	45.1	42.2	49.1	37.1	18°	75.6	51.1	77.4	44.3
62°	45.7	42.5	49.6	37.3	17°	76.4	51.2	78.1	44.4
61°	46.3	42.8	50.2	37.5	16°	77.1	51.3	78.8	44.4
60°	46.8	43	50.8	37.8	15°	77.9	51.4	79.5	44.5
59°	47.4	43.3	51.3	38	14°	78.7	51.5	80.1	44.6
58°	48	43.6	51.9	38.2	13°	79.5	51.5	80.8	44.6
57°	48.6	43.8	52.5	38.4	12°	80.3	51.6	81.5	44.7
56°	49.2	44.1	53.1	38.6	11°	81.1	51.7	82.9	44.8
55°	49.8	44.3	53.6	38.8	10°	81.9	51.7	82.9	44.8
54°	50.4	44.6	54.2	39.1	9°	82.7	51.8	83.6	44.8
53°	51	44.8	54.8	39.3	8°	83.5	51.8	84.4	44.9
52°	51.6	45.1	55.4	39.5	7°	84.3	51.9	85.1	44.9
51°	52.2	45.3	56	39.7	6°	85.1	51.9	85.8	44.9
50°	52.9	45.6	56.6	39.9	5°	85.9	51.9	86.5	44.9
49°	53.5	45.8	57.2	40	4°	86.8	52	87.2	45
48°	54.1	46	57.8	40.2	3°	87.6	52	87.9	45
47°	54.8	46.3	58.4	40.4	2°	88.4	52	88.6	45
46°	55.4	46.5	59	40.6	1°	89.2	52	89.3	45
45°	56.1	46.7	59.6	40.8	0°	90	52	90	45

OUTSIDE CORNER JOINTS

AS A GENERAL RULE, moldings that meet at outside corners must be cut to form a miter joint. For flat stock such as friezes, chair rail, and picture molding, these miter joints are relatively simple: pieces that are mounted to the wall are cut with a bevel cut (through the thickness of the stock) and those that mount to the ceiling are cut with a flat miter (across the width of

the stock). In both cases, the angle cut on each piece is equal to one-half of the total corner angle. For example, if two walls meet at a corner that measures exactly 90 degrees, each piece of molding will be cut at a 45-degree angle; if the corner is 86 degrees, each side must be cut at a 43-degree angle.

To fashion a tight miter joint, it is important that you know the exact angle of the corner. Even though a corner is supposed to be 90 degrees, there are plenty of reasons why this is often not the case.

For the most direct approach, use an angle measuring gauge to get a reading of the corner angle. Then simply divide the total angle in half for your miter setting. As an alternative, you can cut a 45-degree miter on the ends of two scrap boards and hold them in place to test if they fit tightly together. If the joint is open at the outside edge, the angle is greater then 90 degrees; if it is open along the wall, it is less then 90 degrees. In either case, re-cut the angles on both of the scrap pieces and test again. With a little trial and error, you will arrive at the proper miter setting. Remember that both sides of the miter must be cut at exactly the same angle for a proper joint. (See "Installing Outside Corners," page 159.)

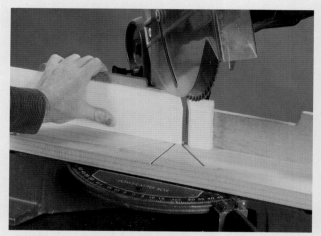

1 To make a bevel cut on a flat molding, hold the molding against the fence and rotate the saw to the desired bevel angle.

2 To make a miter cut on a flat molding, hold the molding flat on the saw table.

3 The most direct method of determining the angle of a corner is to use an angle gauge. Hold the legs of the gauge against the walls and read the angle. The miter angle is one-half of the total measurement.

Crown and Cornice Molding

CALCULATING THE RIGHT ANGLE

YOU CAN USE GEOMETRY to determine the proper miter angle. Begin by taking a reading of the angle using an adjustable bevel gauge. Transfer the angle to a piece of scrap cardboard or plywood. Then use a set of dividers to mark out equal distances from the apex of the angle along each leg. Place the dividers on each of those marks and, using the same distance setting, make two intersecting arcs in the center of the angle. Draw a line from the apex of the angle through the intersecting point to indicate an angle that is one half of the original. Use an angle gauge to measure the resulting angle.

1 To bisect the angle of an outside corner, use an adjustable sliding bevel gauge to copy the angle.

2 Transfer the corner angle to a piece of scrap plywood or cardboard.

3 Use a set of dividers to mark out equal distances from the apex of the angle down each leg.

4 Place the dividers on each of the previously established marks, and using the same setting, scribe two intersecting arcs in the center of the angle.

5 Draw a line that connects the apex of the angle with the intersection of the two arcs. This line divides the original angle into two equal parts.

6 Use an angle-measuring gauge to determine the desired miter-saw setting.

INSIDE CORNER JOINTS

If you are planning to install only a flat band around the room, the inside joints can be simple butt joints. However, once your molding choices get more complex, the joinery also gets more involved. There are some molding materials, such as plaster, and a variety of synthetic cast options that are designed to be joined with miters at the inside corner joints. However, if you plan to install either wood or MDF moldings, arguably the most common materials, the best treatment for inside corners involves cutting a coped joint. A coped joint is one in which one of the intersecting pieces of molding is cut so that its end matches the face profile of the opposite corner piece. Although the process of cutting this type of joint requires more time, effort, and experience than a simple inside miter, the advantages for a quality installation are more than sufficient to justify the effort.

Coped Joints

If you have no experience in fashioning coped joints, it's a good idea for you to practice the basic techniques on some scrap molding stock before attempting your first cornice project. While not particularly difficult, the steps involved are also not exactly intuitive, and manipulating a coping saw can be frustrating at first. Although there are some basic rules that guide the coping process, it is important to remember that a certain amount of trial and error and adjustment are an expected part of most trim carpentry, and these joints will certainly illustrate that principle. In addition to your tools, bring a good bit of patience to the job to ensure the best results and a satisfying experience.

Because a coped profile is cut on the second piece of molding in any inside corner, begin by installing the first piece of stock. For purposes of this example, we'll assume that this molding has a square cut at either end and will fit between two walls. For the coped joint, measure the length of the next wall, and add 4 to 6 inches to that measurement. Begin the coped joint by cutting an open 45-degree miter joint on the end of your molding stock that will abut the already installed piece. This is the same angle you would cut for an inside miter joint, and the cut will clearly expose the molding profile that you need to follow. To make it easier to follow the molding shape, it's a good idea to run the side of a pencil lead over the edge of the cut to outline the profile.

The Bottom Edge. At this point, you have two options as to how to approach the intersection of the moldings at their bottom edges: they can be either mitered or treated with a simple butt joint. (See "Dealing with the Bottom Edges of Sprung Molding," opposite.) There are as many opinions on this issue as carpenters, and either method can yield perfectly satisfactory results. The more conservative tactic is to use a butt joint at the bottom edge. So, assuming you will cut a butt joint, use a small square to mark across the bottom edge of the molding for a straight cut. Use a small dovetail saw or backsaw to make the cut. It's always a good idea to clamp the molding stock to a worktable to keep it from moving around.

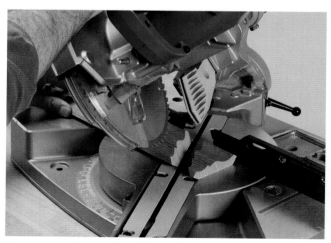

Prepare a piece of molding for a coped joint by cutting an open miter cut to expose the profile of the molding. The molding should be cut at the same angle that you would use for an inside miter joint in the same corner.

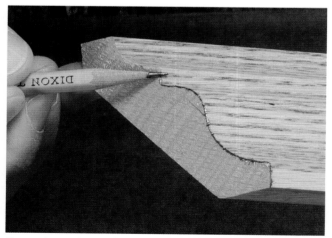

Sometimes it can be difficult to clearly see the cut line for a coped joint, so use the side of a pencil to outline the edge of the molding where it meets the open miter.

DEALING WITH THE BOTTOM EDGES OF SPRUNG MOLDING

WHEN YOU CUT A COPED PROFILE on a piece of sprung molding, first decide how to treat the intersection of the two pieces along their bottom edges. If you strictly follow the profile as it is exposed by the open miter cut, you will end up with a miter joint along the edge. This creates an elegant-looking joint, as the line of the intersecting profiles is continuous. However, you pay a price: the thin, mitered sliver of stock at the bottom edge of the coped joint is extremely fragile and difficult to cut, and is easily damaged. In addition, this type of joint requires that you cut a shallow mortise in the adjacent molding to house the overlapping miter

For an equally acceptable and safer approach, make a square cut at the bottom edge of the molding. This technique simplifies the coped profile and eliminates the need to mortise the adjoining molding.

Mitered Bottom Edge. To accommodate the thin angled return piece, you must cut a shallow mortise in the bottom edge of the mating molding. Use a sharp chisel to pare away the required stock. (Shown upside down.)

Square-Cut Bottom Edge. This is a detail of a coped inside corner joint with a square-cut bottom edge joint. (Shown upside down.)

HOW TO CUT A SQUARE-CUT BOTTOM EDGE

1 At the bottom edge of a sprung molding, it is often best to make a square cut rather than follow the angled profile exposed by the open miter. This will allow the molding to butt cleanly to the adjacent profile. Use a square to mark the cut at the molding's bottom edge.

2 Begin the coped joint by making the short square cut at the bottom edge of the molding. A dovetail saw is the perfect tool for this type of cut—it is small and easy to control.

3 This is a detail of an assembled inside corner joint with a square-cut bottom edge joint. (Shown upside down.)

Crown and Cornice Molding

CUTTING A COPED JOINT

WITH THE OPEN MITER CUT, you can begin to cut along the exposed profile line. Once again, this is a process, and it will take practice to develop a feel for the tool and for how to approach the joint in a logical way. Most carpenters prefer to attach the coping saw blade so it cuts on the pull stroke. Because coping blades are, by necessity, quite thin, this orientation allows you to cut with minimum force, making it less likely that the blade will bind or break. It also permits you to clearly view the cut line and eliminates the risk of chipping out the molding on its face side. The action of the saw should be quite easy; if you find

yourself forcing the blade, you are most likely twisting it. The teeth of a coping blade are set to create a generous kerf, providing ample room for adjustment and change of direction. Position the saw so the angle of the cut is sharper than 90 degrees; the cut should remove more stock from the back side of the molding than from the front. This technique is called back-cutting, and it will

smart tip

YOU CAN CUT THE MOLDING $\frac{1}{16}$ TO $\frac{1}{8}$ INCH LONG (DEPENDING ON ITS TOTAL LENGTH) AND SPRING IT INTO POSITION SO THAT ITS COPED END ACTUALLY DIGS INTO THE ADJACENT PIECE. THIS TECHNIQUE FORMS A TIGHT JOINT, WITH THE ADDED ADVANTAGE OF CAUSING ANY SMALL GAPS IN THE JOINT TO DISAPPEAR.

1 Hold the coping saw at an angle greater than 90 deg. to start cutting the coped profile. Keep the saw blade about $\frac{1}{32}$ in. to the waste side of the layout line.

4 Use a rasp to further refine the shape of the coped joint.

5 It is often necessary to use a variety of abrasive tools to finish shaping a coped profile. Here a round Surform tool is used on the concave portion of the joint.

allow the coped profile to meet the adjacent piece along a sharp edge with no interference. Back-cutting also makes it easier to adjust the profile, as you won't need to remove much stock to alter the shape. Cornice molding shapes can be very complex, and it is usually not possible to cut the entire profile from one direction. Cut as far as you can along the profile, keeping the kerf approximately $\frac{1}{32}$ inch to the waste side of the line. When you reach an impasse, remove the blade from the kerf and make a relief cut from the outside edge to remove some of the stock. Then pro-

ceed with the cut, working from both directions whenever necessary.

As you gain skill with the coping saw, you will find that you can follow the profile line quite closely; however, this is not a precision tool, and you should not expect to cut a perfectly finished joint. Instead, use a selection of rasps and knives to refine the profile.

Hold the molding in place, and check the fit against its mating piece. Use a sharp pencil to mark any areas that need adjustment, and make the alterations.

2 Make relief cuts as necessary to keep the saw blade from binding in the cut. It is sometimes necessary to make several relief cuts, especially for more complex molding profiles.

3 Continue the coped cut after removing some of the waste to free the saw blade. It is perfectly fine to cut from either edge of the molding; just remember to keep the blade angled to create a back-cut.

6 This is a finished coped profile.

7 This is the back side of a coped joint. Notice the clearance provided by the back-cut on the profiled edge. This will allow the adjacent molding to pass by the shaped end of the molding and will make it easy to adjust the profile for a tight fit.

INSTALLING AN INSIDE CORNER

project

Crown profiles sit at an angle to the wall and ceiling known as the spring angle. The most common spring angles are 45/45-degree and 52/38-degree. The first number indicates the angle to the ceiling, and the second indicates the angle to the wall. The spring angle affects how you cut the blocking, how you mount the molding to wall and ceiling, and how you set the miter saw to cut the joints.

TOOLS & MATERIALS

- Hammer ∎ Nail set ∎ Measuring tape
- Chalk-line box ∎ Power drill and bits
- Power miter saw ∎ Coping saw ∎ Files
- Caulking gun ∎ Crown molding
- Blocking material ∎ Wood glue ∎ Caulk
- Finishing nails

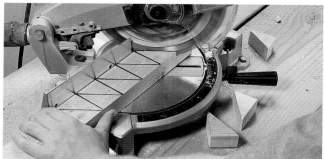

1 Once you've established your guideline location, snap a chalk line for the molding (top). Cut support blocks that match its spring angle (bottom) and that are slightly smaller than the opening behind the molding, so there is a gap between molding and blocks. (This will allow for adjustments needed because of imperfect walls.)

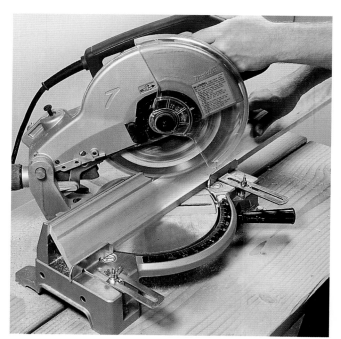

4 Cut the coping miter on another board, and transfer the dimension from Step 3, measuring from the miter tip. If possible, cut this piece several inches long, so you can make corrections if needed. If you are unsure of your skills, practice steps 4 through 8 on a scrap piece first, and then apply the steps to the real thing.

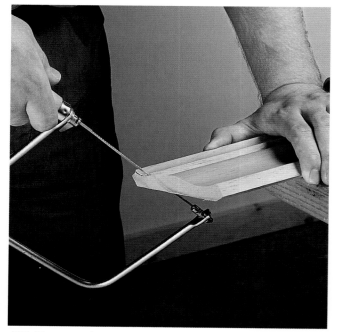

5 Use a coping saw to start the profile cut. Angle the saw to back-cut the coped piece. See pages 152 to 155 for detailed instructions on planning and making this cut. If you need to cut a piece with coped joints in each end, make it $1/16$ inch long, so you have to bend it slightly and spring it into place; this ensures a tight fit.

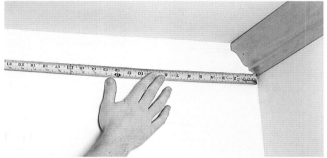

2 Nail or screw the support blocks to wall studs and the wall top plate every 16 inches. You may need to pre-drill pilot holes to prevent splitting the wood.

3 Install the full-length square-cut cornice, fitting it into the corner (top). Don't nail within 3 or 4 ft. of the corner yet; this will allow you to adjust the piece if needed to fit tightly against the coped piece. Measure out from the corner (plus an extra couple of inches) to find the rough length of the coped molding (bottom).

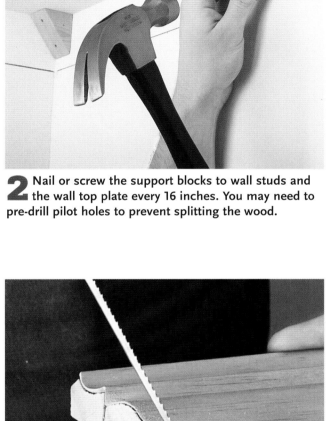

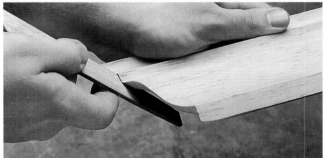

6 Rotate the saw as needed to maneuver the thin blade along the profile of the miter.

7 Use an oval-shaped file (or a round file in tight spots) to clean up curved sections of the profile (top). Use a flat rasp as needed to clean up the upper section of the coped cut or to increase the back-cut angle (bottom). On soft material, you can also use a utility knife to cut away material.

Continued on next page.   **157**

Crown and Cornice Molding

Continued from previous page.

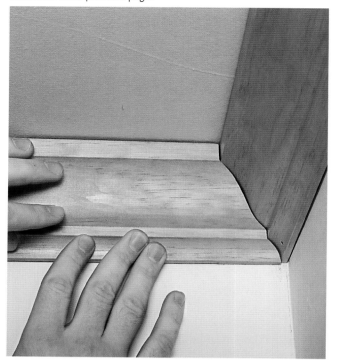

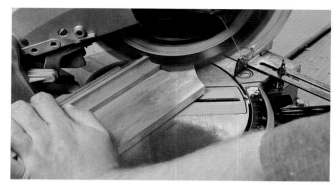

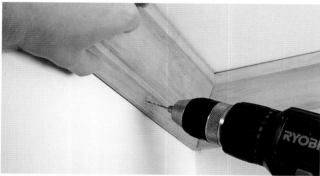

8 Test-fit the coped piece in place, supporting the other end to be sure the board is level. If there is a gap, you may be able to tighten it by shimming out the first piece.

9 Double-check your measurements, and trim off any extra wood from the rough measurement (top). Adjust and fit the pieces, support the coped piece in place, and drill near the coped end to prevent splitting (bottom).

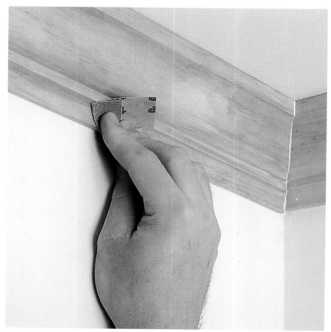

10 Apply wood glue to sections of the coped end that will make contact with the square-end piece.

11 To finish, drive and set finishing nails to secure the corner pieces, and sand or caulk the joint as needed.

INSTALLING AN OUTSIDE CORNER

project

If your room has an outside corner, make it the last joint you fit. Because it is an open-ended joint, you can cut it long, fit the coped corner at the other end first, and then hold the molding in place to mark for the outside miter. Test the corner for square and make the miter cuts accordingly, as shown on pages 146–147. Or, test-cut two pieces out of scraps that are at least 2 feet long, and adjust your saw until you achieve perfection; then cut the actual boards.

TOOLS & MATERIALS

▌ Hammer ▌ Nail set ▌ Measuring tape
▌ Chalk-line box ▌ Power drill and bits
▌ Power miter saw ▌ Crown molding
▌ Blocking material ▌ Wood glue ▌ Caulk
▌ Finishing nails

1 Cut and fit the coped joint first, and then hold the section in place and mark for cutting.

2 Trim the molding, and cut a miter joint on the end. Do the same for the adjoining piece (top). Install the pieces by applying a bead of carpenter's glue to the joint and securing with finishing nails (bottom).

3 Smooth the joint so that the molding appears to be a continuous piece. Use a nail set to knock down the edge. If the back of the cut pieces meet and create a gap in the front, use a knife or a rasp to remove material that will not be visible. If the molding will be painted, apply wood filler, allow to dry, and sand smooth.

BUILT-UP OR COMPOUND CORNICE TRIM

For rooms with high ceilings, or for any situation where you want a more elaborate ceiling molding, consider a built-up or layered approach to the cornice. Even a room with an 8-foot ceiling can accept this type of treatment, providing the cornice is in proper proportion to the scale of the room. The cornice can be as simple as pairing a frieze of inverted baseboard or 1-by pine with a crown molding, or as complex as combining several different profiles that complement each other. A built-up cornice does not need to include an angled crown molding. It can include two or more types of flat molding stock applied to just the wall or both wall and ceiling.

Profile Choices. Common elements that are used in built-up cornices include dentil, egg and dart, cove, bead, bed, and crown molding, although your actual choices are certainly not limited to those options. The best way to proceed in developing a design is to study available molding profiles and draw full-scale cross sections of different combinations so that you can better envision them. Use the samples in the drawings below and on pages 226–229 as a guide in designing your cornice. When you arrive at a prospective design, purchase short sections of each molding, and assemble a sample block of the cornice that is 1 or 2 feet long—you can use nails or even hot glue to hold the parts together—and hold it up to the ceiling. This will allow you to best judge whether the proportions and particular moldings are correct. While this may seem excessively cautious, remember that the investment in both materials and time for a cornice of this type is considerable. The worst case scenario has you completing the job only to realize that the trim seems totally out of place in the room. An additional bonus to making the sample cornice is that you actually go through the assembly process. This can be very helpful in planning the sequence of steps you will go through when installing the molding.

Blocking and Backing. In some cases, you will need to provide blocking to support a built-up cornice, and in other situations, none will be required. In more elaborate designs, continuous backing is often the best choice because it is good practice to stagger scarf joints, and the backer allows you to locate these joints at any convenient spot.

TYPICAL BUILT-UP CORNICE PROFILES

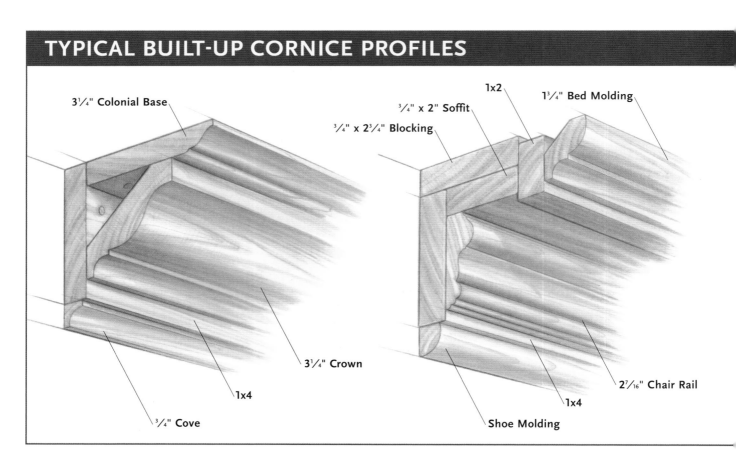

3¼" Colonial Base
3¼" Crown
1x4
¾" Cove

¾" x 2¾" Blocking
¾" x 2" Soffit
1x2
1¾" Bed Molding
2⁷⁄₁₆" Chair Rail
1x4
Shoe Molding

In a built-up cornice, it is always best to establish a level line to define the bottom edge of the trim element against the wall. Then if you encounter deviations in the height of the ceiling from that line, you can take up the difference between two or more molding elements and make the discrepancy less visible. As a general rule, those viewing a finished cornice installation tend not to notice small variations in the reveals between profiles from one part of a room to another—things that can seem quite problematic, and obvious, to the installer.

Most built-up cornices involve some type of frieze that is mounted to the wall and serves as the base for other profiles. The frieze serves as a decorative element as well as blocking to accept the nails to hold them in place. It can be made from 1x4 stock, either with or without a molded edge, or a piece of inverted baseboard molding. Once you have established your level line, it is a simple matter to install the frieze to the wall. If you are using stock without a molded edge, inside corners can be treated with simple butt joints; otherwise, coped joints are required. Outside corners should be treated with miter joints, just as if installing baseboard—only upside down. Whenever possible, use screws to fasten the frieze to the wall studs and top plate, as they provide more strength and less trauma to the wall than nails. Locate the screws where they will be covered by the next layer of molding, and use nails at spots that will be exposed.

If your design requires further blocking, install it next. The specific configuration will depend on the moldings you have chosen. Often 2x4 stock can be ripped at the required angle to form continuous backing for a crown or bed molding. Nail or screw the backer to the frieze board. For those situations that demand blocking on the ceiling, methods of fastening can be a problem. On walls that run perpendicular to ceiling joists, you can use nails or long screws for fastening. However, on walls parallel with the joists, there are often no framing members where you need them. The easiest solution is to get an assistant to help hold the blocking in place on the ceiling, and drill pilot holes for screws through the blocking and into the drywall surface. Then remove the blocking to install spiral anchors in the pilot holes in the ceiling. You can then replace the blocking and use long screws to attach it.

Place marks on the frieze to act as guides in positioning the next layer of molding. Install that layer, nailing it to the frieze and appropriate backing. Proceed with each layer in similar fashion until the cornice is complete.

¼" Reveal

1x4

1x2

1⅞" Bed Molding

2¾" Crown

See pages 162–163 for installation of this profile.

¾" Cove   1x3

Many cornices are made up of a number of molding profiles installed together to form a pleasing design.

INSTALLING A BUILT-UP CORNICE

project

Installing a multipiece cornice calls for the same operations as used for a one-piece crown molding, but you must do them repeatedly. Each visible piece gets bevel- or miter-cut at an outside corner, and each piece (except for flat pieces) must be cope-cut at inside corners. If your walls or ceiling wave, avoid the temptation to bend pieces; this will make wavy lines in the molding. Instead, make a scribe cut.

TOOLS & MATERIALS

▮ Power drill and bits ▮ Hammer ▮ Nail set ▮ Measuring tape ▮ Nail gun and nails (optional) ▮ Miter saw ▮ Spirit level ▮ Screwdriver ▮ Cornice molding stock ▮ 1-by blocking stock ▮ Wood glue ▮ Hollow-wall anchors ▮ Finishing nails

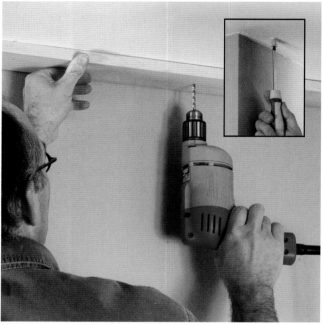

1 Where possible, attach blocking to joists or studs. Where you cannot locate a framing member, hold the blocking in place and drill into the ceiling to mark the location of spiral anchors. Drill a pilot hole, and install the anchor (inset). Reposition the blocking, and drive screws through it and into the anchor.

5 With the soffit and fascia in place, install the crown molding. Fashion coped joints for inside corners. Adjust the fit as required. Cut miter joints for outside corners, and nail the crown to both the soffit and frieze. The crown should cover the fasteners.

6 Nail the fascia to the soffit and backer boards. Position the fascia so that it projects ¼ in. below the soffit.

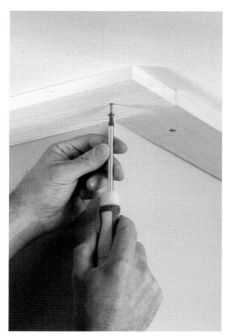

2 Screw through the blocking to fasten it to the ceiling. Drive the screws into ceiling joists or spiral anchors to form a base for cornice trim.

3 Cut flat miters for outside corners of the soffit trim, and nail the soffit to the backer. Mark a level line to indicate the bottom edge of the frieze. Use screws to fasten the frieze to wall studs or to a top plate.

4 Cut an open miter to prepare for cutting the coped profile at an inside corner. Test the fit, and make necessary adjustments.

7 Install bed molding between the fascia and ceiling. If necessary, you can caulk any gaps between the molding and ceiling or wall surfaces.

8 Completed built-up cornice. The goal is to make the multiple components look like one piece of molding.

beams, columns, and pilasters

6

DECORATIVE BEAMS don't actually provide structural support, but they do allow you to dress up an expanse of ceiling with a distinctive design element. Interior columns can elegantly define the transition between two rooms. You can go for a full-bore classical look with fluted columns; a more sedate but still antique-style cylindrical column; or a square-paneled look, which hearkens back mere centuries rather than millennia. Pilasters are basically faux columns that appear to be buried in the wall.

BEAMED CEILINGS

A ceiling beam usually consists of a long U-shaped structure that is fastened to strategically located blocking on the ceiling. Beams run parallel with one another and can be spaced evenly or irregularly across a room. Rooms with tall ceilings can generally tolerate larger beams and closer spacing than rooms with lower ceilings. This type of treatment is not limited to rooms with flat ceilings; some of the most dramatic applications of a beamed ceiling are found in spaces with soaring cathedral ceilings.

Coffered ceilings add a level of complexity to a standard beamed ceiling. Coffers are recessed areas on a ceiling that are the result of intersecting beams, turning the ceiling surface into a virtual grid.

Materials. Like all interior trim, beamed and coffered ceilings can be constructed with either paint- or stain-grade materials. Pine and poplar are the logical choices for work that will be painted, as they are easy to work and are relatively inexpensive. If painted the same color as the ceiling, the beams become more restrained details, and if given a complementary or contrasting color, they become

dominant features. Stained oak makes a strong statement, drawing attention with bold open-grain patterns. Cherry and maple are more subtle choices, contributing warmth and character without overpowering other architectural features. Walnut is associated with elegance and formality; it is a good choice for a more formal public room. (For more information on selecting lumber, see "Lumber for Trimwork," page 222.)

Beam Designs. The simplest design uses butt joints at the bottom; the bottom piece may be flush with the sides or recessed. You may use joining plates to align and reinforce the joints. You can also create miter joints to join the pieces, but a long mitered joint is difficult to make. One solution is to chamfer the miter to make imperfections less noticeable.

Termination Points. Plan how to treat the intersection of the beam ends with the walls. You could just let the beams die into the drywall. A more attractive option is to mount a frieze along the wall to accept the beams. If you size the frieze to be wider than the depth of the beams, it can provide a nice clean transition between the elements. It also provides you with an easier installation by remov-

DECORATIVE BEAM CONSTRUCTION

TRADITIONAL BOX BEAM

Ceiling Joist

Cove Molding

MITERED BOX BEAM

Ceiling Joist

Crown Molding

Chamfered Edge

BEAM LAYOUT

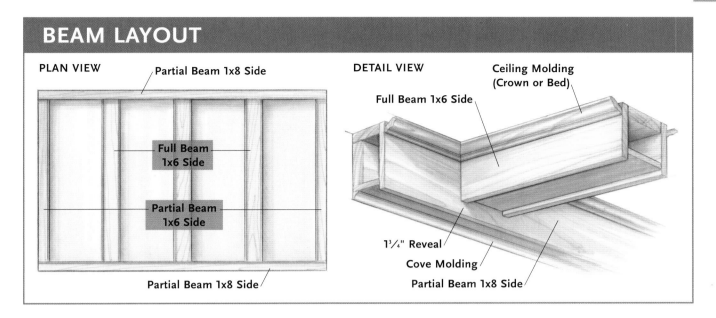

PLAN VIEW

Partial Beam 1x8 Side

Full Beam
1x6 Side

Partial Beam
1x6 Side

Partial Beam 1x8 Side

DETAIL VIEW

Ceiling Molding
(Crown or Bed)

Full Beam 1x6 Side

1³⁄₄" Reveal

Cove Molding

Partial Beam 1x8 Side

ing the necessity of fitting the beams tightly between the drywall surfaces. You can also use the partial beams that are half as wide as the other beams and appear to be partially buried in the wall as a way to treat the beam ends. These provide a convenient way of ending the beams and also create the illusion that the deeper partial beams are supporting those that die into them.

Cut the blocking to length; then have an assistant help you to hold it in place along the chalk lines while you drill pilot holes for screws through both blocking and ceiling.

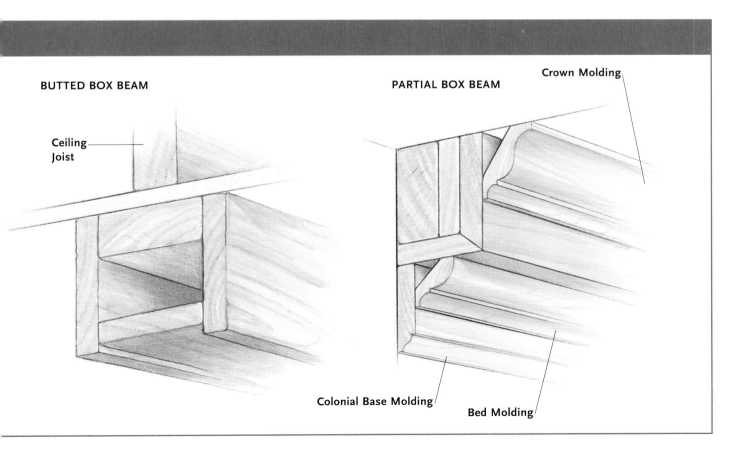

BUTTED BOX BEAM

Ceiling
Joist

PARTIAL BOX BEAM

Crown Molding

Colonial Base Molding

Bed Molding

Beams, Columns, and Pilasters

INSTALLING A BEAMED CEILING

Choose a beam design from the drawings on pages 166–167. Draw a cross section, indicating the sizes of each part. You may need to rip some boards. If you use ¾-inch-thick stock to construct the beams, the edge of the blocking must be ¾ inch inside the finished beam.

Lay out for the blocking. Lightly mark the ceiling, next to each end wall, to indicate the outside edges of each piece of blocking; then strike chalk lines between the marks.

TOOLS & MATERIALS

- Hammer ▌ Nail set ▌ Plate joiner
- Power miter saw ▌ Drill with screwdriver tip ▌ Spirit level ▌ Nailing gun and nails
- Clamps ▌ 1-by stock ▌ Finishing nails
- Joining plates ▌ Wood glue ▌ Screws

1 Rooms are rarely perfectly square, so measure the length for each beam. Rip and crosscut the parts to size. Clamp the side pieces, and cut plate slots. To recess the bottom panel, support the plate joiner on a spacer. Glue slots and plates; then place the plates into the slots and assemble the beam (inset).

4 Install blocking for all the beams. If your plan includes either a frieze or partial beams as end details, begin your installation there. If beams run across the joists, just drill pilot holes and drive screws into joists. If beams are parallel with joists, attach using spiral anchors in the drywall.

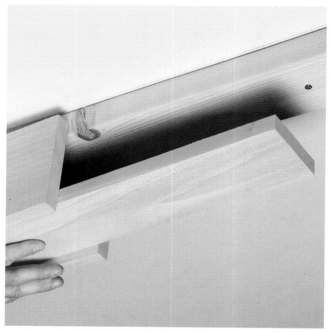

5 Slip the first section of a beam over the blocking, and push it tight to the ceiling. It usually helps to have a helper holding one end.

2 Nail the beam sides to the bottom to hold the parts together while the glue sets. If you have lots of clamps, use them instead of nailing; this will save you from filling and sanding later.

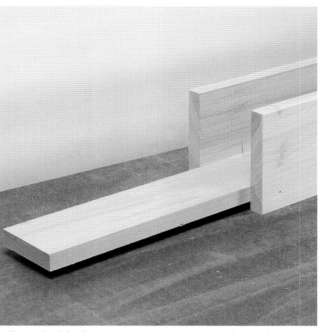

3 To build a beam in sections, stagger the end joints. Extend the bottom panel by about 12 in. on one section, and recess it by the same amount on the adjacent section.

6 If you plan to install a ceiling molding, use screws to fasten the beam to the blocking, as the molding will cover screw heads. Or drive nails with a gun. Hand nailing is somewhat difficult, because the pieces are long and the blocking may vibrate while you hammer.

7 After you install all the beams, install crown molding or other molding at the top of the beam. This provides another level of detail and can cover gaps between the beam and an uneven ceiling. Treat the beams as you would any wall surface, and cope all inside joints as needed.

COLUMNS

Columns have been used as both structural and decorative elements in buildings since ancient times. And their clear reference to those classical traditions makes them very effective in creating a sense of elegance and dramatic flair when used in a home environment. Columns are powerful elements, though, and their use must be considered carefully so that they do not become an unwelcome and overly dominant feature in a room. The scale, style, particular detailing, and finish of a column all contribute to the overall effect.

Column Materials. While the columns of antiquity were carved from stone, today you have a choice of a wide variety of materials. Of course, stone columns are still available, and for interior use, shorter stone columns

Square paneled columns add distinction to an upstairs hallway. Note the arch to the right.

might be appropriate as stands for plants or sculpture. However, the expense of stone columns, as well as the difficulty in moving and installing them, makes them an unlikely choice for most homes. For columns that will be painted, the selection of materials includes wood, MDF, fiberglass, polyurethane, concrete, aluminum, and polystyrene foam. These can be treated with a variety of finishes, including faux-painting techniques that mimic marble or other stone surfaces. You can also purchase stain-grade wooden columns that are designed to take a clear finish. There are suppliers that offer a variety of stock column designs and those that specialize in custom items. You can specify the material, height, diameter, and style for the particular column that will fit your situation.

Column Styles. Many people tend to think of columns as round, but square wooden columns also have a long history; they are appropriate for use in many situations, including contemporary, traditional, and Arts and Crafts interiors. These can be constructed entirely from solid wood or a combination of solid wood and veneered panels. And while round columns must be purchased from a manufacturer, you can easily construct square columns in your home shop using basic trim techniques.

Although most interior columns are purely decorative,

smart tip

VISUAL BALANCE

HISTORICALLY ACCURATE COLUMNS INCORPORATE A FEATURE CALLED *ENTASIS*. FROM THE TIME OF ANCIENT GREECE, IT WAS NOTED THAT IF THE SIDES OF A COLUMN ARE STRAIGHT, THEY HAVE THE TENDENCY TO APPEAR CONCAVE. TO COUNTER THIS ILLUSION, THEY MODIFIED THEIR COLUMNS TO INCLUDE A SLIGHT BULGE ALONG THE LENGTH OF THE SHAFT, AND THIS IS KNOWN AS ENTASIS.

there are situations where load-bearing capability is important. For example, if you want to replace a weight-bearing post or support wall with a header and column, it is critical that the column be rated to carry the appropriate load—and that the entire alteration conforms to local building codes. In these cases, consult with an architect or structural engineer. You might also seriously consider having a contractor make the structural changes to your home, reserving the decorative projects for yourself. Columns that are rated for load-bearing applications are available in limited material choices.

Parts of a Column. There are three primary parts to a column—base, shaft, and capital. Most manufactured columns provide these parts separately to simplify installation and give you maximum flexibility in selecting individual parts. Bases and capitals for columns can be relatively simple or extremely ornate. They can be constructed to strictly follow a classical order, or they can be of a more free-form derivative design. Round column shafts can be either smooth or fluted, and most taper from bottom to the top.

Prefabricated Columns. Column manufacturers vary their construction methods depending on the materials used, as well as proprietary considerations that make their operation more efficient. The particular installation procedure you must follow will depend on the column you purchase, so it is important to read and follow any instructional material that comes with your column. The instructions should advise as to the best method of fastening the parts together, as well as what type of fasteners are recommended between column parts and the building structure.

CLASSICAL COLUMN STYLES

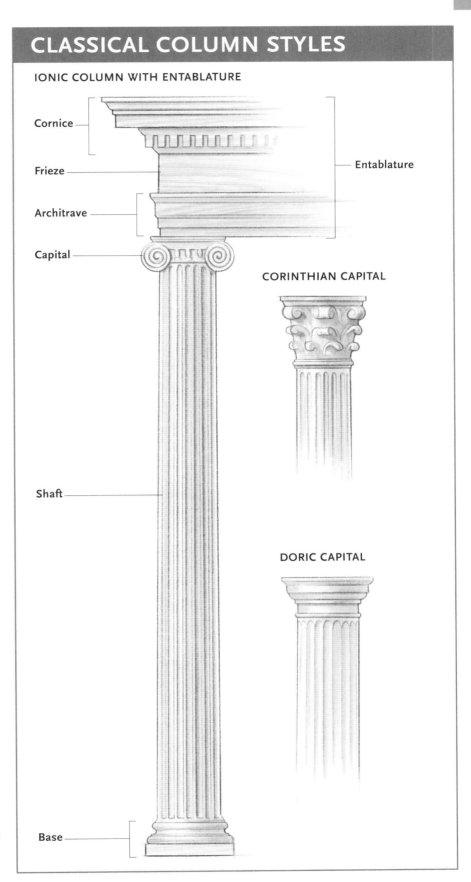

IONIC COLUMN WITH ENTABLATURE

Cornice

Frieze

Architrave

Capital

Shaft

Base

Entablature

CORINTHIAN CAPITAL

DORIC CAPITAL

Square columns mounted on pedestals help define a living room in an open floor plan.

SIMPLE COLUMN CONSTRUCTION

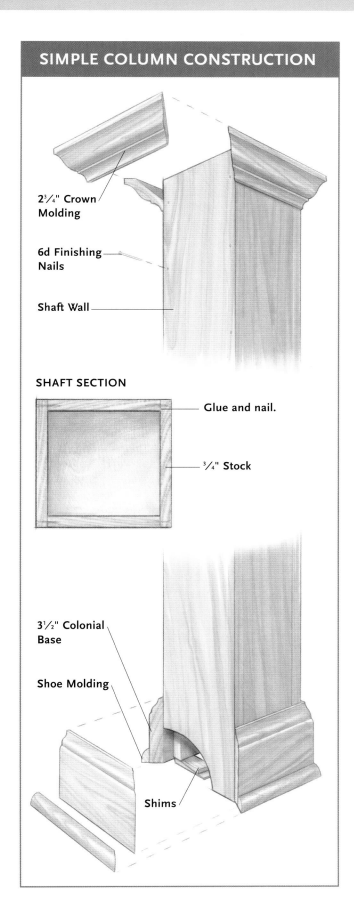

2³⁄₄" Crown Molding

6d Finishing Nails

Shaft Wall

SHAFT SECTION

Glue and nail.

³⁄₄" Stock

3¹⁄₂" Colonial Base

Shoe Molding

Shims

PANELED COLUMN CONSTRUCTION

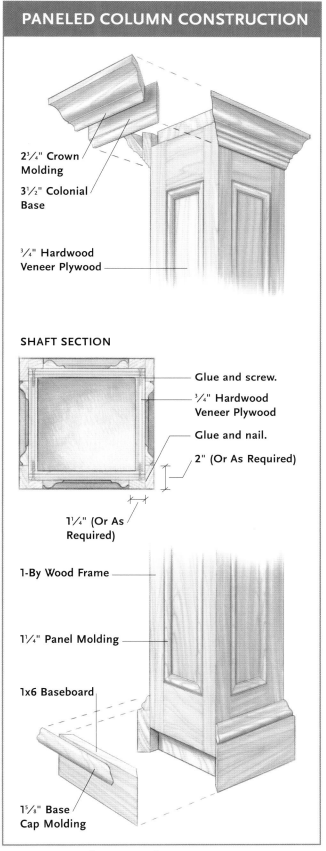

2³⁄₄" Crown Molding

3¹⁄₂" Colonial Base

³⁄₄" Hardwood Veneer Plywood

SHAFT SECTION

Glue and screw.

³⁄₄" Hardwood Veneer Plywood

Glue and nail.

2" (Or As Required)

1¹⁄₄" (Or As Required)

1-By Wood Frame

1¹⁄₄" Panel Molding

1x6 Baseboard

1⁵⁄₈" Base Cap Molding

See page 174 for construction sequence of this project.

BUILDING A PANELED COLUMN

Building a column's shaft is not difficult, because it's a straightforward arrangement of four straight-cut pieces. But take care to get it perfectly square and straight; otherwise, trimming it out will be difficult. Embellish your column by adding frames and molding stock as shown here. Build the shaft about ¼ inch shy of the ceiling or beam height so that you can lift it into position; add shims for a tight fit.

TOOLS & MATERIALS

▪ Hammer ▪ Nail set ▪ Table saw
▪ Power miter saw ▪ Nailing gun and nails (optional) ▪ Plate joiner ▪ Clamps
▪ Power drill and bits ▪ Stock for frames
▪ Molding stock ▪ Finishing nails
▪ Wood glue ▪ Joining plates

1 To build a shaft, use a table saw or a circular saw with a guide to cut four plywood panels that are perfectly straight and about ¼ in. short of the ceiling. Drive nails or finishing screws to assemble (top). Take care when positioning plywood panels to keep the edges perfectly flush (bottom). Also check for square as you work.

4 After fastening the two narrow frames to the shaft, apply the wider frames. Spread glue along the joints, and use clamps to hold the parts while you nail the frames together. Carefully mark panel molding to length, and cut to size with miter joints at the ends. Use brads to fasten the molding to the plywood column shaft (inset).

5 Position the column, and check for plumb in both directions. Use a pry bar to lift it to bring its top tight to the ceiling or beam. Place shims under each corner to support the column. Use a utility knife to trim. Drill angled pilot holes into the bottom of the shaft for toenailing it to the floor. Use finishing nails to lock the column in position. Set the nailheads below the wood surface.

2 Cut slots for joining plates in the edges of frame stiles and rails (inset). Apply glue to both the slots and plates before assembling the parts. Allow for the proper exposure above the base trim. Apply clamps to pull the frame joints tight. Leave the clamps in place until the glue sets—at least one hour.

3 Nail a narrow frame to one side of the plywood column shaft. Keep the edges of the frame flush to the shaft's edges all along its length.

6 Apply base trim to the column using the same techniques you would for a wall. In this example, a small piece of trim is placed on top of the base. After the finish flooring is installed, a base shoe may be attached at the bottom of the column.

7 Apply cornice trim around the top of the column. Follow instructions for cutting and installing crown molding. (See "Crown and Cornice Molding," page 139.) If the molding is large, you may need to install blocking first. If the column is truly square, you can cut all the pieces to the same length, and at exactly 45-deg. bevels.

PASSAGEWAY TREATMENTS WITH COLUMNS

The following type of installation requires a comprehensive understanding of woodworking tools and skills—and takes a lot of time to install and finish. But the design provides delineation between rooms laid out in an open plan while retaining an open feeling, and it creates a striking passageway.

You also can build columns on podiums to stand alone in a passageway. In fact, many of the details you'll find on the next few pages can be scaled back if, for example, the adjacent walls do not have wainscoting. But the most complete installation includes many trim components. The ideal treatment extends the wainscoting in a room around into the passageway, but only at the height of the paneling.

The extension forms a knee wall, sometimes called a podium because it supports a decorative column. You can use many styles of columns. Typically, you don't need the column to provide structural support. That job is handled by a header that's usually dropped below the ceiling.

But a column on a podium on each side of a passageway provides the classical appearance of a supported opening. It defines a passageway and adds decorative detail while allowing you to see past the columns into the next room.

Columns and podiums create an elegant passageway.

TYPICAL PODIUM PLAN VIEW

Stile · Rail · End Stud · End Rail · Return · Mitered Stile · House Wall · End Stud · Drywall

PODIUM · WING WALL

Stile · Rail · Plywood · Shoe · Podium Stud · Double Wing-Wall Studs · Shoe

TYPICAL PODIUM ASSEMBLY

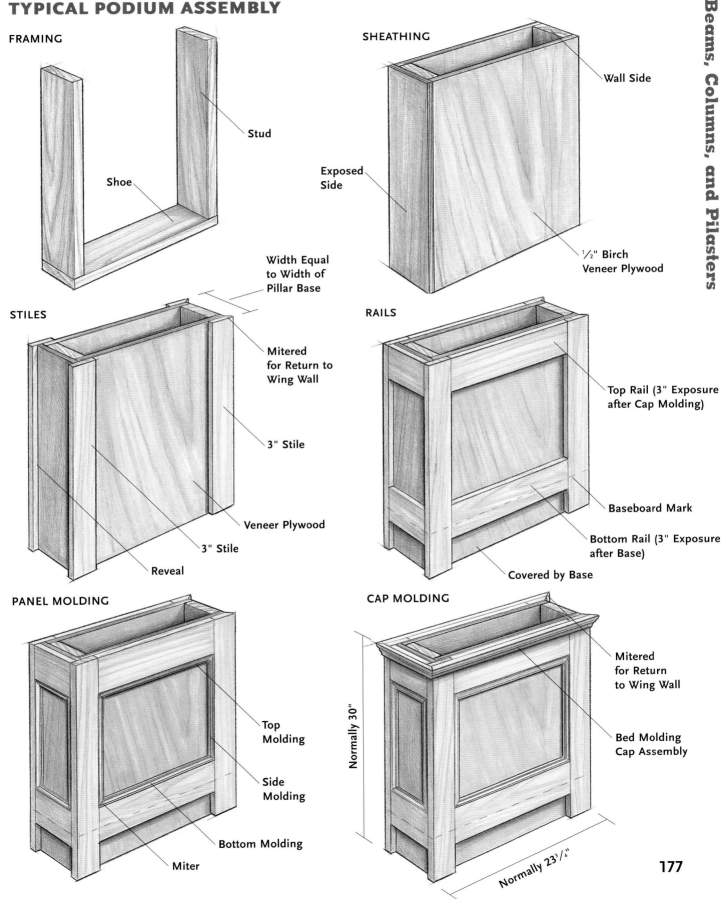

FRAMING

Stud

Shoe

SHEATHING

Wall Side

Exposed
Side

½" Birch
Veneer Plywood

STILES

Width Equal
to Width of
Pillar Base

Mitered
for Return to
Wing Wall

3" Stile

Veneer Plywood

3" Stile

Reveal

RAILS

Top Rail (3" Exposure
after Cap Molding)

Baseboard Mark

Bottom Rail (3" Exposure
after Base)

Covered by Base

PANEL MOLDING

Top
Molding

Side
Molding

Bottom Molding

Miter

CAP MOLDING

Mitered
for Return
to Wing Wall

Bed Molding
Cap Assembly

Normally 30"

Normally 23¾"

177

Beams, Columns, and Pilasters

Squaring Up Passageway Walls

One of the most accurate ways to square up walls relies on a simple bit of mathematics you may remember from school. The idea is to use the proportions of a 3-4-5 triangle. Here's how it works: when the three sides of a triangle are in the proportion of 3 : 4 : 5, one of the corners has to be exactly 90 degrees, no matter what unit of measurement you use, inches or feet, or how long the measurements are.

Start from an initial point where you want the passageway wall to join the existing house wall at a right angle. (See the illustration "Squaring Up Walls," below.) Measure a 3-foot leg along the wall and mark that point. Then measure a 4-foot leg extending into the passageway using a string and a pencil to swing a short arc along the 4-foot distance. You can also do this holding a pencil at the end of a ruler, or cut a board to the 4-foot length and use it to control the measurement mark.

Then move to the end of your 3-foot leg, and swing a 5-foot arc back into the passageway. This is the long leg, or hypotenuse, of the triangle. The point where the arcs intersect will be square with your initial point where the passageway wall joins the house wall. Connect the starting point with the intersecting arcs, and your passageway wall will be square. For larger areas, you can change the proportions—6 : 8 : 10, for example.

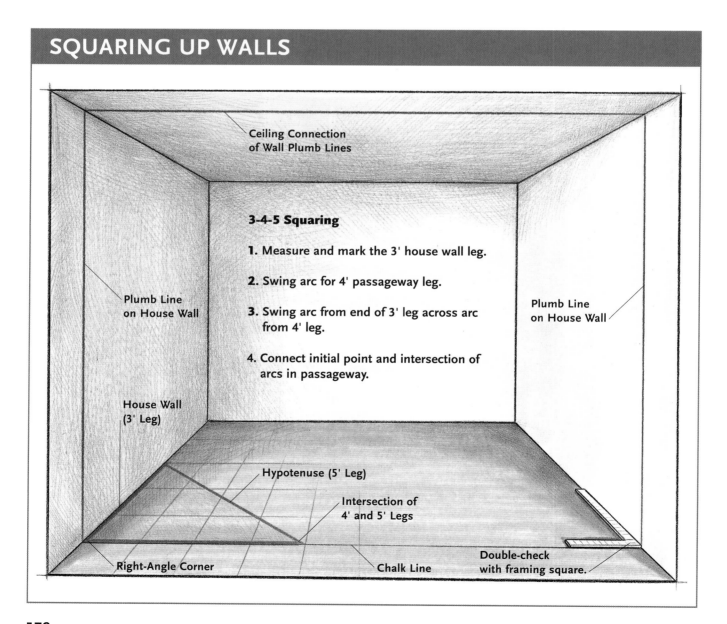

SQUARING UP WALLS

Ceiling Connection of Wall Plumb Lines

3-4-5 Squaring

1. Measure and mark the 3' house wall leg.

2. Swing arc for 4' passageway leg.

3. Swing arc from end of 3' leg across arc from 4' leg.

4. Connect initial point and intersection of arcs in passageway.

Plumb Line on House Wall

Plumb Line on House Wall

House Wall (3' Leg)

Hypotenuse (5' Leg)

Intersection of 4' and 5' Legs

Right-Angle Corner

Chalk Line

Double-check with framing square.

Creating a Faux Header

Some passageways have walls on each side that go all the way to the ceiling. Others have a header across the top that's dropped down from the ceiling. (See the photo below.) If a header is already installed, you can make the standard checks for square and level and start trimming. There will be studs to support the molding along the sides and a large built-up timber such as two 2×10s to support the molding across the top.

If you need to fill in the space between the side walls, you can box in the space using a long rectangular frame reinforced with short studs. Set horizontally at the top of the opening, the frame creates a faux header.

Build the box frame on the floor using 2×4s for the perimeter frame and short (say, 6¼-inch) 2×4 studs nailed at least every 16 inches. This will imitate a 2×10 header. You might want to use screws to make the box frame even stronger and to fasten it to the ceiling joists and wall studs before you cover it with drywall.

If you want to enlarge a passageway or build a new one altogether, you should probably hire a contractor to handle the structural alterations. That's because load-bearing headers (unlike a nonload-bearing box frame) carry the weight of ceiling joists and other loads, and you can seriously damage your house's structure if you don't install the header properly.

Podiums with columns separate an entryway, even without wainscoting in the adjacent room.

PILASTERS

A pilaster is a vertical molding assembly applied to a wall surface in the form of a column. The design of a pilaster is meant to suggest that it is embedded in the wall and performing a structural function. It normally features both plinth base and molded capital details, and it can extend from floor to ceiling or only part of the way up a wall. Pilasters can be used alone or in combination with other architectural features, such as doors or mantles, and they are often employed as part of a wainscoting installation to create a transition between the paneling and door or window casings. You can place two pilasters on the same wall, flanking a door, window, or fireplace, or locate them on opposite walls in a hallway to create a colonnade.

Types of Pilasters. Most pilasters employ fluted columns. You can purchase material that already has a fluted profile, or use your router and a core-box bit to make your own stock, as shown at right.

But the column need not be fluted. Almost any wide, symmetrical casing stock can be an appropriate choice; you could also use a plain flat board for a shaft or apply a surface molding to give it another level of detail.

Creating a Pilaster. Building a pilaster involves the same techniques used in installing base trim, cornices, and casing. Install a plinth block of ¾ material that is high enough to allow the adjacent base trim to neatly die into it on either side. You could also make the plinth an extension of the base trim. In this case, miter three pieces of baseboard to form a column base, and install them around the shaft. If you have a wall stud directly behind the shaft, nail the shaft to the framing. However, a wide shaft should be fastened along each edge to keep it tight to the wall. Use panel adhesive or hollow-wall anchors and screws to fasten it. Make sure to counterbore pilot holes for the screws, and plug the holes over any screw heads.

If you plan to install a chair rail in the room, you can add a pilaster block at chair-rail height to provide a way to terminate the adjacent molding. The block divides the length of the shaft into discrete upper and lower sections. You can fashion these blocks from solid ¾ stock, or you can miter 1-by stock to assemble a block. Chair rail or panel moldings make a nice transitional detail between the block and pilaster shaft.

To complete the pilaster, install crown molding or a built-up cornice around the shaft, just as you would any cornice trim.

ROUTING FLUTES

project

The most common pilaster design includes a fluted shaft. If you choose to shape your own stock, you have the advantage of being able to customize the size and frequency of the flutes. You can design a shaft that has either small flutes spaced close together or larger but fewer flutes. If you have a plunge router, you can cut flutes that stop shy of the board ends all in a line or at staggered end points. With a fixed base router you need to gradually tip the bit into the stock to achieve a stopped flute.

TOOLS & MATERIALS

- Combination square
- Plunge router and bit
- Clamps
- Knot-free 1-by stock

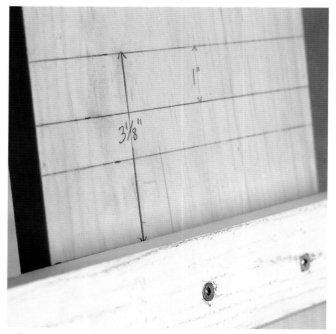

3 Measure the distance between the edge of the router base and the bit. Using that dimension, screw a stop block at each end of the board to limit the travel of the router and the length of the flutes. If you want some flutes to be longer than others, you will need to move the stop.

1 Once you mark the locations of the flutes, split each one with a centerline to guide your router alignment. Note: For a complicated operation like fluting, it's a good idea to first practice on scrap boards until you get the hang of it. In particular, stopping the flutes at the correct locations can be tricky.

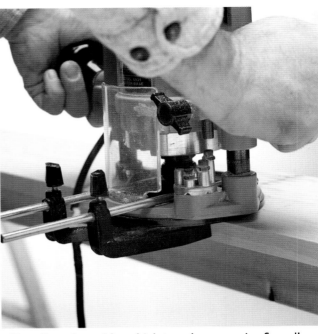

2 Adjust the guide, which travels on a pair of small rails so that the bit point lines up with the flute centerline. You will need to make this adjustment for each of the flute grooves.

4 With a firm grasp on the router, plunge the bit just enough to make contact and leave a mark on the line. Experiment on scrap pieces to get the depth adjustment just right.

5 With practice, you can get the knack of gradually plunging the router to create a tapered end to the flutes.

PASSAGEWAY SURROUNDS

Passageway surround systems combine many aspects of trimwork, including fluted pilasters with base, mid, and cap features, cornice trim, and paneled molding treatments. The overall concept is to extend the idea of using pilasters in an assembly where they appear to support a large decorative crosshead. You will need to borrow from several other sections of the book for a project of this scope. And, as always, there is no one correct way to design and install the assembly.

But you can use the overall sketch below as a guide, making proportional adjustments to fit your work area. You can also refer to the details at right that show how different types of molding are joined together to form the most crucial components of a surround.

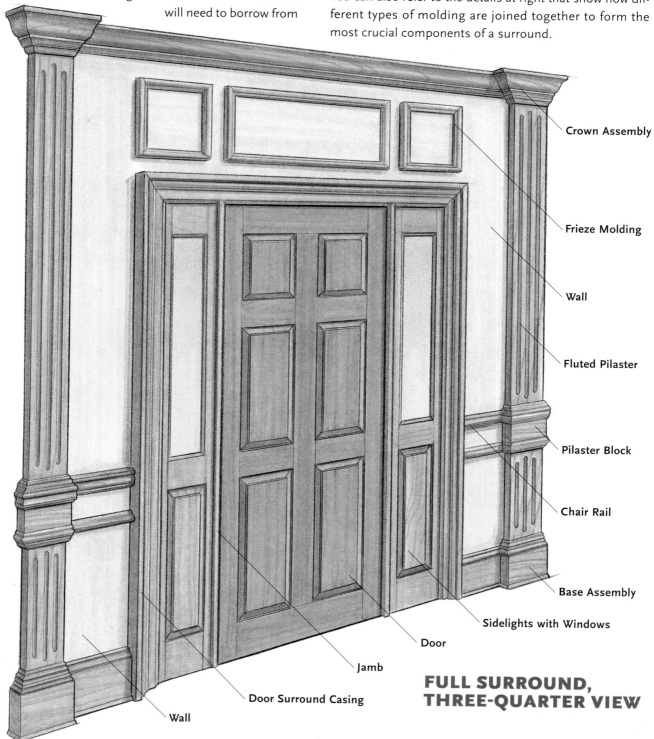

Crown Assembly

Frieze Molding

Wall

Fluted Pilaster

Pilaster Block

Chair Rail

Base Assembly

Sidelights with Windows

Door

Jamb

Door Surround Casing

Wall

FULL SURROUND, THREE-QUARTER VIEW

CROWN DETAIL

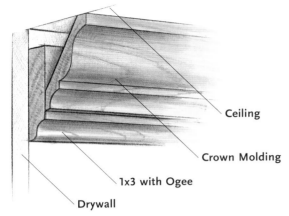

Ceiling

Crown Molding

1x3 with Ogee

Drywall

ALTERNATIVE HEAD DETAIL

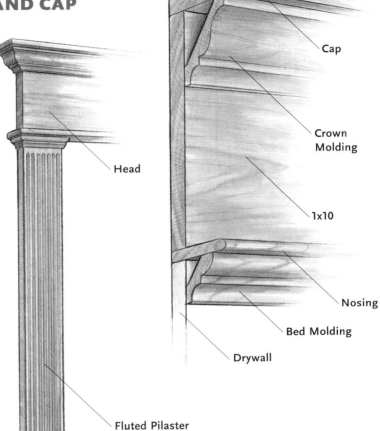

Cap

Crown Molding

1x10

Nosing

Bed Molding

Drywall

ALTERNATIVE PILASTER AND CAP

Head

Fluted Pilaster

Block

Base Assembly
(See detail at left.)

PILASTER BLOCK DETAIL

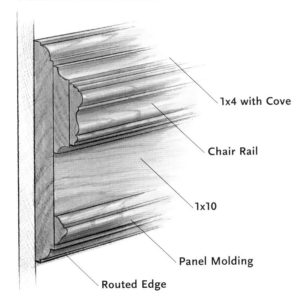

1x4 with Cove

Chair Rail

1x10

Panel Molding

Routed Edge

BASE DETAIL

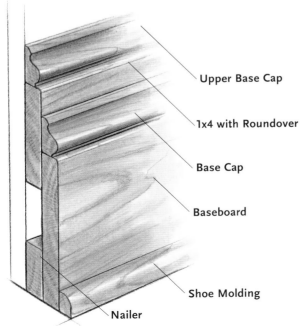

Upper Base Cap

1x4 with Roundover

Base Cap

Baseboard

Shoe Molding

Nailer

ALTERNATIVE PILASTER BLOCK DETAIL

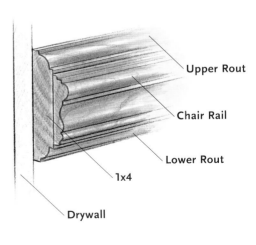

Upper Rout

Chair Rail

Lower Rout

1x4

Drywall

183

staircase details

7

STAIRCASES ARE BOTH practical and an important element in interior design. Ascending at dramatic angles from floor to floor, traditional staircases proudly display fine materials and elegant lines—appropriate as the first thing one sees from a home's entrance. When considered in parts, a staircase is full of architectural details, each contributing to the significant visual impact of the whole. While the balance between beauty and function has shifted toward the practical over the years, even the most ordinary modern staircases can be made over with a variety of upgrades and additions that do not require rebuilding the staircase.

ANATOMY OF A STAIRCASE

A notable characteristic of staircase design is that the finished product reveals very little about its basic construction. Without careful inspection, you can't see the supports and all the little joints and fasteners that hold the parts together. Identifying the standard parts and learning a little about how your staircase is built are the first steps to redecorating.

The supporting structure of a staircase is made up of a stringer on each end (and sometimes a carriage in the middle), typically 2x12 boards that span from floor to floor. The stringers either are cut in a sawtooth fashion and support the steps from below (known as a notched stringer) or have grooves cut into their side faces and support the steps from their ends (known as a housed stringer).

Treads and Risers. Each step of a staircase has two parts: the tread is the horizontal part that you walk on, and the riser is the vertical part between the treads. The tread and riser may be connected with dado (grooved) joints or may simply be butted together. With notched stringers, the treads and risers are nailed in place; with housed stringers, their ends are secured within the stringer grooves by glued wedges. Some staircases also have a starting step, a wider, sometimes deeper first step that typically has one or more rounded ends and often supports the newel. (See opposite.)

A grand staircase, above, is often the first thing that meets people when they enter a house. The landing of this staircase has become a handy place to display art.

Grand historic homes often included decoration on the undersides of multistory staircases, below left. This Craftsman-inspired design features trim bands along the undercarriage and landing newels with decorative pendants extending below the stair structure.

Steep, compact staircases, below, were common in Colonial homes, where they were often placed in unobtrusive locations. The fine balustrade details and applied trimwork are typical of late-period designs.

STAIRCASE CONSTRUCTION

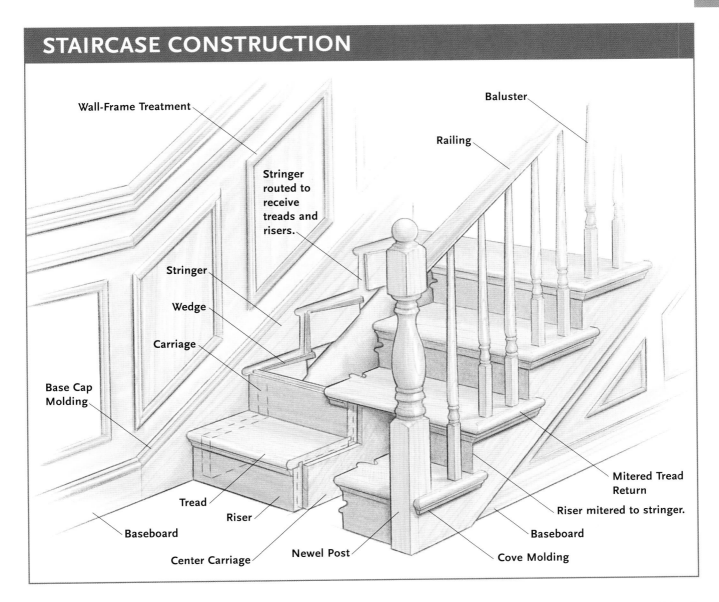

Wall-Frame Treatment

Baluster

Railing

Stringer routed to receive treads and risers.

Stringer

Wedge

Carriage

Base Cap Molding

Tread

Riser

Baseboard

Center Carriage

Newel Post

Mitered Tread Return

Riser mitered to stringer.

Baseboard

Cove Molding

Skirtboards. Where steps run along a wall, many staircases have a decorative skirtboard, which serves the same purpose as a baseboard. Modern staircase construction typically includes a continuous 2x4 spacer fixed between the stringer and the wall framing, providing a 1½-inch gap for installing drywall and in some cases, a skirtboard. If your stairs have no skirtboard, the gap between the stringer and wall makes it fairly easy to install one.

Balustrades. Staircase railing parts are known collectively as the balustrade, which includes the newels (or newel posts), the balusters, and the railing. Newels are the primary supports for the railing, while the balusters provide secondary support and create a barrier.

Traditional wooden staircases with uncarpeted or partially carpeted steps are generally referred to as "finish" stairs, because their exposed parts have to be of finish quality. Steps intended to be fully carpeted are typically built with construction-grade materials.

Staircase Evolution

The fundamental design of the staircase has changed little over the years, but its architectural stardom has seen some ups and downs. Stairs in modest Colonial homes were often concealed behind a door in the fireplace wall. Late-Colonial and Georgian builders brought the staircase out into plain view in the central hallway. The prominent placement naturally led to more embellished decoration and a greater architectural significance for the staircase. Staircases in modern homes seem to follow the whim of the architect or the confines of the floor plan more than the tides of fashion.

Staircase Details

Building Codes

The staircase is one of the most closely regulated elements of a house, and any changes that you make to yours must conform to the local building code. Everything from the steps to the stairwell width to the size and strength of the railing must meet strict specifications, and with good reason. Most of the time, stairs are climbed unconsciously—or blindly, when arms are full of laundry—and any irregularity, such as a shorter or longer step, or one with an excessive overhang, can cause a fall. Even if everyone in the home has gotten used to a known tricky spot, it will always be a hazard for guests. Most cosmetic changes won't require a permit, but it's a good idea to start your planning process by getting a copy of the staircase code from the local building department.

Treads and Risers

The treads and risers may be the most practical parts of a staircase, but they also have a significant impact on its appearance. Traditional finish stairs have polished hardwood treads and hardwood or paint-grade risers. If not left bare, they usually receive a carpet runner, a narrow strip of carpet with finished edges that leaves the attractive ends of the treads exposed. You can renew a worn set of finish stairs by adding a runner and refinishing the ends of the steps. One of the most dramatic staircase makeovers is turning a modern, carpeted version into a beautiful finish staircase by removing the carpet and adding new hardwood treads and riser panels. With some staircase configurations, you can also add an all-hardwood starting step to enhance the foot of the staircase.

Staircase Details

A fine, winding staircase, opposite, demonstrates the simple elegance of stained hardwood treads over painted risers.

Rich, contrasting finishes bring out the beauty of traditional stair parts, above left.

The charming staircase above features square-nosed oak treads, stenciled risers, and a simple, painted skirtboard. Slender balusters echo the spare newel detailing, and the railing is visually anchored at the wall by a square rosette.

Tread and Riser Makeovers

Replacing unfinished, construction-grade treads with hardwood is a good do-it-yourself project, but it's not for all types of staircases. It does not work with housed stringers, where the ends of the treads are seated in grooves and are too difficult to remove. Also, if the balusters rest on the treads, replacing the treads involves replacing or removing and reinstalling the balusters. Hardwood treads are available in one-piece versions for a full finished step, and in economical two-piece types made of particleboard with a specially cut end that receives a hardwood cap. The latter is used when you're also installing a carpet runner that will cover the particleboard. Commonly available hardwood species include oak, cherry, and maple, but others can be special-ordered. Some companies carry treads with wood-inlay decoration.

Riser Panels. An easy method for adding a finished look to risers is to cover them with ¼-inch-thick pieces of hardwood-veneer plywood or, if you want to paint them, paint-grade plywood. Using thicker plywood is not recommended, as this will limit the tread depth too much. Traditional finish steps look best with a skirtboard, and this project presents a good opportunity for adding one.

smart tip

STAIRCASE MAKEOVER

To add new treads and riser panels, carefully pry up the old treads. Measure and cut each riser panel individually; then test-fit each; finish as desired; and install with glue and finishing nails. Measure for each tread, and cut it to length. Test-fit the treads; then finish them as desired. Secure the treads to the stringers with adhesive and finishing nails driven through pilot holes. If desired, add scotia molding underneath the tread overhangs.

189

Stair Runners

Carpet stair runners essentially offer the best of both worlds: the quiet, comfort, and sure footing of carpeted stairs and the natural wood beauty of finish stairs. Runners are traditional accents that add warmth and a finishing touch to bare wooden staircases. You can buy machine-made runners in the standard synthetic- and natural-fiber materials, specifying the length and width to fit your stairs.

Runner Installation. Installing a runner is not difficult with most staircases, but it does require carpet-laying tools. For comfort and to prevent wear, professional carpet installers recommend adding a firm, nonfoam pad at least ¼ inch thick applied over the top and nosing of each stair tread. Use tackless strips to secure the runner at the backs of the treads. For straight runs of stairs, you can install a runner in a single, continuous piece; winders (steps that turn a corner) require a specially cut piece for each step.

Stair Rods. These are a popular traditional embellishment for carpet runners. Available in various styles and metals, stair rods fit over the crease where each stair tread meets the bottom of the riser and are secured at the ends by decorative brackets. In the past, stair rods were used to hold carpet runners in place, but today they are purely ornamental.

Starting Steps

When added as an accent, a starting step is a finished hardwood step that replaces the first riser and tread of a mitered-stringer staircase. Starting steps are wider than regular steps—48 inches wide or more—and so create a kind of decorative platform suggestive of grand staircases that widen toward the bottom. They typically are rounded on their exposed end: if only one end is rounded (the other end abuts a wall), it's a single-bullnose step; if both ends are rounded, it's a double-bullnose. When a staircase has a newel, it is typically installed in the center of the starting step's bullnose end.

You can add a starting step as part of a tread replacement project; if there's no newel, it's like installing a new tread and riser at the same time. Incorporating a newel is fairly complicated, and you would probably need some professional help with the installation. Like treads, starting steps are available in various hardwood species and paint-grade materials, so you can match the other steps or choose a contrasting style for the starting step. One of the most elegant uses of a starting step is as a base for a scrolling volute newel.

A frame-and-panel wainscot with chair rail, opposite top, integrates this well-decorated stairwell into the surrounding decor.

Two hardwood starting steps, opposite bottom, give this enclosed staircase a more open, welcoming feel. The custom steps have square ends rather than the standard bullnose.

An unusual feature, above, this bottom landing is framed by a grouping of newels with finials.

Carpet stair runners offer opportunities for creative decorating, right. Here, the playful scene displayed on each riser gains definition from a simple brass stair rod.

Staircase Details

SPIRAL STAIRCASES

SPIRAL STAIRCASES have a romantic history, but in modern homes, building codes prohibit the use of spiral staircases as the only means of access between full stories. However, they can serve as secondary staircases between main levels or provide access to lofts and other private places. Factory-built spiral stairs are available in a variety of wood and metal designs, including complete, one-piece units and do-it-yourself assembly kits.

BALUSTRADES

The balustrade is undoubtedly the most ornamental and visually dramatic part of a staircase. The eye delights in taking it all in: the stately newel, the graceful curves of the railing, the polished surfaces, the balusters in perfect repetition. Today, as in the past, a staircase balustrade is often the most ornate and finely crafted built-in feature of the home. The main balustrade elements (newels, railings, and balusters) are offered by stair parts manufacturers both separately and as sets. Common materials include hardwoods such as oak, maple, cherry, mahogany, and poplar (usually considered paint-grade because of its color variation), and iron and steel. Replacing any or all of the main parts can bring a dramatic change to your staircase. However, aside from replacing individual balusters, installing balustrade parts is not a job for amateurs.

Newel Posts

Newels anchor the staircase railing and are the primary stylistic elements of the balustrade. They appear in an endless variety of styles, but the most common types available today are made of wood and are categorized as either "solid" or "box" type. Solid newels are just that—solid pieces of wood (although some are laminated) that are milled or turned on a lathe for a decorative profile. They are typically more slender than box types and often have square ends, a turned midsection, and an ornamental top. A volute newel is a traditional style consisting of a central solid newel supporting a scrolling railing end and surrounded by a column of balusters.

Box Newels. Box newels are hollow wood boxes topped with a molded wood cap and sometimes a finial ornament. The classic box is four-sided and may have embellishments such as flutes, chamfered corners, or levels of applied molding. Some newel designs combine a box-style base with a turned solid post. One interesting feature of box newels is their mounting hardware: traditional types are held in place with a long metal rod with threaded ends that extends from a plate affixed near the top of the newel down through the floor; nuts at either end of the rod are tightened to secure the post.

Railings and Balusters

Together, railings and balusters provide architectural definition to a staircase, in addition to their obvious functional roles. From a design standpoint, the two parts are related to the extent that the baluster's top end must conform to the hole or groove in the underside of the railing. Likewise, the bottom end of the baluster must fit with the tread or curb design. But beyond that, there's little that limits the decorative possibilities of a baluster or a railing and baluster combination.

Material Choices. Most railings are made of hardwood, but iron and steel are not uncommon. Railings are categorized as either over-the-post, which means the railing runs over the tops of the newels, or post-to-post, meaning the railing ends butt into the sides of the newels. The differences are primarily aesthetic, although with post-to-post railings you have to remove your hand from the railing at transitions. Where railing ends do not meet newels, decorative options include curved or mitered wall returns, decorative blocks called rosettes that receive the railing end at a wall, and half newels—a partial newel installed flush to a wall.

Balusters. Installing most balusters is fairly straightforward but does require careful cutting and measuring. Balusters with rounded top ends fit into holes in the underside of the railing, while square-top styles are nailed into a groove and have thin wood plates, called fillets, applied between the balusters. Most wood balusters have square bottom ends and attach to the treads or to a low curb with nails or by means of a dowel or tenon that fits into a hole in the tread. Some treads have a little piece of applied nosing trim covering the dowel or tenon. New baluster blanks have elongated top ends that you cut to match the slope of the railing.

The combination of wood and metal is a popular treatment for custom balustrades. This modified volute-style newel employs a deep starting step.

The advent of household electricity inspired some architects to incorporate light fixtures into their newel designs.

STAIRCASE ACCENTS

In addition to upgrading its essential parts, you can enhance the appearance of a staircase with a number of applied features that can be added without altering the basic staircase parts.

Skirtboards and Tread Brackets

Skirtboards can be added to unfinished basement or attic staircases and to carpeted stairs that have gaps between the rough tread and the wall. In these applications, the installation involves cutting the ends of the skirtboard to follow the top riser and the floor at the foot of the staircase and slipping the board between the treads and the wall. Without the gap at the wall, you would face the monumental task of making a cutout for each step.

Skirtboards come in standard dimensions of $^{11}/_{16}$ x 11 inches, in 8-, 10-, 14-, and 16-foot lengths. They usually are made of particleboard with a hardwood veneer. Architecturally, a skirtboard performs the same role as a baseboard. At the bottom and top of the stairs, the skirtboard should be joined by a matching baseboard or terminated at a decorative transition block that abuts the baseboard.

Tread Brackets. A good way to embellish the ends of treads on the open side of a staircase is to install tread brackets. They were especially popular accents in Georgian and later Colonial homes, but are found in all styles of historic homes. These purely decorative details are very easy to install, requiring a little glue and a few small finishing nails to keep them in place.

Stair Seats

Stair seats are built-in features that were born out of the custom of placing furniture, such as a bench or settle, against the wall next to the bottom of a staircase. They are found in Colonial-style homes, country farmhouses, and some Victorian homes, but they were favorite details of Craftsman-style designers, who liked the stair seat for its practical use of space. More importantly, the built-in seat promoted the concept of turning hallways and staircases into living spaces rather than service areas.

In design, stair seats are similar to window seats. Corners and alcoves created by L-shaped stairs are ideal locations, but you can add a stair seat under any open-sided staircase. Like window seats, a stair seat can be made with a flip-up lid concealing a handy storage space.

Shadow Railings. A novel variation of the paneling treatment involves using trim to create a "shadow railing" on the staircase wall. A shadow railing is not a functional railing, but merely projecting trimwork that mirrors the lines of the balustrade railing. A popular decoration in Georgian and some Colonial homes, shadow railings were often enhanced with half newels placed at the appropriate locations. Their decorative effect is an interesting combination of formal and playful characteristics, and they add a strong linear element that increases the visual impact of the staircase.

smart tip

FINDING STAIR PARTS

YOU CAN FIND A LIMITED SELECTION OF THE MAIN PARTS AT HOME CENTERS AND LUMBERYARDS, BUT STAIR PARTS MANUFACTURERS CARRY A LARGER SELECTION. OTHER SOURCES INCLUDE MILLWORK COMPANIES AND ARCHITECTURAL PRODUCTS DEALERS. YOU CAN ALSO FIND SOME PARTS, SUCH AS NEWELS AND VARIOUS ACCESSORIES, AT SALVAGE YARDS AND ANTIQUE SHOPS.

Used as a decorative shelf, this traditional stair seat, opposite, dresses up an entryway. The feature works well in traditional and Craftsman-style homes.

A shadow railing with half newels, above, is a classic molding treatment. Here it creates a striking profile against a stark white background.

Tread brackets, right, traditionally concealed the exposed ends of stair risers. These historic examples are enhanced further by a thin band of decorative ogee molding.

mantels 8

IF A ROOM contains a fireplace, the fireplace and its mantel are usually its focal point. The term "mantel" refers to the entire decorative surround and not just the shelf. In historic homes, the quality of a mantel indicated the homeowner's status, and its form was a showpiece for the architect's personal art and the handiwork of many local craftsmen. Today, it remains as the social and aesthetic focus of any room it occupies—from grand living rooms used for entertaining guests to more private family rooms and bedrooms. Replacing an old, skimpy mantel or embellishing a bland brick surround not only transforms the appearance of your fireplace but can change the architecture of the entire room. You can also enhance a room by adding mantel to fireplace kit.

ANATOMY OF A MANTEL

The classic decorative mantel was a product of the Italian Renaissance, and its basic structure is still used today. A mantel includes four main parts: the field, the pilasters or columns, the mantelshelf, and the decorative molding. Some mantels also include an overmantel—a decorative treatment applied to the wall above the mantelshelf, often intended to receive a framed picture or painting.

The field is the inverted "U" frame of the mantel, made up of two vertical side boards and a horizontal frieze board. It is the foundation to which the other mantel parts are attached. With a traditional masonry fireplace, the field covers a portion of the brick opening and overlaps onto the surrounding wall surface. The band of brick left exposed is called the slip; it is often kept plain or decorated with a non-combustible finish, such as ceramic tile, marble, or metal.

Columns and Shelf. Standing at each side of the opening, a pilaster or column adds a sense of structure to the mantel and visually carries the mantelshelf above. In the classical mode, pilasters and columns may be mounted atop plinth blocks or bases and crowned with a capital or block. The mantelshelf traditionally is a solid piece of wood measuring 1 to 2 inches in thickness, with a milled front edge or molding added for a decorative profile. Support for the shelf can come from molding, blocks above pilasters or columns, brackets, or any kind of decorative projection centered along the frieze.

Mantel Moldings. Molding finishes the mantel. As with a built-up cornice, a combination of relatively simple

Marble mantels are popular in traditional-style homes. Although wood is the most popular material, stone, tile, and even solid surfacing are used on mantels.

While less common than pilasters, a nearly full-radius column provides a deep projection to the mantel's profile and adds a strong visual feature.

trim pieces can add up to a deceptively complex treatment. Cove, bead, half-round, crown molding, or a simple astragal band or carved frieze trim are used to add rich detail to the mantel while cleverly hiding gaps, fasteners, and joints. In addition to trimwork, friezes and blocks are often adorned with carved wooden plaques and appliqués.

While most mantels are made of wood, marble, stone, brick, river rock, iron, copper, and plaster were also commonly used for historical mantels. Modern mantels can include concrete, glass, cast-stone, stucco, and polymers.

MANTEL ANATOMY

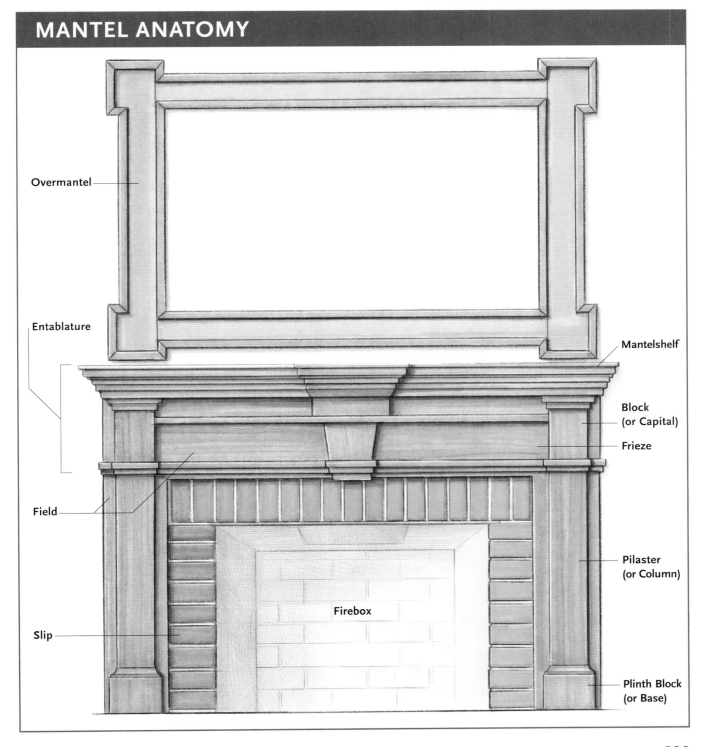

Overmantel

Entablature

Mantelshelf

Block (or Capital)

Frieze

Field

Pilaster (or Column)

Slip

Firebox

Plinth Block (or Base)

PERIOD MANTELS

As powerful symbols of domestic life, mantels have received special attention by designers throughout history and remain as some of the best examples of the major architectural periods.

Colonial Mantels. Decorative mantels weren't common in American homes until later in the Colonial period, mostly because the early settlers did little to beautify their large, utilitarian fireplaces. As the colonies developed and homes became more refined, mantels appeared in simple forms of wooden trimwork surrounding coarse brick openings. Some versions had a narrow mantelshelf. In the eighteenth century, fireplace openings were often surrounded by wood paneling that extended over the entire fireplace wall.

Georgian Mantels. The grand homes of the Georgian period featured the mantel as an important showpiece of bold, classical styling. Large pilasters led up to a carved or molded mantelshelf, which was not deep but often quite high. An overmantel was very common and often included a rectangular frame and a second set of pilasters or columns supporting a broken pediment above. The mantel detailing frequently tied into the room's ceiling cornice. Moldings carried deep profiles of classical design: egg-and-dart, acanthus leaf, key, and dentil motifs.

Federal Mantels. The restrained classical detailing of the Federal period created exceptionally elegant mantels. Their basic form and proportions have become a standard for much of traditional mantel design. Evolving out of the Georgian model and influenced heavily by the decorative designs of the English Adam style, Federal mantels included the basic parts in refined forms and typically had no overmantel. Frieze panels decorated with garlands, urns, and carved appliqués are characteristic features, as are delicate moldings of classical motifs and the use of built-up molding treatments.

Colonial fireplace mantels were of plain design and usually integrated into the surrounding room decor.

A richly decorated overmantel with broken pediment was a key characteristic of Georgian fireplaces.

This ornate Victorian mantel, left, shows a creative mix of elements typical of the period, including tall pilasters that rise from floor level to support a cornice at the top of the overmantel. A set of three mirrors completes the overmantel. A painted-tile slip separates the wooden trimwork from the firebox.

The brick-faced mantel shown above in a sedate Craftsman-inspired interior has an organic texture and sports a medieval arch motif over the fireplace opening. The fine yet plain mantelshelf is consistent with the room's trimwork.

Narrow frieze panels, below, with delicate swags and finely carved plaques are sure signs of Federal-style mantels.

Victorian Mantels. Victorian mantel design is characterized most markedly by its break with classical rules of composition. While many versions employed classical elements, such as pilasters, columns, entablatures, and classical moldings, these were mixed liberally with Gothic shapes, spindle work, and Asian and other "exotic" imagery. Typical examples have ornate, imaginative designs and often include overmantels with display shelves and inset mirrors.

Craftsman Mantels. Craftsman-style mantels are simple and organic, relying on the natural beauty of raw materials rather than formal ornamentation. The classic wood frame facing of previous styles is replaced by flat fields of brick or tile, the latter usually with a monochrome, earth-tone finish or storied pattern. Many examples include a heavy wood mantelshelf with simple brackets or modillion blocks for support, often with a recessed nook above for displaying decorative items. Use of molding, if any, is minimal. A novel feature of the Craftsman style is the fireplace inglenook—an alcove housing the fireplace in the center with bench seating on either side.

DESIGNING YOUR MANTEL

There are no strict guidelines for mantel design, but traditional wooden mantels tend to follow a few basic design criteria. The one specification that you must include is proper clearance between the fireplace opening and any combustible parts of the mantel.

Most fire-safety codes require 6 inches of clearance to combustible materials that project up to ¾ inch from the face of the fireplace, and 12 inches of clearance to projections equal to or greater than 1½ inches. Other design considerations are based on the type of fireplace you have, the mantel's style, and whether it will be custom-built or ordered as a kit.

Traditional Designs

For a traditional wooden mantel, a good model with which to start is the basic four-part type shown in "Mantel Anatomy," page 199. This style of mantel has a field with vertical side boards that are 7 to 13 inches wide. The frieze board of the field should be between 1 and 2 times as wide as the side boards—enough room for the moldings and a flat area below for additional decoration. The mantelshelf may be anywhere from 5 to 12 inches deep, but it should fit the proportions of the mantel overall and not overhang its supporting moldings by more than a few inches.

smart tip

FIREPLACE CARE

IF YOUR FIREPLACE HAS NEVER WORKED PROPERLY, HAVE IT CHECKED BY A PROFESSIONAL BEFORE YOU START THE COSMETIC WORK. SOMETIMES A POOR DRAW CAN BE REMEDIED BY SOMETHING AS SIMPLE AS ADDING A LAYER OF BRICKS THAT RAISES THE FIREBOX FLOOR.

Classical architecture receives a modern interpretation in the elegant mantel design shown left. Streamlined pilaster forms intersect a simple crown molding below the mantelshelf. A fine band of molding subtly creates the look of an entablature.

The combustible parts of a mantel, above, should be placed at least 6 in. from the firebox opening.

This elaborate yet refined mantel, opposite, employs Georgian-style features to enhance a projecting fireplace wall: a surround full of classical detailing, an overmantel framing a decorative mirror, and fluted pilasters starting at a paneled wainscot and extending up to the ceiling cornice.

Mantels

Columns and Pilasters

Pilasters or columns extend from the floor to the under-side of the shelf and are narrower than the vertical field boards, even with molding applied. The middle sections of pilasters can be fluted, reeded, recess-paneled, or left plain, while columns look especially ornate when wrapped with vines or floral strands. Plinths and bases add archi-tectural weight to pilasters and columns, as do top blocks and capitals. Square-edged plinths and blocks also serve as projections for wrapping with molding. Frieze panels can receive almost any type of decoration, but traditional styling always calls for symmetry and balance. A central block helps break up the frieze and can project for addi-tional molding detail.

Mantelshelves. Most mantelshelves are between 52 and 62 inches above the floor, although this varies based on the size of the fireplace and whether the hearth is raised or flush with the floor. For best appearance, the sides of the mantel should be aligned with or extend just beyond the sides of a flush hearth; for a raised hearth, the mantel should equal the hearth width or be slightly narrower.

If you're adding tile to the slips around the fireplace opening, choose a tile size that will result in a minimum of cuts. Above the opening, start with a full tile in the cen-ter rather than a grout joint, and place any cut tiles along the side slips at the bottom. Cover the outside edges of the tile with a small molding, or mill a rabbet into the field boards to receive the tile edges.

This simple wooden mantel, opposite far left, features a clever departure from conventional design.

A cabin-style setting would be incomplete without a rustic fireplace, opposite top. The craftsman who built this custom mantel added a secondary mantelshelf for decorative items.

Before central heating systems, all rooms were heated by fireplaces, opposite bottom. Those in bedrooms and other private areas were smaller and decorated more simply than fireplaces in public rooms.

A massive stone mantel, above, epitomizes the decorating term "anchor." The Gothic arch and projecting emblem are medieval features.

BUILDING YOUR OWN MANTEL

The best thing about building a mantel is that you can construct almost all of it in your workshop, then install it as one piece. A few power tools that will make the job go smoothly are a biscuit joiner for assembling the field boards, a power miter saw for making all the miter cuts on the trim molding, and a pneumatic finish nailer for attaching the molding.

There are a number of places to find mantel designs, including woodworking books and magazines. Another option is to find a mantel you like and duplicate its design. Sketch the overall design on graph paper; then break down the design into individual components. You can reproduce most wooden mantels with standard molding profiles. After removing your old mantel, take measurements and make a scaled drawing of the new mantel from which to work. If you're adding tile, select the tile before building the mantel to be sure the dimensions are correct.

Installing the Mantel. Center the mantel over the fireplace opening, and fasten it to the wall studs with screws or 16d casing nails. Countersink the fasteners and plug or putty the holes. Add thin edge molding along the outside edges of the field boards and along the tile or brick inside the field. If necessary, plane or trim the molding to follow wall contours. Also add molding along the back edge of the shelf if there are any large gaps.

Careful planning has greatly improved the look of this simple fireplace, below left. Two rows of tile visually extend the hearth up to the bottom of firebox, while two more rows cover the black metal case along the top. A traditional wooden surround adds an attractive frame and a built-in appearance.

The handsome Federal-style mantel shown below may seem impossible to duplicate, but you can come fairly close by using standard materials. In addition to using moldings for the mantel, install marble tiles on the slip area.

MANTEL CONSTRUCTION

THE ILLUSTRATION BELOW shows a basic four-piece mantel made with ¾-inch MDF, which is a good choice for a mantel you'll be painting. The shelf is made from two layers of MDF laminated together with glue and screws. If you prefer a natural-grain finish, use a finish-grade plywood with a hardwood veneer and cover all of the exposed edges with molding.

The Main Pieces. To build the mantel, cut the side field boards and frieze board, and join them with biscuits and glue. Assemble the shelf, and attach it to the top edges of the field with glue and screws, making

sure it is perpendicular to the field. Attach the pilasters and any blocks at the ends by screwing through the back of the field. Install an entablature block the same way.

Molding Applications. You can add molding that won't come in contact with the wall or fireplace opening while the mantel is still on your bench. Install other molding to hide gaps after you have mounted the mantel to the wall. However, you might choose to hide the mounting fasteners behind some molding, and therefore would leave off the appropriate pieces until later.

MANTEL CONSTRUCTION

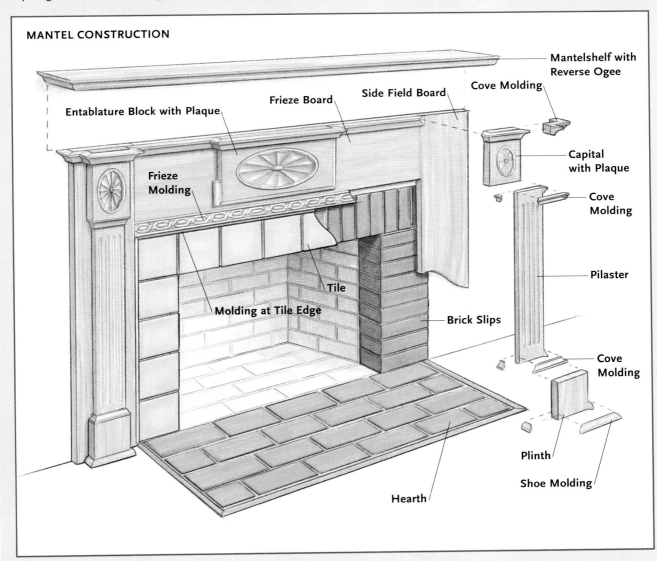

MANTEL KITS

Install-it-yourself mantel kits are a great option for those who don't want to build a custom mantel. Complete mantels are available in wood, cast-stone, iron, plaster, and other materials. You can also order elements a la carte, such as overmantel decorations, columns and pilasters, mantelshelves, corbels and brackets, decorative blocks, and appliqués. Most manufacturers offer mantels in various traditional and contemporary styles in a few different materials and sizes, or you can order custom sizes and designs for an extra fee.

Kit Installation. Kit mantels are typically shipped in three pieces, plus trim and accessories. Assembly and installation are simple: attach the side pieces to the mantelshelf; install a mounting board to the wall; then fasten the shelf to the mounting board and the sidepieces to the wall. If you plan to paint the mantel, choose a model made of MDF, pine, or poplar, which are less expensive than hardwood versions. You can buy mantel kits through fireplace retail stores or through manufacturers' catalogs or Web sites.

MANTEL MAKEOVERS

Sprucing up an old fireplace might involve as little as changing the paint color or as much as remodeling the entire fireplace wall. Budgets vary, of course, but there are a lot of materials and design possibilities with which to work, for both do-it-yourself and professional projects.

If you've updated the rest of your house and the fireplace looks a little neglected and out of touch, paint the mantel to match the surrounding decor. For a slightly more invasive approach, update the mantel's trimwork or replace it altogether. To help generate decorating ideas, look to other design elements in your home. Some architects of the past liked to mimic exterior details in their mantel designs. In a modern home, a clever carpenter might use leftover railing stock from the home's main staircase to create custom molding under a mantelshelf.

In addition to classic rectangular forms, mantel kits are available in styles that break with traditional standards, opposite top. The curvilinear detailing and splayed pilasters of this kit mantel bring a touch of eighteenth-century France to a modern room.

Victorian mantels, with their rich wood hues and charming decoration, opposite bottom, are the epitome of domestic comfort. This relatively plain example bears an overmantel mirror and patterned-tile slips that are typical period features.

With a four-sided surround and continuous metal frame, below left, this bedroom fireplace assumes the aspect of a wall hanging. The position of the fireplace allows it to be viewed from the bed.

Heavy curved molding, below, serves as a strong border for this tiled mantel. The mantel, framed print, and matching wall sconces create an appealing composition.

Mantels

TAKING THE HEAT

WHEN ADDING TILE TO A MANTEL SUR-ROUND, USE A HEAT-RESISTANT THINSET AND MORTAR. STANDARD THINSET, OR-GANIC MASTICS, AND STANDARD MORTAR CAN CRACK UNDER EXTREMELY HOT TEM-PERATURES.

Adding Tile. Adding tile is one of the best ways to make over an old brick surround. Because tile is non-combustible, you can install it right up to the fireplace opening. A complete tile treatment might include covering a raised brick hearth or extending a flush hearth to cover a larger floor area. A flush mantel treatment with a tile field surrounding the fireplace opening and no shelf above has a clean, contemporary feel. Newer homes with original gas fireplaces often have a simple tile decoration and perhaps a small hearth. Remodeling these is relatively easy—you can replace the old tile with a more appealing style, add some bold trimwork for greater definition, or change the look entirely by installing a traditional wooden mantel with narrow slips of tile around the opening.

Stone Mantels. At the other end of the spectrum from molded wood and decorative tile surrounds is the cabin-style warmth of a mortared stone fireplace. By using ve-neer-stone, you can create the look of a real stone fireplace without even calling a mason. Veneer-stone is a molded cement product with natural pigments that convincingly imitates the appearance and texture of natural stone. Indi-vidual "stones" have flat back surfaces that install easily over the wall and a layer of metal mesh. The pieces are mortared into place in a random arrangement; then the spaces in between are filled with mortar and tooled. The most authentic-looking stone treatments include a pro-jecting fireplace with veneer-stone running all the way up to the ceiling, imitating a stone chimney.

A fireplace remodel offers a good opportunity to add details to the fireplace wall. Built-in bookcases or cabinets set into recesses made by a projecting fireplace are a typi-cal embellishment. When there's no space to the sides, you can add shallow bookcases or shelves to create a re-cess for the fireplace itself.

Adding built-in bookcases and cabinets, opposite top, is an excellent way to fill the recesses that often flank a traditional fireplace.

The overmantel, opposite bottom, is often forgotten in modern designs. Here, a simple framed mirror makes an elegant design statement.

Veneer-stone, above, creates the look of traditional mortared stone at a fraction of the cost of real masonry. Special corner pieces effectively replicate the depth of actual stones.

Hand-painted tiles, right, add a personal touch to fireplace slips. You can buy professionally made tiles at tile stores or through art dealers, or do it yourself at a paint-your-own pottery studio.

ZERO-CLEARANCE FIREPLACES

Before the advent of zero-clearance fireplaces, homes that were built without hearths stayed that way. Adding a new masonry fireplace simply is not an option for most home-owners. But today's gas- and wood-burning zero-clearance units are so simple to install that they've become a viable option for even minor remodeling projects. Made of metal with a masonry lining, these self-contained fireplaces are lightweight enough to sit on a standard framed floor and can be surrounded by a wooden frame to within ½ inch of the main box (hence the name). A two-piece vent pipe draws outside air into the unit for combustion while exhausting smoke out of the house.

One clear drawback of zero-clearance fireplaces is that without the right decoration, they can look conspicuously artificial. Here are a few ideas that can help make one of these modern wonders look like a real masonry fireplace:

■ Choose a model with a minimum of brass or other decorative metal features on the front panels.

■ Cover the front of the box with ceramic tile; then surround the tile with a traditional mantel.

■ Recess the unit into the floor so that the bottom of the firebox is flush with the floor surface, or build a raised hearth that is flush with the firebox. (Check with the manufacturer to make that sure the installation is safe for your model.)

The stone surround and raised hearth, above, complement the design of this rustic-style room. The built-in wood box is a useful accessory.

Zero-clearance units, above right, open up a number of design possibilities. This contemporary treatment does away with the traditional mantel.

A contemporary flush tile treatment, right, adds plenty of life to this fireplace without being obtrusive.

ZERO-CLEARANCE FIREPLACE INSTALLATION

ZERO-CLEARANCE UNITS are great choices for remodeling projects. They are light enough for standard floor framing, and they can be installed within inches of drywall-covered walls. But their biggest advantage is the fact that there is often no need for a standard chimney or flue. With direct-vent units, the flue can exit the top, back, or sides of the firebox. That means you can install a unit against a wall and have the flue go through the wall directly to the outdoors. This opens up your design options. For example, with a direct-vent fireplace it is possible to install a unit under a window.

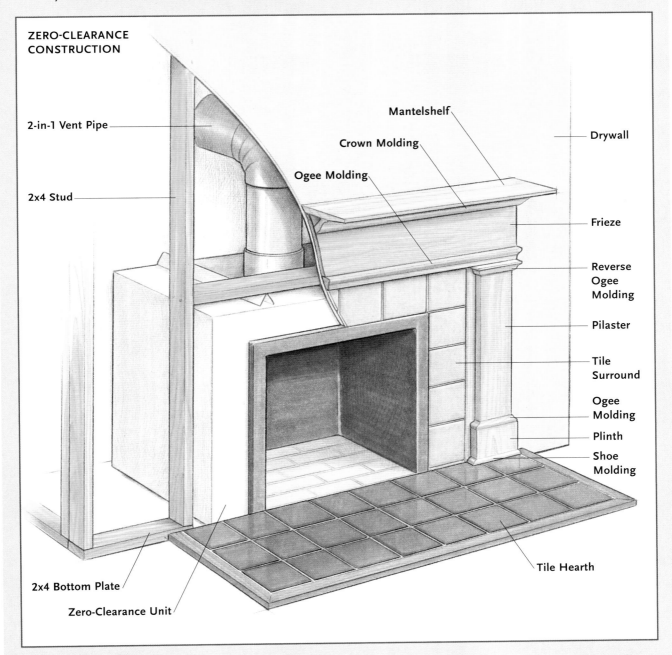

ZERO-CLEARANCE CONSTRUCTION

2-in-1 Vent Pipe

2x4 Stud

2x4 Bottom Plate

Zero-Clearance Unit

Mantelshelf

Crown Molding

Ogee Molding

Drywall

Frieze

Reverse Ogee Molding

Pilaster

Tile Surround

Ogee Molding

Plinth

Shoe Molding

Tile Hearth

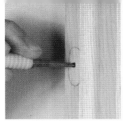

finishing trimwork

9

ONE OF THE LAST THINGS you will do when installing trimwork is apply some sort of finish to the material. You can either paint the molding or apply a clear coating. Paint can be a latex or oil-based formula, and paints are vailable in a variety of sheens. Clear finishes cover a range of materials, including oil, shellac, varnish, and lacquer, and with these too there are both water- and solvent-based products. While it may be the last step in a project, deciding on a finish should be one of the first decisions you make because the material you select often determines the types of finish that are possible.

PAINTED FINISHES

Because paint is an opaque coating, it makes sense that it is the more forgiving category of finish. You can fill and sand small smooth gaps in joints and defects in the trim surface prior to applying the final coats of paint, and if well executed, they will not be visible. A painted finish allows you to select from a wider choice of trim materials. You can apply a painted finish to finger-jointed or select pine, poplar, MDF, resin, plaster, or polystyrene foam trim elements, and you can mix materials as well. It is important to remember, though, that paint is not an opaque curtain that will hide a poor installation; sloppy, ill-fitting joints and carelessness in implementing your design will still be apparent. And you may be surprised to see how paint will make some problems visible that you do not even notice in the raw wood surface. So do not approach a paint-grade job as an opportunity to relax your high standards of workmanship. Painted finishes, especially those with glossy sheen levels, can telegraph irregularities in a surface much more than you might expect. Fill any nail holes with wood filler, and sand until the area both looks and feels perfectly smooth. Apply primer to all natural wood surfaces before painting.

Inspect Surfaces. Use a bright light to illuminate the wood surfaces as you inspect them for defects and mill marks. Even though most boards and moldings feel rather smooth if you run your hands over the surface, it is common for there to be parallel knife marks left from the manufacturing process. In some cases, these marks are so subtle that a painted finish will make them invisible. But sometimes, they are readily visible and will telegraph through the finish. If you have some doubt as to how the finish will appear, apply a test finish on scrap material. Examine the finished sample in bright light to judge whether the stock requires sanding before applying the paint.

Choosing Paint. Many trim pieces, including casing and base moldings, get bumped and brushed up against more often than a typical wall surface. For that reason, it is most common to use flat paint for a wall and semigloss paint for trim. Latex paints are usually sufficiently durable for these uses. However, some trim pieces, such as window sills and tops of chair rails, may experience plenty of wiping and handling. High-quality water-based paints, including "waterborne" and 100 percent acrylic types, offer greater durability and "scrubbability" than standard latex types. For the highest resistance to scratches and deglossing, a high-gloss oil- or alkyd-based paint is still the best choice, but those paints may be prohibited in your area. If you use acrylic or waterborne paints for these areas, you may need to repaint every few years.

SOLVENT-BASED PAINTS

IN RESPONSE to pressures to reduce VOCs (volatile organic compounds), which contribute to ground-level ozone, several states—California, New York, New Jersey, Pennsylvania, Delaware, Maryland, and the District of Columbia—now have regulations in force that limit the content of VOCs in household paints. Similar legislation is being considered in a number of other states. As a result, in these areas most solvent-based coatings will likely disappear from the market and be replaced by waterborne products. Traditionalists may be dismayed by this prospect, as oil-based paints have long had the reputation of better appearance and performance when compared with latex formulas. However, paint manufacturers are quick to assure the consumer that water-based coatings have greatly improved over the last few years and will perform as well, or better, than their solvent-based equivalents.

Four types of paint finishes from left to right—flat, eggshell, semigloss, and gloss. They range from matte to shiny.

REMOVING DENTS

Trim that has been hand-nailed will often show "smiles" or "frowns" created by mishits. These dents will telegraph through any type of finish and can ruin an otherwise-excellent job. Fortunately it's not hard to eliminate hammer marks and other dents. The technique shown here will work on fairly shallow dents and will work better on softwood than on hardwood. If you find that you cannot raise the dent using these instructions, you may need to fill the dent with wood filler.

TOOLS & MATERIALS

- Hammer ▮ Nail set
- Household iron
- Small brush ▮ Cotton cloth ▮ Sandpaper

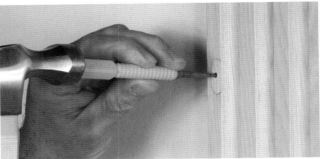

1 A hammer mark will stand out on a piece of newly installed trim (top). This mark will telegraph through the finish. Make sure that the nailhead is set about $1/8$ in. below the wood surface before beginning the repair (bottom). Place the tip of a nail set onto the nailhead, and tap with a hammer.

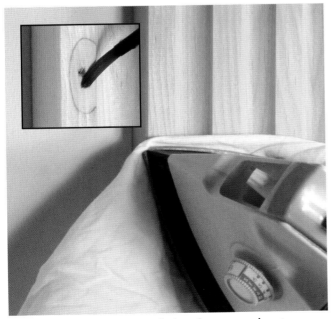

2 Use a small artist's paintbrush to spread water on the surface of the dent, covering the entire area. Let the water soak in for just a minute, and then repeat the application (inset). Place a clean cotton cloth over the dent, and use a household iron on the highest setting to heat the dented area. The steam will force the wood cells to swell.

3 Wait a few minutes for the area to dry. Use sandpaper and a block to remove the raised grain from the area of the repair. Repeat the process if necessary. The nailhole is now ready for filling (inset).

smart tip

CAULKING INSIDE CORNERS

TO FILL GAPS IN INSIDE CORNERS, USE A GOOD-QUALITY ACRYLIC LATEX CAULK—ONE THAT CONTAINS SILICONE—TO FILL THE SPACES IN THE JOINT. REMEMBER, THOUGH, THAT CAULK IS NOT EFFECTIVE AS A REMEDY FOR LARGE GAPS, THOSE LARGER THAN 1/16 INCH. IMMEDIATELY AFTER YOU FILL A JOINT, USE A WET FINGER OR PUTTY KNIFE TO SMOOTH THE SURFACE OF THE CAULK AND REMOVE EXCESS MATERIAL. YOU CAN ALSO USE CAULK TO FILL GAPS BETWEEN TRIM AND THE WALL OR CEILING SURFACE. FILL AND TOOL ONE JOINT AT A TIME BEFORE THE CAULK STARTS TO FORM A SKIN ON ITS SURFACE.

Filling Nailholes. Because trim relies primarily on nails, and lots of them, to hold the individual elements in place, one of your main concerns will be to fill the holes over the nailheads. If you used a nail gun for installation, the nails should all be properly set. If you have been nailing by hand, go over your work to check that all heads are set. In order for filler to hold well in a hole, the nail should be set about 1/8 inch below the wood surface.

For paint-grade work, fillers come in two primary types—drying and flexible putty varieties. Of the two types, drying filler will do the better job, but it also requires more work because it must be sanded after application. Drying fillers come in one and two-part formulas. For trimwork, the one-part product is fine and simpler to use. Use a small putty knife or a finger to fill each nailhole. For best results, slightly overfill each hole, because most fillers shrink slightly as they dry. Let the product dry according to the directions on the package; then use sandpaper and a backer block to level the filler flush to the surrounding wood surface. You can also use a drying filler to repair scratches, dents, or natural defects in the wood surface. If the defect is large, you should plan to use two layers of filler, allowing the first layer to dry completely before applying the second.

If you want to use flexible painter's putty to fill nailholes, it is best to prime the wood first. When the primer is dry, lightly sand it to remove any roughness. Knead a golf-ball size piece of putty until it is soft and pliable; then apply the putty using a knife or your finger. Wipe any excess putty from the surrounding wood surface with a clean rag before applying the first coat of paint.

For filling nailholes in polystyrene molding, the best material to use is drywall compound. Slightly overfill the holes to allow for shrinkage, and when dry, sand off the excess.

Stained finishes, left, allow the natural beauty of the wood to show through.

Use clear lumber, opposite, for any type of clear finish, as defects will become apparent.

CLEAR OR STAINED FINISHES

Trim that will receive a stained or clear finish requires a different level of care. With a clear finish, even small gaps in joints are hard to hide, so it is inevitable that the installation process will be slower and more demanding. Whether your trim is pine or one of the hardwood species, you should keep in mind that the application of stain will emphasize any defect in the wood surface. Scratches or dents act as magnets for stain, and it will settle in these areas and inevitably draw your eye. Mill marks and cross-grain sanding scratches are also areas that will be accentuated by stain.

Trim Prep. If you're putting a stained or clear finish on your trim, lightly sand the material before you install it to remove many manufacturing defects. As a general rule, 120-grit sandpaper is appropriate for this type of sanding. Use a backing block for the sandpaper whenever possible. Always move the sandpaper parallel with the wood grain. Avoid cross-grain scratches, as they are particularly visible in stained finishes. Power sanders may be useful for sanding flat stock, but if you use an orbital sander, always follow up by hand sanding. Orbital sanders leave small swirl marks on the wood surface, and these can become visible when you apply stain. To remove these marks, use the same-grit paper to give the surface a light sanding, working parallel with the wood grain.

Finishing. You can fill nailholes either before or after you apply the first coat of finish. If you want to use drying filler under a clear unstained finish, you should find one that closely matches the color of the wood. It is best to make up a finished wood sample and use it when selecting the color of the filler because all woods change color when a finish is applied—and various finishes will color the wood differently. Solvent-based finishes tend to lend a warm amber cast to the wood tone, while water-based finishes are clear. Nondrying fillers are available in two types, both intended for use after the finish has been applied. Soft, putty-type fillers are available in a wide variety of colors to match different species and stains. Knead the filler until it is soft, and work it into the holes. Crayon and pencil-style fillers are waxy and quite hard. Rub the stick over the nailhole until it is filled, and then wipe away the excess. Some of these colored fillers will accept a top coat of finish; others are intended for use after the final coat.

For final touchup after the last coat of finish has cured, use colored markers that are matched to different color finishes. These are handy for small scuffs and scratches that might result from routine life around the house.

PART II:
Fundamentals

trim materials 10

THE PROJECTS IN THIS BOOK can be completed using solid wood, medium density fiberboard, or one of the new resin products. When selecting one, consider the look you hope to achieve, the workability of the material, and the cost. While there are limits, it is safe to say that you will be able to realize almost any design you dream up or any design you wish to copy using the materials available. Home centers and lumber-yards stock many of the most popular molding profiles in both pine and selected hardwoods, as well as plastic resins. If you can't find what you are looking for locally, consult an online woodworker's supply site.

LUMBER FOR TRIMWORK

If you stroll down the lumber aisles at the local home center, you will see racks of interior moldings and boards in pine, red oak, and poplar. These species are the most common choices for interior millwork, and most stock molding profiles are available in these woods. Millwork is the term used to describe lumber that has been machined into particular profiles. This can include flat stock for door jambs, as well as intricate molding.

Pine

Pine has long been the default choice for interior millwork for a number of reasons. Because pine trees grow faster than many other species, manufacturers have a source of lumber that can be renewed, keeping the cost of materials more manageable. Door and window manufacturers have used pine because of its high resin content, which makes it more resistant to rot than some other species. Builders like pine because it is relatively lightweight, it is easy to install, and it takes a nice finish.

Lumber Grades. Most interior trim jobs use a combination of molded stock and flat lumber. When you shop for pine lumber, you will find that it is available in either *clear* or *common* grades. While the details of lumber grading can get somewhat technical, a functional approach is simple. Clear, or select, grades have relatively few defects such as knots or pitch pockets, while common-grade lumber can include more of these defects. The difference in price in these material grades can be substantial, but for most trim work you should choose clear, or select, stock. The reasons for using clear grades have to do with more than just the appearance of the job. The additional labor involved in cutting around defects, and the inevitable waste, makes the efficient use of lesser grades questionable, even for a painted finish. And knots that are left in place will usually become visible after a time, even through a first-quality paint job.

Molding Types. When it comes to choosing molding, the choices are slightly different. It is difficult, if not impossible, to find molding profiles cut from common-grade lumber. Clear-grade lumber is used for most profiles because knots and sap pockets would create inevitable holes in the molding and can dull expensive cutters. Clear-grade material is suitable for both stain-grade and painted finishes.

Finger-Jointed Molding. If you are looking to save some money, and your job is definitely to be painted, you can consider *finger-jointed* molding. This term describes molding stock that has been built up of short lengths of lumber. The ends of each short piece are machined in an interlocking finger profile and glued together. The built-up lumber is then run through a molder, just like clear stock, and the profile is cut.

The use of short pieces of lumber saves money. In this process, no effort is made to match the color or grain of the lumber, but knots and other defects are excluded. As a result, you can use this stock for paint-grade work and save quite a bit on the cost of material; however, finger-jointed stock is usually only offered in the most common molding profiles. Many suppliers now apply a primer coat to their finger-jointed stock, so you can save both money and labor by using this material.

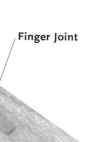

Finger Joint

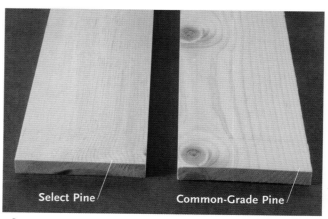

Select Pine   Common-Grade Pine

Clear, or select, pine, left, has few defects; common-grade pine, right, contains more knots and pitch pockets.

Material and finish go hand-in-hand when designing a trim package. In this room, white-painted wainscoting complements the wall color.

STOCK MOLDING PROFILES

MOST LUMBERYARDS and home centers provide a display with a sample of available molding profiles. Each retailer has a selection of moldings that they carry as stock items, and while most are similar, you may find more profiles at one dealer over another. Moldings that are manufactured by one of the large millwork suppliers will be identical from one source to another, but those that are turned out by a local millwork house might not exactly match those of another manufacturer. In other words, a colonial casing from your local home center may not match the one from Johnny's Lumber Barn, despite having the same descriptive name. Because of this possible discrepancy, it is best to purchase all of each molding profile from one supplier.

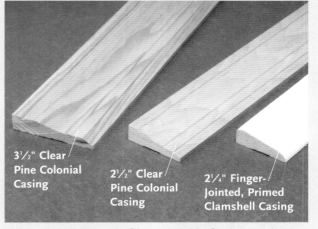

3½" Clear Pine Colonial Casing

2½" Clear Pine Colonial Casing

2¼" Finger-Jointed, Primed Clamshell Casing

Typical molding profiles available from most home centers include the casings shown above.

IF YOU DON'T SEE IT, ASK

IF YOU DO NOT SEE A MOLDING PROFILE ON DISPLAY THAT FITS YOUR NEEDS, IT IS STILL POSSIBLE THAT YOUR RETAILER CAN OBTAIN WHAT YOU WANT. MOST DEALERS HAVE ACCESS TO A MORE EXTENSIVE SELECTION OF PROFILES THAN THEY CHOOSE TO STOCK, SO IT'S WORTH ASKING IF THEY HAVE A CATALOG OF AVAILABLE MOLDINGS. OF COURSE, EXPECT TO PAY A PREMIUM FOR SPECIAL ORDERS, BUT IN MOST CASES, IT WILL BE LESS EXPENSIVE THAN COMMISSIONING A CUSTOM MOLDING.

Poplar

Although pine is the primary softwood that is used for interior trim, poplar is a hardwood species that shares many of the qualities of pine, and it can be used in similar situations. Poplar is soft enough so that you can nail it without drilling pilot holes, and its closed-grain structure finishes well. The natural appearance of poplar can range from a warm cream color to a quite distinct green or purple, and it has a rather bland grain pattern, so it is most often painted. But if the material is carefully selected, you could use it with a stained finish. Poplar is frequently used by millwork houses for their custom paint-grade molding. It is a fast-growing species, and it is one of the least expensive hardwoods.

Red Oak

When home builders decide to provide an upgraded trim package, red oak is often their first choice of materials. Its open-grain structure can create bold contrast, especially when the wood is stained. But red oak also has a pleasant reddish-brown natural color, leaving open the option of treating it with a clear finish and no stain. Depending on the way the lumber is cut from the log, it can display a grain that is linear, with long parallel grain lines, or graphic, with peaked cathedral shapes that run the length of a board.

Because it is used extensively for interior trim, many of the stock profiles that are available in pine are also available in red oak.

THE BACK SIDE OF MOLDING

WHEN YOU EXAMINE most commercial molding, especially those pieces wider than 2 inches, you will notice that the back side has been slightly hollowed out. This relief cut serves two purposes. First, by reducing the thickness, it helps to lessen the tendency of the stock to cup. And second, it allows the molding to bridge any irregularities in the wall surface and stay tight at the outside edges—where it counts.

Wide moldings often have relief cuts on the back. The hollowed-out sections help reduce cupping.

Relief Cuts

HARDWOOD VERSUS SOFTWOOD

IN A HOME CENTER, poplar and other hardwood boards are often sold according to the same system that is used for softwood lumber. In this convention, boards are given a nominal size description, 1x2, 1x4, etc., that corresponds to the size of the board that is rough-sawn at the mill before it is planed smooth. The actual size board that you purchase is always less than the nominal size. For instance, the 1x2 and 1x4 boards are actually ¾ x 1½ inches and ¾ x 3½ inches. These boards are sold in even foot lengths from 6 to 16 feet.

If you shop for material at a hardwood lumberyard, however, you will find another classification system. Hardwood lumber is also classified according to the thickness of the material before it is planed smooth, but the descriptive categories are different. Trees are sawn at the mill into boards of varying thickness measured in quarters of an inch. For example, a board that is 1 inch thick would be called 4/4 stock and one 2 inches thick would be 8/4 stock. These rough-sawn boards are then dried and sold to a wholesaler or end user who planes them to a finished thickness. In addi-tion, hardwood lumber is normally sold in boards of random width and length. So specifying the amount of material needed for a particular job requires a bit more effort and results in a greater amount of waste.

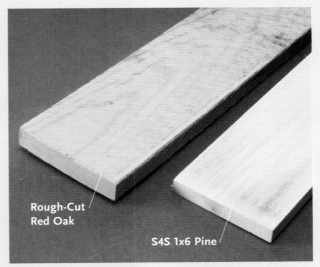

Rough-Cut Red Oak

S4S 1x6 Pine

Hardwood and softwood have different classification systems that denote stock size.

HARDWOOD LUMBER THICKNESS CHART

SIZE NAME	ROUGH THICKNESS	PLANED THICKNESS
4/4	1"	$^{13}/_{16}$"
5/4	1¼"	$1^{1}/_{16}$"
6/4	1½"	$1^{5}/_{16}$"
8/4	2"	$1^{3}/_{4}$"
10/4	2½"	$2^{5}/_{16}$"
12/4	3"	$2^{3}/_{4}$"

Painted finishes, opposite, are usually applied to molding made from softwood.

Stains and clear finishes, right, are usually reserved for hardwoods.

Selecting Wood Moldings

Keep in mind that although each molding profile usually has a particular use associated with it, you are not bound to use it in any specific way or in any specific place. For example, it is not unusual to find a baseboard profile used as a frieze board in a cornice.

In addition, you can cut a stock molding apart and use just part of the profile, either alone or in combination with other pieces. This technique may require additional modification, such as planing the back flat, but it provides another tool for expanding your design options.

Built-Up Designs. Another option is to create designs using two, three, or even four common profiles in one assembly. Some examples are shown on the opposite page, but you can easily create your own designs with a little experimentation. By varying the use of moldings and combining them in layered assemblies, you can achieve a wide variety of effects that create extravagant architectural details or may go well beyond the obvious applications.

Custom Profiles. If you find that you cannot achieve the look you desire with stock molding, even by combining profiles, you can turn to a custom molding supplier.

COMMON MOLDING PROFILES

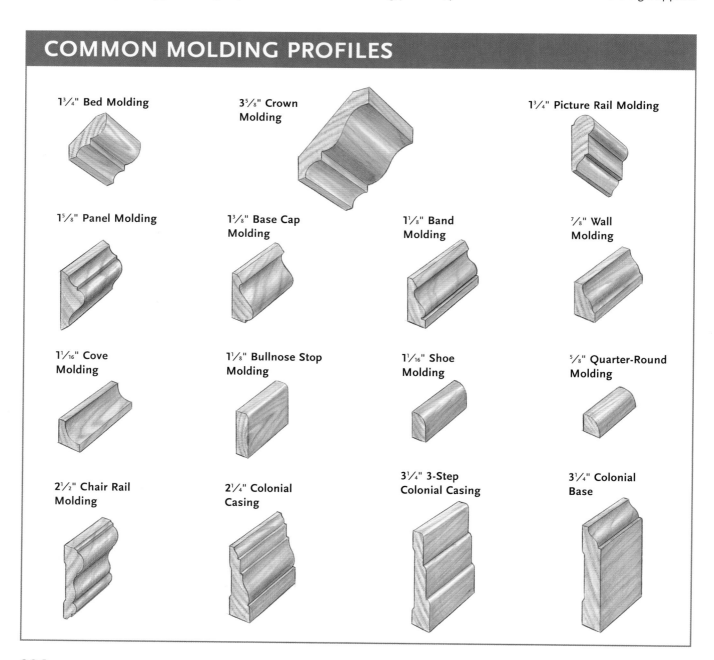

1³⁄₄" Bed Molding

3⁵⁄₈" Crown Molding

1³⁄₄" Picture Rail Molding

1⁵⁄₈" Panel Molding

1³⁄₈" Base Cap Molding

1¹⁄₈" Band Molding

⁷⁄₈" Wall Molding

1¹⁄₁₆" Cove Molding

1¹⁄₈" Bullnose Stop Molding

1¹⁄₁₆" Shoe Molding

⁵⁄₈" Quarter-Round Molding

2¹⁄₂" Chair Rail Molding

2¹⁄₄" Colonial Casing

3¹⁄₄" 3-Step Colonial Casing

3¹⁄₄" Colonial Base

Most areas of the country have custom millwork shops that offer a wide selection of profiles, as well as the capability to match an existing molding or a drawing that you provide. (See "Custom Molding Profiles," on pages 228–229 for a sample.) Most have Web sites, so you can see molding samples and profile drawings to help you select your profiles.

As you might expect, having custom moldings made can be expensive—especially if a new cutter must be ground for the job. The cost for these services is based on a combination of material and labor costs to install the knives and run the molder—knife grinding is additional and is based on the size of the knife and depth of profile. Most of these shops have an extensive collection of molding cutters from past jobs that they can use. You would be well advised to examine their list of available profiles before spending the money to have a new knife ground.

Once you enter the realm of custom molding, you open the door to a large world of material choices. Of course, for paint-grade work, poplar would be the first choice. But if you are attracted to a natural finish, you can consider any of the native or imported hardwoods.

Text continues on page 231.

BUILT-UP MOLDING PROFILES

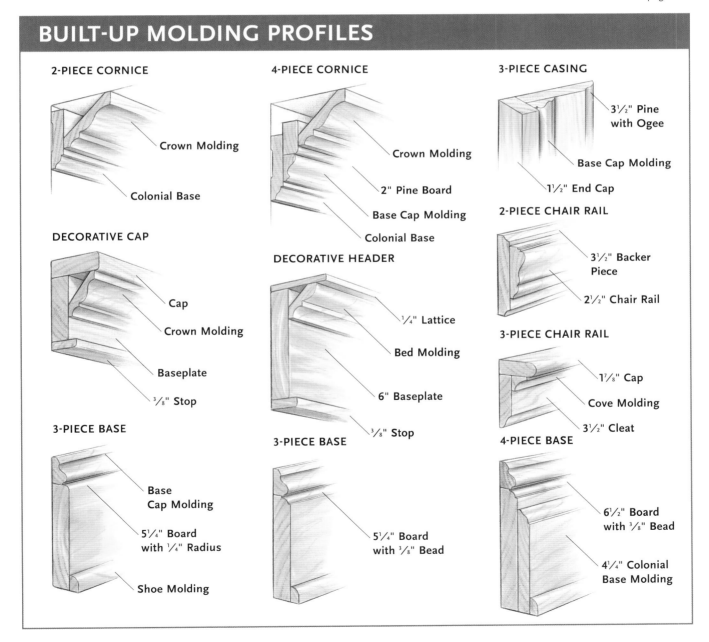

2-PIECE CORNICE
- Crown Molding
- Colonial Base

DECORATIVE CAP
- Cap
- Crown Molding
- Baseplate
- $3/8$" Stop

3-PIECE BASE
- Base Cap Molding
- $5^1/4$" Board with $1/4$" Radius
- Shoe Molding

4-PIECE CORNICE
- Crown Molding
- 2" Pine Board
- Base Cap Molding
- Colonial Base

DECORATIVE HEADER
- $1/4$" Lattice
- Bed Molding
- 6" Baseplate
- $3/8$" Stop

3-PIECE BASE
- $5^1/4$" Board with $3/8$" Bead

3-PIECE CASING
- $3^1/2$" Pine with Ogee
- Base Cap Molding
- $1^1/2$" End Cap

2-PIECE CHAIR RAIL
- $3^1/2$" Backer Piece
- $2^1/2$" Chair Rail

3-PIECE CHAIR RAIL
- $1^7/8$" Cap
- Cove Molding
- $3^1/2$" Cleat

4-PIECE BASE
- $6^1/2$" Board with $3/8$" Bead
- $4^1/4$" Colonial Base Molding

Trim Materials

CUSTOM MOLDING PROFILES

CORNICE

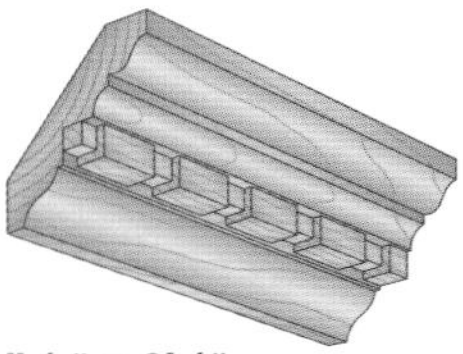

$^{11}/_{16}"$ x $3^{1}/_{4}"$

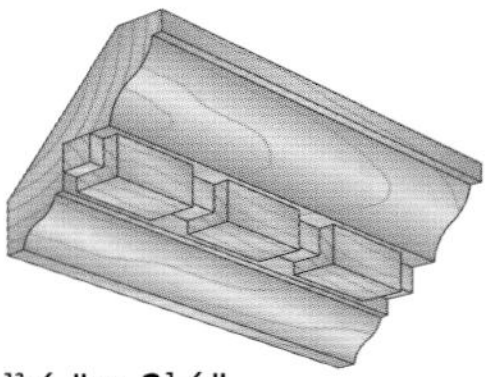

$^{13}/_{16}"$ x $3^{1}/_{2}"$

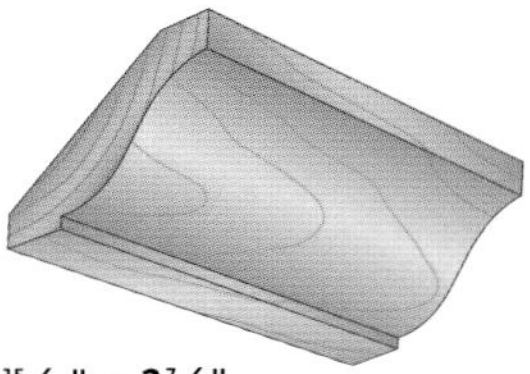

$^{15}/_{16}"$ x $3^{7}/_{8}"$

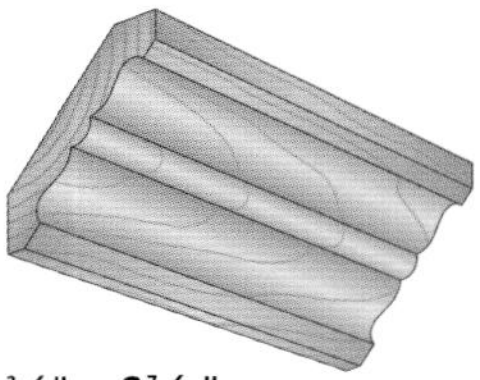

$^{3}/_{4}"$ x $3^{7}/_{16}"$

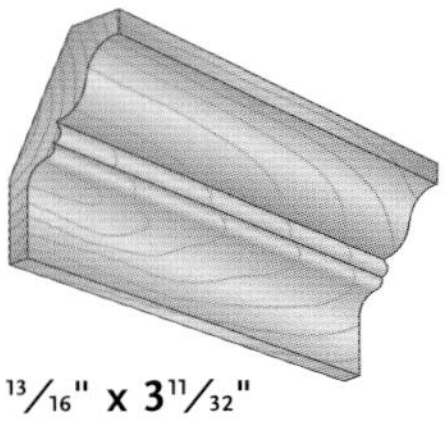

$^{13}/_{16}"$ x $3^{11}/_{32}"$

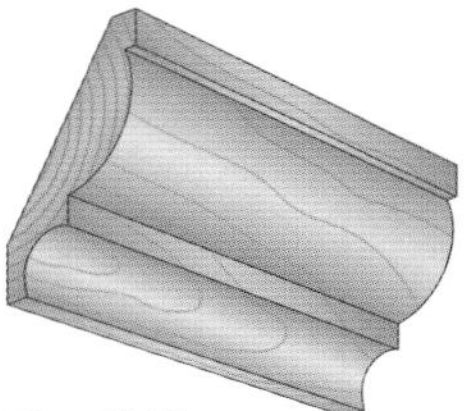

$1"$ x $3^{7}/_{8}"$

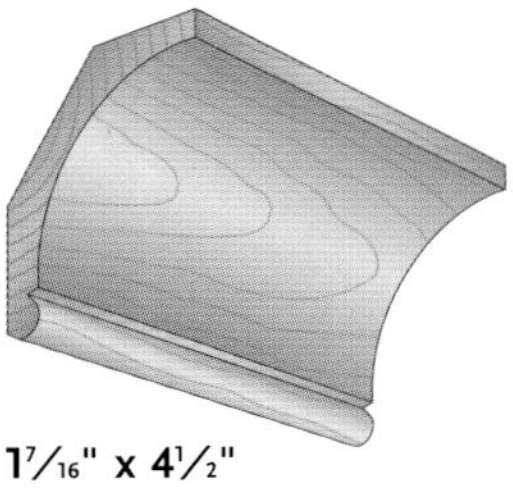

$1^{7}/_{16}"$ x $4^{1}/_{2}"$

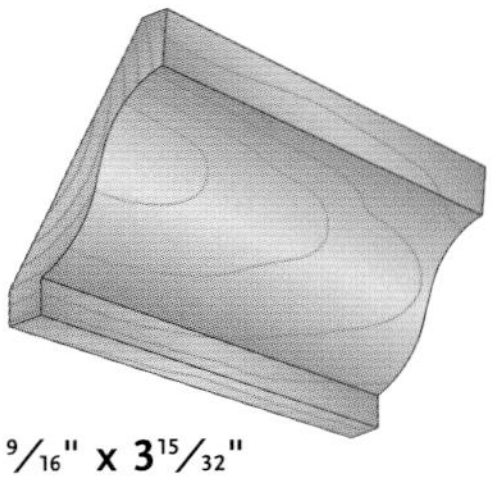

$^{9}/_{16}"$ x $3^{15}/_{32}"$

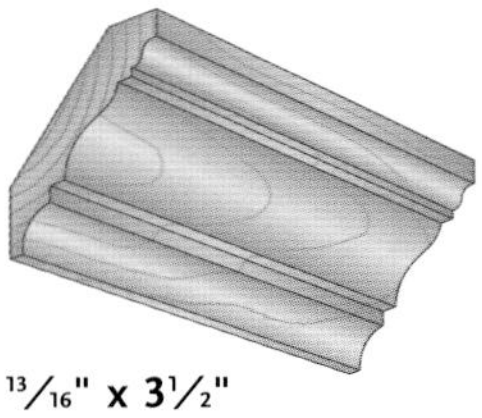

$^{13}/_{16}"$ x $3^{1}/_{2}"$

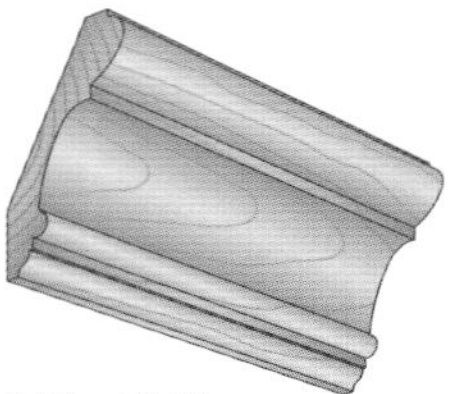

$^{3}/_{4}"$ x $3^{1}/_{2}"$

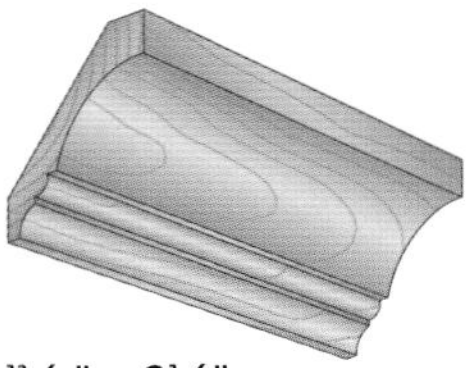

$^{13}/_{16}"$ x $3^{1}/_{4}"$

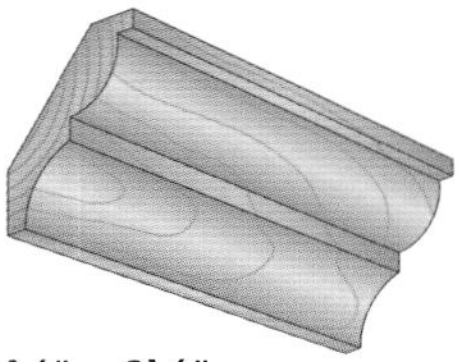

$^{3}/_{4}"$ x $3^{1}/_{8}"$

CHAIR RAIL

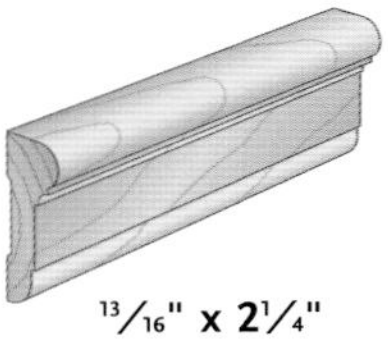

$^{13}/_{16}"$ x $2^{1}/_{4}"$

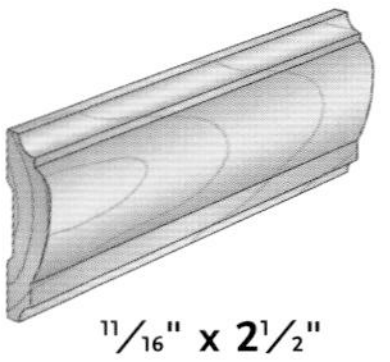

$^{11}/_{16}"$ x $2^{1}/_{2}"$

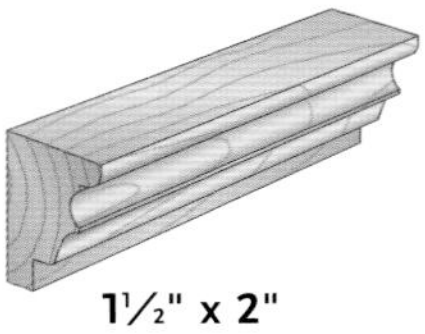

$1^{1}/_{2}"$ x $2"$

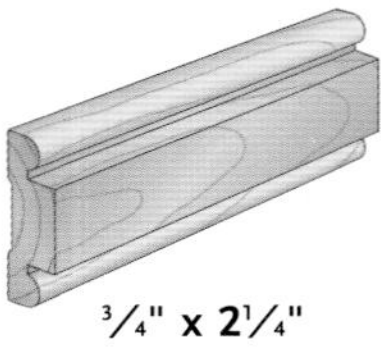

$^{3}/_{4}"$ x $2^{1}/_{4}"$

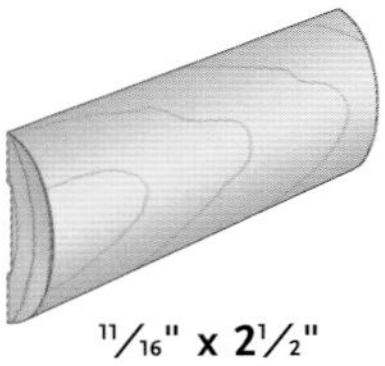

$^{11}/_{16}"$ x $2^{1}/_{2}"$

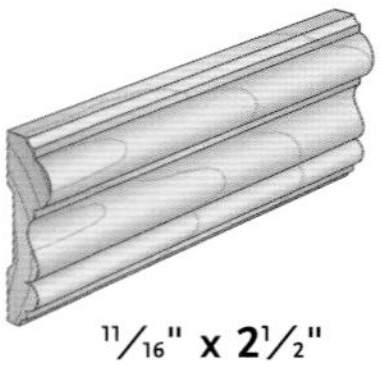

$^{11}/_{16}"$ x $2^{1}/_{2}"$

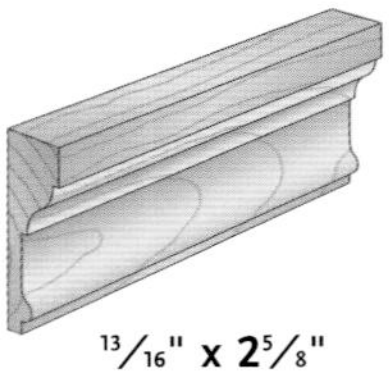

$^{13}/_{16}"$ x $2^{5}/_{8}"$

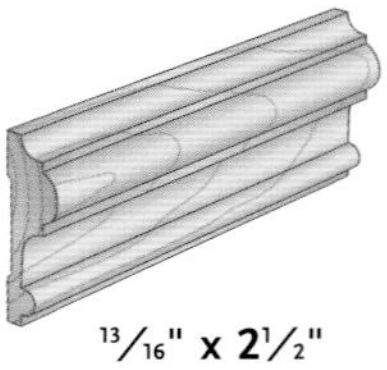

$^{13}/_{16}"$ x $2^{1}/_{2}"$

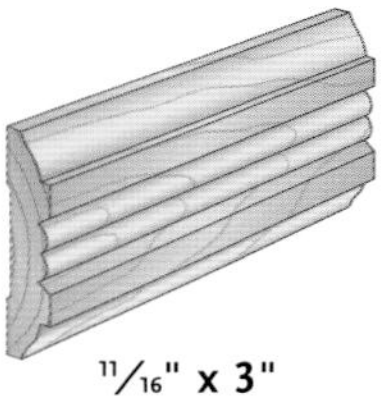

$^{11}/_{16}"$ x $3"$

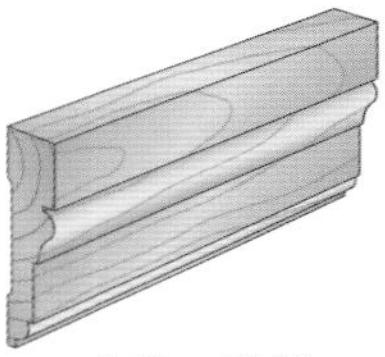

$^{3}/_{4}"$ x $2^{7}/_{8}"$

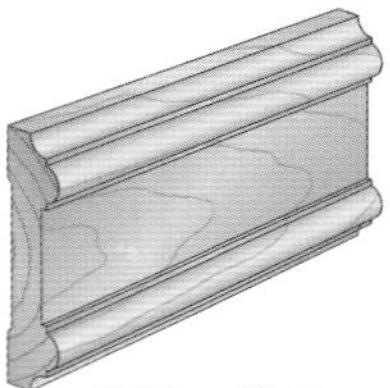

$^{13}/_{16}"$ x $3^{3}/_{8}"$

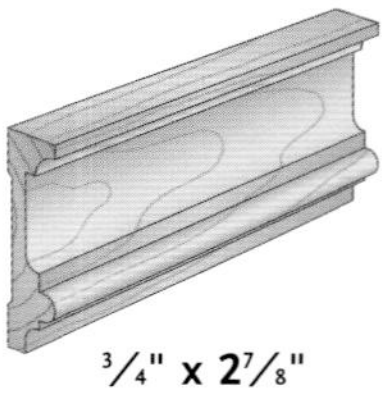

$^{3}/_{4}"$ x $2^{7}/_{8}"$

CASING

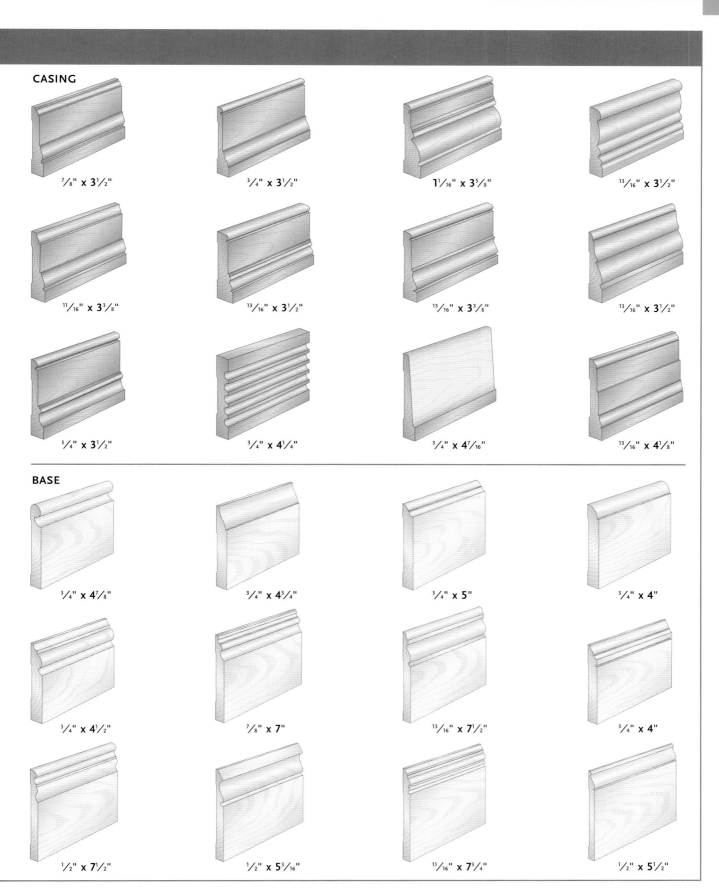

$^7/_8$" x $3^1/_2$"

$^3/_4$" x $3^1/_2$"

$1^1/_{16}$" x $3^5/_8$"

$^{13}/_{16}$" x $3^1/_2$"

$^{11}/_{16}$" x $3^3/_8$"

$^{13}/_{16}$" x $3^1/_2$"

$^{13}/_{16}$" x $3^3/_8$"

$^{13}/_{16}$" x $3^1/_2$"

$^3/_4$" x $3^1/_2$"

$^3/_4$" x $4^1/_4$"

$^3/_4$" x $4^7/_{16}$"

$^{13}/_{16}$" x $4^1/_8$"

BASE

$^3/_4$" x $4^7/_8$"

$^3/_4$" x $4^3/_4$"

$^3/_4$" x 5"

$^3/_4$" x 4"

$^3/_4$" x $4^1/_2$"

$^7/_8$" x 7"

$^{13}/_{16}$" x $7^1/_2$"

$^3/_4$" x 4"

$^1/_2$" x $7^1/_2$"

$^1/_2$" x $5^3/_{16}$"

$^{11}/_{16}$" x $7^3/_4$"

$^1/_2$" x $5^1/_2$"

Trim Materials

OPEN- AND CLOSED-GRAIN HARDWOODS

IN BROAD TERMS, hardwoods are divided into those with an open grain and those with a closed-grain structure. Woods with open grain include ash, red and white oak, walnut, butternut, elm, and mahogany. Some of these species feature a distinct difference in the density of the early and late seasonal growth that makes up each annual ring. As a result, when the wood is sliced, it displays a characteristic coarse appearance with alternating dense and porous grain. When these woods are stained, the open grain readily absorbs the color, while the dense areas are more resistant. This can create a striking effect, but for some situations it may appear too busy. Other open-grain woods have a more uniform grain, but one which is nonetheless porous, causing uneven absorption of the finish. When preparing an open-grain wood for a smooth finish, you should apply paste grain filler to fill the more porous areas of the wood surface. This technique prevents the finish material from being absorbed into the grain, which would otherwise leave a textured coating on the surface.

Closed-grain woods include birch, cherry, hard and soft maple, poplar, gum, and sycamore. These are woods of more uniform density and, except for figured varieties, generally present a quieter and more reserved appearance than the open-grained woods.

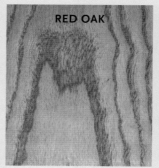
RED OAK

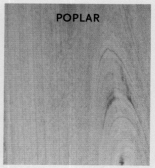
POPLAR

Open-grain wood absorbs stains more readily than closed grain. Red oak is open grain; poplar is closed grain.

Text continued from page 227.

Matching Lumber. If you select a custom hardwood molding, you may need some matching lumber as well. In most cases, your local home center won't be much help in this regard. Sometimes a custom millwork house will supply lumber in a matching species, but some are not equipped to provide sales of plain lumber. The alternative source is a dedicated hardwood supplier. These dealers are often a bit more difficult to locate, since most of their customers are cabinet and furniture shops, but many are willing to sell to retail clients. And if you only need a small amount of lumber, you can always approach local wood-workers—more often than not they are happy to help out an enthusiastic do-it-yourselfer. When all else fails, there are many lumber dealers who will ship material anywhere in the country. Just remember to factor in the cost of shipping when you put together your budget.

Painted finishes, opposite bottom, work well on both softwood and hardwood.

Finding matching lumber, below, is required on some trim projects.

CHARACTERISTICS OF LUMBER

Whether you are dealing with molding or flat lumber, wood is a dynamic material. Although it is solid and hard, it is not a static substance, and it responds to fluctuations in temperature and humidity by expanding, contracting, cupping, and warping. The degree to which any piece of wood reacts to changing conditions is dependent on a number of factors, and the study of this subject has filled many volumes. But for the purpose of trim installation, some basic knowledge can be useful.

Quarter-Sawn Lumber. When boards are cut from a log, the orientation of the grain in the boards is determined by the way that the growth rings intersect the board surface. At one extreme is a *quarter-sawn* board in which the rings are perpendicular to the surface; this is also called vertical grain. To manufacture quarter-sawn lumber, the boards are sawn perpendicular to the exterior of the log. In this process, the yield from the log is reduced and the boards are relatively narrow. The stock displays straight, parallel grain lines on a board surface and, in some species like oak, characteristic rays become visible. These boards resist cupping and warping, and they are less likely to swell and contract than flat-sawn stock. Because there is more waste and also higher labor costs involved in cutting quarter-sawn lumber, it commands a premium price.

Flat-Sawn Lumber. In *flat-sawn* lumber, the boards are cut parallel with one side of a log, and the growth rings intersect the surface at a more acute angle. This technique provides the best yield from a log, but the lumber is less stable than quarter-sawn, and the grain patterns are more variable. In practice, much lumber falls somewhere between true vertical grain and flat-sawn patterns. If you have the luxury of examining a pile of lumber to make your selection, you can often select boards with similar grain for a particular project.

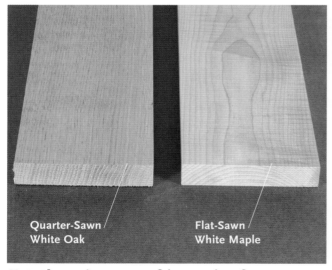

Quarter-Sawn
White Oak

Flat-Sawn
White Maple

Note the grain pattern of the samples of quarter-sawn and flat-sawn lumber shown above.

Expansion and Contraction. Movement due to expansion or contraction occurs almost exclusively across the grain of a board, and not along its length. For practical purposes, the majority of trim applications will not be greatly affected by this movement, as most details are constructed of narrow pieces where the movement is negligible. However, you will notice that wooden doors and windows tend to swell in the hot and humid summer months and then contract in the winter. Another case where wood movement must be taken into account is when you install a shoe molding around a hardwood floor. In this situation, it is important that you nail the molding to the baseboard instead of the floor boards so that the boards can expand and contract independent of the molding. And if wide, solid wood panels are used in a wainscot application, it is also important to design the installation so that the panels can expand and contract without cracking or showing gaps.

smart tip

BACK PRIMING

WOOD EXPANDS AND CONTRACTS AS MOISTURE IS ABSORBED OR LOST FROM ITS CELL STRUCTURE. AND WHEN YOU USE ANY WOOD IN A PROJECT, ANYTHING YOU CAN DO TO MINIMIZE THAT MOVEMENT WILL RESULT IN A BETTER RESULT—LESS SPLITTING OF THE STOCK AND TIGHTER JOINTS. ONE SIMPLE TECHNIQUE YOU CAN USE IS TO MAKE SURE THAT ALL SURFACES OF YOUR TRIM ARE SEALED. FOR PAINT-GRADE WORK, SIMPLY APPLY A COAT OF PAINT OR PRIMER TO THE BACK SIDE OF THE STOCK BEFORE INSTALLING IT. FOR PARTS THAT WILL RECEIVE A STAINED OR CLEAR FINISH, APPLY A COAT OF VARNISH OR POLYURETHANE— STAIN ALONE IS NOT A GOOD SEALER. THIS TECHNIQUE IS ESPECIALLY IMPORTANT IN AREAS THAT ARE SUBJECT TO HIGH HUMIDITY, SUCH AS KITCHENS, BATHROOMS, AND UTILITY ROOMS.

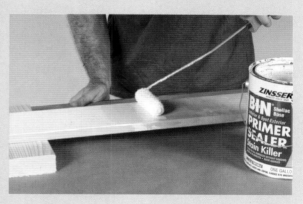

Complementary trim is used to highlight the newel posts, opposite.

Back primed trim is destined for high-humidity areas, above.

Molding details enliven simple square columns, right.

Trim Materials

DEFECTS IN LUMBER

WHEN YOU SHOP FOR LUMBER, it is important that you pay careful attention to the quality of the stock. As a natural material, wood is subject to a number of defects, and these can present problems in a job where straight edges, flat surfaces, and tight joints are important. Defects in lumber can be due to natural causes that arise during the growth of a tree, or due to the way it is cut, dried, and handled.

For most small trim projects, you will probably be able to select the material you will be using by going through the bin at the home center or the local lumberyard. If you order through a reputable millwork shop, you should receive good-quality stock.

Knots. *Knots* in a board are an indication of where a branch grew off the trunk of the tree. Small, solid knots are usually not a problem for trimwork, and they are allowable defects in even select stock. Large knots, however, are not features that you generally want to include in your work, so think carefully about the yield you will get after cutting around them. Keep in mind that stock with knots should be primed with a good-quality primer before painting. Unprimed knots will eventually bleed through any paint job.

Bark Inclusions. Sometimes trauma to a tree during its growth cycle can cause *bark inclusions* in the interior portion of the tree. These areas are too soft and unstable to be used as finish lumber and should always be dis-

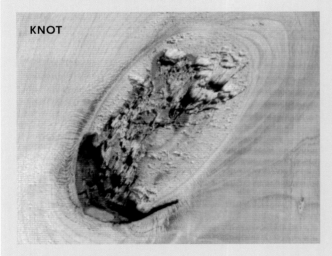

KNOT

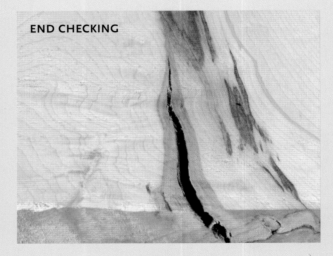

END CHECKING

BARK INCLUSION

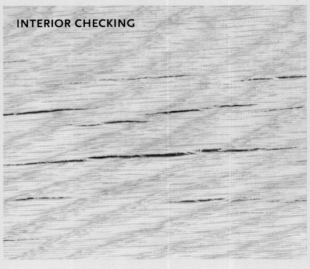

INTERIOR CHECKING

carded. *Pitch pockets* and *worm holes* are also seen in some lumber species. If these are small and infrequent, you can generally work around them, but if too prevalent, you could end up with a large pile of firewood. Keep in mind that particular defects are more common in some types of lumber than in others. Pitch pockets are quite common in cherry lumber, and walnut boards often show more knots than other species.

Checking and Spalting. *Checking, splitting, honeycombing,* and severe *warping* are symptoms of improper drying. Checks, splits, and honeycombing occur because of different rates of shrinkage between the surface and core of a board.

Warping can occur because of improper stacking of lumber in a kiln or because of naturally occurring stress in the wood.

Sometimes, especially in lighter materials like maple and ash, stains will appear cross the wood surface. These can be caused either by a fungus or by the use of wet *stickers,* which are the strips used between adjacent boards as the lumber dries.

Spalting is caused by a fungus that affects maple, causing a dark stain. Spalting is technically a decayed state, and material affected with this condition is not generally used for trim. However, spalted maple is highly valued by bowl turners for its spectacular visual effects.

WORM HOLES AND SPALTING

smart tip

DEALING WITH PLANER AND MOLDER MARKS

WHEN LUMBER IS FIRST CUT FROM A LOG, IT IS ROUGH-SAWN INTO BOARDS AND THEN DRIED. IN MOST CASES, BEFORE IT REACHES THE RETAIL OUTLET, IT IS PUT THROUGH A SURFACE PLANER, WHICH USES A SPINNING CUTTERHEAD TO YIELD AN EVEN FACE AND UNIFORM THICKNESS. THE SAME GENERAL PROCESS APPLIES TO MOLDING STOCK, WHICH IS SHAPED BY A SERIES OF PROFILE KNIVES. BOTH PROCESSES LEAVE A PRETTY SMOOTH SURFACE ON THE WOOD, BUT IF YOU LOOK CAREFULLY, YOU WILL USUALLY BE ABLE TO SEE A FAINT SERIES OF PARALLEL KNIFE MARKS DOWN THE LENGTH OF A BOARD OR MOLDING. SOMETIMES THESE MARKS ARE NOT VISIBLE UNTIL YOU APPLY THE FIRST COAT OF FINISH TO THE WOOD—AND THEN IT'S A BIT LATE.

WHEN BOARDS ARE RIPPED TO WIDTH OR CROSSCUT TO LENGTH, EITHER AT THE LUMBERYARD OR IN YOUR HOME SHOP, THE SAW BLADE INEVITABLY LEAVES A TRAIL OF MARKS ON THE CUT SURFACE. ONCE AGAIN, IF YOU DO NOT SMOOTH THESE SURFACES, THE MARKS WILL BE VISIBLE ONCE THE FINISH IS APPLIED AND ARE THE SURE SIGN OF SHODDY WORKMANSHIP.

THE REMEDY FOR THESE CONDITIONS IS SIMPLE, BUT LABOR INTENSIVE. EXPECT TO SAND ALL WOOD SURFACES IN PREPARATION FOR FINISHING, EVEN IF THEY FEEL SMOOTH TO THE TOUCH. ALSO MAKE IT A PRACTICE TO LIGHTLY EASE ALL SHARP EDGES WITH A SANDING BLOCK SO THAT EVERY SURFACE HAS A FINISHED LOOK AND FEEL.

Surface planers leave their mark on finished boards. Sanding is the only remedy.

OTHER TRIM MATERIALS

Although most people think of wood when the subject of trim arises, these days there are other options. When a job is destined to be painted, you can consider molding made of composite wood materials or even plastics.

Medium Density Fiberboard. *Medium density fiberboard,* or MDF, is a product that is made from ground wood fibers bound with adhesive under pressure. The resulting material is uniformly dense and very stable. Manufacturers can mill the raw material, much like wood, into various profiles, and the resulting moldings have an exceptionally smooth surface. Most of these moldings are primed at the factory, providing an excellent base for a painted finish. The extreme density of MDF makes it quite a bit heavier than a comparable piece of wooden molding; and it must be treated much like hardwood, in that you need to drill pilot holes before nailing. Because it has no grain structure, the edges of cuts tend to be pretty delicate, and the material can chip easily when fitting an intricate joint; use extra care in those situations.

Resin Moldings. *Polyurethane* and *polystyrene* moldings provide another option for paint-grade jobs. These products are especially attractive for ceiling moldings because they are extremely lightweight and install very easily.

Plastic moldings can be cast in a wide variety of shapes, and extremely large and elaborate profiles are easy to achieve. For the installer, you eliminate the need for cutting coped joints at inside corners, as the plastic resin cannot be worked like wood. Instead, these intersections are treated with miter joints, and any gaps must be filled with joint compound or caulk.

Some resin moldings are designed for use in curved applications. They are flexible enough so that you can bend them to fit a concave or convex wall surface. There are also manufacturers that will cast these moldings to fit an arched or elliptical opening. For these situations, you would need to specify the dimensions of the opening, or send a template, to have the pieces made. Most of these systems use a combination of adhesives and nails to hold them in place, and they generally come primed to accept either a painted or opaque stain finish.

If you are looking for columns or ornamental pedestals to bring classical style to a room, you might look at some in fiberglass instead of wood. In most cases, a polymer column is less expensive than one of wood, and it typically requires less maintenance—especially if you are considering a damp location such as the kitchen or bath. These products are offered in both stock and custom sizes so that almost any situation can be accommodated.

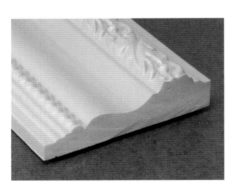

Resin molding can be installed with nails and glue like traditional wood molding.

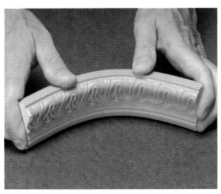

Flexible resin molding can be bent to match most curved walls—either concave or convex surfaces.

Resin moldings come in hundreds of profiles and designs. This room contains resin crown, casing, and panels.

MAKING YOUR OWN MOLDING

COMMERCIAL MOLDING MANUFACTURERS use heavy-duty molders and shapers to produce the different profiles they offer. Working at home, you cannot expect to duplicate that capability. However, with a router and small table saw, you can produce a modest selection of moldings to function as elements of window and door trim, chair rail, baseboard, or wainscoting.

For a few small pieces of molding, use a hand-held router to cut the profile. Clamp a board to the worktable to keep the stock secure while routing. You may need to place spacer blocks beneath the board to provide clearance for the ball-bearing pilot. Allow the router to get up to full speed before starting the cut. Then advance the tool along the edge to cut the molded shape.

Router Tables. If you need a lot of molding, the easier method is to mount the router in a router table. Commercial router tables are available in a variety of prices and configurations, some for tabletop use and others that are freestanding. Whatever type of table you use, make sure that it is either clamped firmly to a worktable or screwed to the floor to keep it from moving around while you work.

If you examine a catalog of router bits, you might be surprised at the number of different profiling bits that are available. Some of the larger bits are only available with a ½-inch-diameter shank, and require a heavy duty router for safe use, but many are suitable for smaller routers that accept bits with a ¼-inch-diameter shank.

Mount your chosen bit in the router, and install the router in the table. Adjust the height of the tool, and then set the fence to expose the desired profile. Even though many bits have a ball-bearing pilot guide, it is safest to use a fence on the router table—the face of the fence should align exactly with the bearing. Adjust the guard on the table to cover the spinning bit, and install finger-board hold-downs to keep the stock pushed tight to the table surface.

For the safest procedure, do not attempt to cut a molding profile on a narrow board. Instead, cut the molding on the edge of a wide board, and then use the table saw to rip the profile off the edge. Then repeat the procedure for each piece you need. When the board gets too narrow, put it aside for another use.

TOOLS & MATERIALS
▌ Router and bit ▌ Clamps ▌ Table saw ▌ Push stick
▌ 1-by stock

1 To make a narrow molding, first rout the desired profile on the edge of a wide board. Use a bit with a ball-bearing guide, or install an accessory edge guide to determine the position of the bit. Make a test cut on some scrap stock to be sure that adjustments are correct; then cut the profile on the edge of the stock.

2 Use the table saw to rip the narrow molding from the edge of the wide board. If possible, use a finger-board hold-down jig to exert even pressure on the board and prevent kickbacks. The hold-down jig also eliminates any need to position your fingers near the blade. Always use a push stick as you reach the end of the cut.

MATERIALS FOR WAINSCOTING

Wainscoting is the term used to describe a solid wood or paneled treatment of the lower part of a wall. This treatment can cover a wide range of styles and materials, from simple painted boards to intricately molded hardwood panels. While the installation and design options for your wainscoting will be treated elsewhere, the materials you require are related to those for the rest of your trim projects—and the suppliers are generally the same.

Bead Board. The simplest wainscoting, and one of the most popular, is an application of narrow tongue-and-groove boards with a beaded profile to the lower section of a wall. The material for this treatment is often made of fir lumber and sold either under the name of "bead-board wainscoting" or "beaded porch ceiling boards," after one of the more popular uses for the stock. You can usually find this material in bundled packages at home centers or in random lengths at a traditional lumberyard. Similar profiles are also available in a wide range of hardwood species from specialty suppliers.

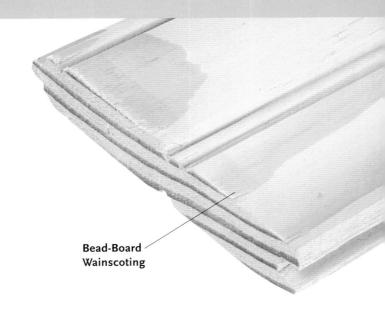

Bead-Board Wainscoting

Plywood Panels. To achieve the same general look, but with less labor, some people use plywood panels with a grooved design cut into the surface instead of individual boards. Although there is some sacrifice in detail, these panels have the advantage of eliminating potential gaps at the board seams as boards dry out. As with most plywood panels, these are manufactured in 4 x 8-foot sheets, but some home centers offer smaller, precut panels.

Classic Wainscoting. More-formal wainscot systems involve a combination of wood frames and either solid wood or plywood panels. Frame stock is typically the same type of material that you would purchase for other trim applications, such as pine, poplar, or oak boards. If you want to embellish the panels with molding, and to cap the top of the installation, there are many profiles that can be used to add depth and character.

Flat panels are usually formed from manufactured panel stock. The advantages of this material over solid wood are considerable. First, plywood panels are almost always less expensive than an equivalent amount of solid wood, especially when you factor in labor and waste. Second, manufactured panels are much more stable than solid wood; they usually stay flat and do not expand and contract with seasonal changes in humidity. These materials have a smooth, sanded face that requires minimal preparation for finishing, and if you want a clear finish, the grain of the face veneer is more consistent from panel to panel than solid wood.

Wainscoting, opposite bottom, can be created from a number of materials, including solid wood and plywood.

Bead-board wainscoting, right, fits in with a number of traditional design schemes.

CONSRUCTION-GRADE VERSUS HARDWOOD PLYWOOD

FOR INTERIOR TRIM, it is usually best to avoid construction-grade plywood. This material is made from layers of softwood veneers and typically has defects and voids in the core. The veneers used for the core are quite thick and the number of laminations is relatively few, resulting in an inherently unstable panel. Even though it is offered in A and B grades with smooth faces, it is just not made to standards comparable to that of hardwood panels, and can yield a poor surface, even for paint-grade work. Save this material for exterior jobs or utility applications.

Hardwood plywood generally features many thin laminations and a void-free core. Although this material also can exhibit a tendency to warp, especially when cut, the surface quality of the face veneer and ability to hold fasteners is far superior to construction-grade stock.

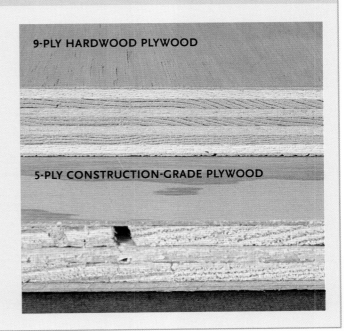

9-PLY HARDWOOD PLYWOOD

5-PLY CONSTRUCTION-GRADE PLYWOOD

PANEL MATERIALS

PANEL STOCK is most often carried in thicknesses of ¼-, ½-, and ¾-inch, although it is manufactured in sheets as thin as ⅛ inch and as thick as 1½ inches. When you shop for this material, you will find that a variety of core options are available. Traditional plywood has a *veneer core*—formed from thin layers of wood pressed together—with a decorative veneer on each face. The grain of each layer is arranged at 90 degrees to that of the adjacent layer, so the panel is dimensionally stable. One drawback to traditional plywood is that these panels often do not stay flat, especially after they are cut. In a wainscot application where the material will be fastened to a wall, this is usually not a problem, but for other jobs this can be troublesome.

PANEL DIMENSIONS

STANDARD DIMENSIONS FOR A PLYWOOD PANEL ARE 48 x 96 INCHES, BUT THOSE WITH A PARTICLEBOARD AND MDF CORE ARE SLIGHTLY LARGER, 49 x 97 INCHES. MOST HOME CENTERS SELL PANELS THAT HAVE BEEN CUT TO SMALLER DIMENSIONS, AND IF YOU PURCHASE YOUR MATERIAL AT A LUMBERYARD, THEY WILL USUALLY CUT PANELS INTO MANAGEABLE SIZES FOR YOU, BUT EXPECT TO PAY A CUTTING CHARGE.

MANUFACTURED PANEL CORE MATERIALS

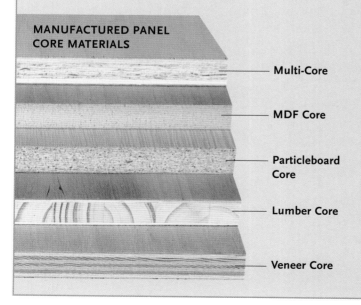

- Multi-Core
- MDF Core
- Particleboard Core
- Lumber Core
- Veneer Core

MDF Panels. Some panels are made with a *medium-density fiberboard* (MDF) core. A mixture of wood fibers and glue that is pressed together and heated, MDF is extremely smooth and uniformly dense. An MDF panel without a face veneer is considerably cheaper than a sheet of plywood and provides an excellent surface for a painted finish. The price of an MDF panel with a face veneer is usually close to that of a plywood panel, but it is more likely to remain flat when cut into workable parts. If you are buying MDF panels for a job, you should plan to have a helper to handle the material, as it is extremely heavy. Also, the nature of the core is such that machining it yields a lot of very fine dust. So be prepared with dust masks, eye protection, and a good shop vacuum.

Particleboard Cores. Panels with a *particleboard core* are another option. The construction of these panels is similar to that of MDF-core stock, except that the core consists of flakes of softwood lumber and glue. These panels are also formed under heat and pressure, and while quite stable, they do not feature a particularly uniform core. As with MDF panels, these are sold with and without a face veneer, but the raw panels are not as well suited to paint-grade use. In general, these are a less desirable choice for a wainscoting application.

Lumber-Core Panels. *Lumber-core* panels are the elite class of manufactured panel stock. Strips of solid lumber are glued together and covered with a thick layer of veneer called cross-banding. The face veneer is then applied to each side of this sandwich to yield the finished product. Since this is a premium product, and is most often used in furniture manufacture, you would need to obtain this type of panel by special order—and expect to pay a premium price. It is not unusual for a lumbercore panel to cost twice the price of a comparable plywood panel.

Advances in technology have yielded a number of composite *multi-core* panels, which mix different materials in the core in an effort to reduce weight and cost while maintaining a stable product. One of these products uses the idea of traditional plywood, but alternates layers of wood and MDF. Another panel features a core of particleboard covered by thick cross-bands under the face veneer.

PANEL FACES

THE VENEERS that are applied to panel faces can display various patterns, depending on the way that they were cut from the log and joined together. Some veneers are peeled from a log that is mounted on a huge lathe. These are called *rotary-cut* veneers, and they show a characteristic grain pattern that is rather wild. In some species, a rotary-cut veneer can feature grain that moves in a zig-zag pattern down the sheet. Rotary veneers can be very large, and often one sheet can cover an entire panel.

Some veneers are sliced or sawn into sheets that are parallel with one side of a tree; these are called *plain-sliced* veneers, and they usually show cathedral shaped grain patterns. Plain-sliced veneers are often *book-matched,* or joined together, so that symmetrical patterns appear across the panel. *Quartersawn* veneer is cut parallel with the radius of the log. These veneers show straight grain, and in some oak species, characteristic ray flake.

When shopping for panel stock, pay close attention to the veneer on the face. If you need more than one panel, try to select them so that the veneers are close in color and grain pattern. Whatever type of panel you select, inspect the face for any defects such as torn out veneer, wood-filler patches, and deep scratches. For use in wainscoting, you only need material with one good face, so if available, purchase stock with a back veneer of inferior grade to save some money.

Materials and finish selection contribute to the distinctive look of this staircase.

ROTARY-CUT MAPLE VENEER FACE

BOOK-MATCHED CHERRY VENEER FACE

QUARTERSAWN WHITE OAK VENEER FACE

FASTENERS

Fasteners are an essential part of trim work. Almost every process demands that you use some type of mechanical fastener to hold a molding to a surface or join two pieces of wood. The primary fastener for trim is the *finishing nail*. These nails feature a relatively narrow shaft with a slightly larger head. Typically, the head has a small dimple in the top surface to engage the tip of a nail set. Select an appropriately sized nail for each task—for example, for fastening trim boards to framing members, the nail should enter the framing member at least 1 inch. Remember to take the thickness of the drywall or plaster surface into account.

For fastening small pieces of molding, wire nails, or *brads,* are often used. These are essentially very fine finishing nails available in sizes between ⅝ and 1½ inches long.

The nails that are used in nail guns are classified in the same manner as traditional finishing nails, but they are slightly different in configuration. With normal nails, as the length of a fastener increases, the diameter also gets larger. But the nails for a nail gun are of one constant diameter, regardless of the length. Consequently, a nail gun can drive a long nail and still leave a relatively small diameter hole.

Screws. Screws are another important fastener. For many years, brass screws with slotted heads were the norm for woodworking, but the expense and relative soft nature of brass have made these obsolete except for decorative applications. And the popularity of power screw drivers has almost eliminated the slot head, replacing it with the more reliable Phillips and Robertson (square drive) styles.

Finishing nails have a dimple in top to hold a nail set. When installing molding, the nail should penetrate into the underlying framing by at least 1 in.

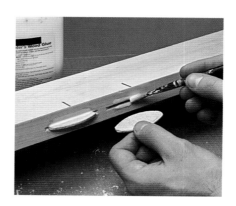

When covered with glue and inserted into the slot cut by a plate joiner, joining plates provide a reliable fastening option.

TYPES OF SCREWS

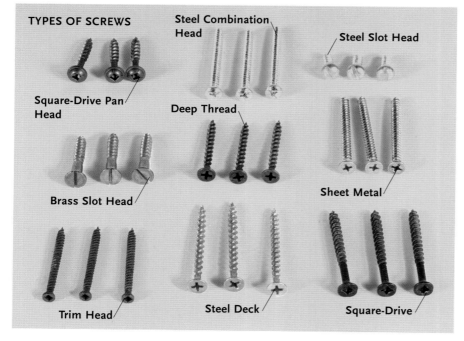

Square-Drive Pan Head

Brass Slot Head

Trim Head

Steel Combination Head

Deep Thread

Steel Deck

Steel Slot Head

Sheet Metal

Square-Drive

NAIL SIZES

NAIL SIZE	LENGTH
3d	1¼"
4d	1½"
6d	2"
8d	2½"
10d	3"
12d	3¼"
16d	3½"

Screws are available with round, oval, flat, and bugle-head styles. If you need your screw to sit flush with the wood surface, or want it completely hidden by a plug or filler, you should choose flat or bugle-head styles. Next, select the screw material. Plain steel screws are the least expensive alternative, but hardened steel offers a tougher screw that is less likely to snap under pressure or strip out if the driver slips. Finally, consider the style of the screw body. Traditional wood screws have a body with threads that only extend about two-thirds of the way up the shank, and the body tapers from the head to the tip. Sheet metal and deep-thread styles have bodies of constant diameter, and the threads extend farther up the screw. Trim-head screws have small diameter heads that can be used like finishing nails.

Dowels. Dowels are wooden cylinders of a specific diameter that are coated with glue and inserted in matching holes in the two sides of a joint. For commercial applications, dowels are available in precut lengths with either spiral or longitudinal grooves down the dowel length. These grooves provide a means for excess glue to escape the hole. If you are using plain dowel stock, it is a good practice to carve one or two shallow grooves down the length of each dowel with a knife or chisel.

Joining Plates. These are football-shaped wafers of compressed wood. They are designed to fit into matching semicircular slots that are cut in each side of a joint using a plate joiner. Joining plates come in three standard sizes, and there are also other plates available for specialized uses.

USING HOLLOW-WALL ANCHORS

IT'S ALWAYS PREFERABLE to fasten trim parts to the framing inside a wall or ceiling, but there are times when there is no stud, plate, or joist where you need one. In those situations you have two options. You can rip into the wall and install some blocking, or you can use one of the various hollow-wall anchors to install your part.

TOOLS & MATERIALS
▎Power drill and countersink bit ▎Pencil ▎Screwdriver ▎Wall anchors ▎Wood plugs ▎Glue

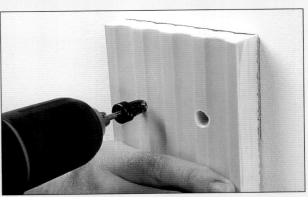

1 Drill through the piece to be installed using a countersink bit. The bit will mark the drywall for drilling.

2 Remove the molding, and drill pilot holes. Insert anchors into the pilot holes.

3 Attach molding, and cover screw heads with dowels. Trim the dowels, and finish the workpiece.

GLUE AND CONSTRUCTION ADHESIVES

In the pursuit of tight, strong joints, woodworking adhesives are an important addition to your arsenal of tools. The standard glues for most joints are *polyvinyl acetate (PVA) adhesives,* known casually as *white* and *yellow* glues. While the white variety can be used for most porous materials, the yellow variety—also called aliphatic resin glue—has been specifically formulated for woodworking applications. Brown-colored versions are available for use with woods of darker tone. For applications that need water resistance, there are formulations of yellow glue that are rated as *waterproof.* These glues are technically known as cross-linking PVA. They are easy to use, nontoxic, and clean up easily with water before curing.

Polyurethane adhesives also offer water resistance and are compatible with a number of different materials. One unique feature of this glue is that it requires moisture to cure, so it is often recommended that you slightly dampen the wood surface before applying the glue. This glue tends to foam up as it cures, and it can be difficult to clean up a joint without leaving a residue. In addition, polyurethane glue will stain your skin, so you need to wear gloves when working with it.

Epoxies are available in a variety of formulas with different strengths and setting times. These adhesives require that you mix a hardener with a resin to start the chemical reaction that cures the epoxy. Quick-setting versions are sold in convenient double-tube dispensers that provide the proper ratio of hardener to resin. For joints that require the highest bonding strength, especially in varied materials, epoxy is the best choice. But epoxy is also a toxic material, so be sure to wear gloves and a respirator to protect yourself from exposure.

Instant-bonding adhesives, sometimes called "super glue," have limited use in woodworking, but there are times when this can be a life-saver. Technically called cyanoacrylate adhesive, this glue sets in a matter of seconds, so clamping is virtually unnecessary. This adhesive can be very useful to repair small chips and torn-out grain in a wood surface.

Construction adhesive is a thick-bodied substance that comes in a tube for use in a caulk gun. There are different formulations of adhesive for specific uses such as bonding paneling or drywall, or resin molding installation.

TYPES OF GLUE

Yellow PVA Glue

White PVA Glue

Waterproof PVA Glue

Polyurethane Adhesive

Instant-Bonding Adhesive

Construction Adhesive

Epoxy

For tight joints, apply a bead of glue to miter cuts. Complete the job using finishing nails.

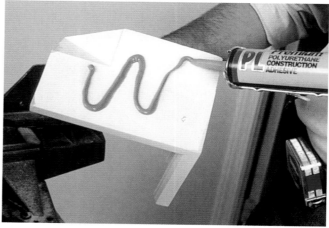

Standard construction adhesive is often all that is required for applying resin-type moldings.

Sandpaper

It's rare to find someone who truly enjoys sanding, but it is an important part of most woodworking projects, and if approached methodically, it need not be a particularly tedious or difficult task. The first step is to have the right material for the job, and that means sandpaper.

You will see sandpaper that is manufactured with different abrasives, and each has its preferred use. Garnet paper is best for sanding by hand. Machine sanding requires a longer lasting, tougher abrasive, and aluminum oxide is generally considered the best choice. Silicone carbide paper is a good choice for sanding finishes between coats as it holds up well in fine grits.

Sandpaper is rated according to the coarseness of the abrasive particles and type of backer. Lower grit numbers correspond to coarser abrasive. You can find papers rated from 40 to 1500 grit, but for general trim projects, your most frequent selections will fall between 100 and 220 grit. Backers for sandpaper can be either cloth or paper, with paper more common in sheets and discs, and cloth most prevalent in belts. The weight of the backer is classified from "A" to "X" with "A" being the thinnest and most flexible. For hand sanding, "A" weight is most appropriate, and for orbital machine sanding "C" weight is best.

Sandpaper is sold in full sheets of 9 x 11 inches, as well as in ¼- and ½-sheet sizes for pad sanders. You will also find discs and belts of various sizes to fit different types of power sanders. Most discs come with a backing of Velcro or pressure-sensitive adhesive for mounting to the sanding pad.

Caulk

For jobs that are destined to be painted, caulk can be the trim carpenter's best friend. But it's also important to realize that caulk is not a replacement for doing a careful job of fitting and assembling joints. Although we generally think of walls and ceilings as flat, in most cases you will find dips and humps in these surfaces. And when trim is applied, there is sometimes a small gap between the two materials. These are the places where caulk is an indispensable tool. A judicious application of caulk can blend an applied molding to a wall or ceiling surface, creating a seamless appearance. Small gaps in trim joints, especially at inside corners of baseboards and cornices, can also be filled with caulk.

Acrylic latex caulk is the best all-around choice for interior trim work. This material is easy to apply, and you can shape a caulk joint with a wet finger or putty knife. It cleans up with water while still fresh, and it readily accepts a painted finish after proper curing. Expect latex caulk to shrink a bit as it cures, so for wide joints you might have to reapply the material before painting. For best results, prime the woodwork and wall or ceiling surface before applying the caulk.

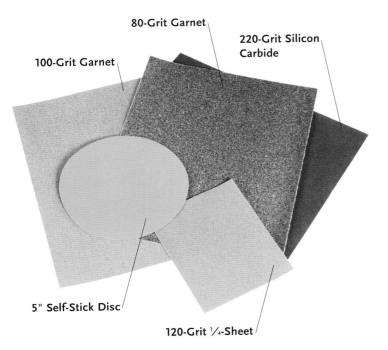

100-Grit Garnet
80-Grit Garnet
220-Grit Silicon Carbide
5" Self-Stick Disc
120-Grit ¼-Sheet

Paintable Latex Caulk
Caulk Release Pin

tools and techniques 11

TRIMWORK PROJECTS REQUIRE both common carpentry tools and some more specialized items. But don't feel the need to purchase the more advanced tools all at once—you will be able to complete the majority of projects with hand tools. The best approach is to master a few basic items before moving on to the advanced power tools. Don't shy away from using power tools, however: they will speed up the work and help you obtain professional-like results. Installing trimwork also requires some building techniques that you may not have used for other home improvement projects. Mastering them will lead to the best job possible.

MEASURING AND LAYOUT TOOLS

Your choice of measuring tools for any task depends, at least partially, on the scale of the job and tolerances you must keep. The secondary factor has to do with personal preference, for often there is a choice of appropriate tools. As you work with a variety of tools, you will naturally gravitate toward some over others. Just make sure that your preference for comfort or convenience does not result in a sacrifice of accuracy.

When it comes to marking stock to be cut to size, or laying out more complex joints, the accuracy of your marks is critical. Although the tool most associated with carpentry layout is the flat carpenter's pencil, this tool is really not very useful for trimwork. The thick, soft lead of the pencil and its fat body make it awkward to use and prone to rapid dulling; the result is a wide, vague mark. For trimwork, the better choice is a hard pencil—#3 is perfect—that can be sharpened to a very fine point. If you keep a fine point on the tool, it will provide you with an extremely precise mark.

For the finest work, even a sharpened pencil mark can be too vague. In those situations where you want the highest degree of accuracy, a knife mark is the best choice. The type of knife you use is not important—an inexpensive utility knife will work as well as a fancy rosewood-handle layout knife—but the edge and tip should be razor sharp.

Measuring Tapes

A *measuring tape* is a great device for estimating materials and laying out a job. The most common sizes of steel retractable tape are ¾ inch wide by 12- or 16-feet long and 1 inch wide by 25 feet long, although reel-style tapes are available to 100-foot lengths. For room measurements and all-around general use, the 1-inch by 25-foot model is your best bet. The wide blade will support itself over a long span, and most rooms are less than 25 feet in length. Most have a locking lever that keeps the blade from retracting. Tapes usually have each "foot" mark clearly delineated as well as arrows or other indications for 16-inch spacing—this is especially handy for stud locations. You will typically find graduations down to ¹⁄₁₆ inch, with some models having ¹⁄₃₂-inch graduations for the first foot of the tape.

Folding Stick Rules

The *folding stick rule* is one of carpentry's oldest measuring devices and still very useful. These come in 6- and 8-foot lengths that fold into a compact 8-inch-long package. A stick rule is great for those situations where you need to measure something that is just out of reach, and you need to suspend the ruler over an unsupported space. It is also handy to gauge the extent of an overhanging detail or to measure the inside dimension of an opening. Most models have a sliding extension at one end for easy inside measuring. For easy folding, periodically apply a tiny drop of oil to each folding joint.

smart tip

ADD AN INCH

AFTER SOME USE, THE HOOK ON THE END OF THE TAPE CAN BECOME BENT, WORN, OR HAVE EXCESS PLAY, RESULTING IN LESS THAN ACCURATE READINGS. WHEN CLOSE TOLERANCES ARE INVOLVED, TRY A PROFESSIONAL CABINETMAKER'S TRICK. RATHER THAN MEASURING FROM THE END OF THE TAPE, START YOUR MEASUREMENT AT THE 1 INCH MARK. JUST REMEMBER TO SUBTRACT THAT INCH FROM THE READING AT THE OPPOSITE END.

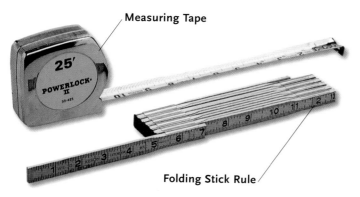

Measuring Tape

Folding Stick Rule

Steel Rulers

Steel rulers usually come in sizes from 6 inches to 24 inches, although a yardstick could easily be included in this category. For the most accurate measurements, it's hard to beat a steel ruler because the graduations are scribed or etched into the surface, and they are, typically, finer lines than those painted on a wooden ruler or tape. In addition, it's easy to find rulers that have graduations as fine as $\frac{1}{64}$ inch.

Squares

A *square* is the primary tool for testing that two edges are perpendicular, but it is also important for layout. Squares are available in different sizes and configurations for various uses.

Framing Square. This tool is made of steel or aluminum and has legs of 16 and 24 inches. In addition to inch measurements along each blade, you will find a chart for determining the angles for rafters of various slope roofs. A framing square is handy for laying out stud walls, but it is also useful in trimwork to check that larger panels are square or for testing door and window openings. The long blade of the square is also valuable as a straight edge.

Sliding Combination Square. In addition to being a precision square, this tool has a milled edge on the body that sits at 45 degrees to the blade for testing miter cuts. The body can slide along the graduated blade and lock in place at different settings so that you can use it as a depth or marking gauge. Most models also include a steel scriber and a small level vial on the body.

Try Square. This tool has a 6- or 8-inch blade with a fixed body. These are convenient for testing the accuracy of cuts on small parts. For the highest degree of accuracy, you can purchase an *engineer's precision square*. These steel squares are available in blade sizes from 6 to 12 inches and are guaranteed to conform to extremely fine tolerances (typically .016mm).

Speed Square. Although designed as a rafter layout tool, a *speed square* is valuable in trim work. You can use the speed square as a crosscutting guide for the circular saw to help in making square cuts on narrow lumber.

smart tip

PARALLEL LINES

IF YOU NEED TO MARK A LINE PARALLEL WITH A STRAIGHT EDGE, REACH FOR YOUR SLIDING COMBINATION SQUARE. SLIDE THE BODY ALONG THE BLADE UNTIL YOU REACH THE DISTANCE YOUR LINE NEEDS TO BE FROM THE EDGE. HOLD THE BODY ALONG THE EDGE AND YOUR SHARPENED PENCIL AGAINST THE END OF THE BLADE. SLIDE BOTH SQUARE AND PENCIL DOWN THE EDGE TO SCRIBE YOUR LINE.

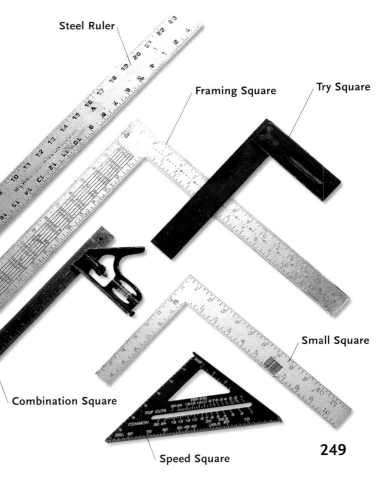

Steel Ruler

Framing Square

Try Square

Small Square

Combination Square

Speed Square

Tools and Techniques

Angle Guides

Things would be much simpler in trim work if all angles were either 90 or 45 degrees, but life is just not like that. So, in order to be able to work with various angles you will need a *protractor* or *angle gauge*. The particular configuration of your tool is not critical, but it's worth investing in a steel tool rather than a plastic model.

Adjustable Sliding Bevel. An adjustable sliding bevel has no graduations to indicate particular angle measurement, but it is a great device for copying any angle. Simply loosen the nut; hold the body against one side of the angle; and slide the blade until it rests against the opposite side of the angle. Tighten the blade to retain the setting. You can then use the gauge to trace the angle onto another surface for direct cutting or bisecting with a protractor.

Chalk Line

A *chalk-line box* is a simple, but very valuable, tool for marking a long straight line between distant points on a wall, floor, or ceiling. It consists of a metal or plastic enclosure with a reel that holds a cotton string; the string has a metal hook on its free end. Pour powdered chalk into the box, and extend the string between the points you wish to connect. Hold the string taut, and gently lift and release it so that it snaps once against the surface to mark the straight line.

Levels

The concepts of plumb and level are primary to good trim carpentry work. In carpentry terms, something is level when it is perfectly parallel with the ground, with no slope. Something is plumb when it is perfectly vertical. Plumb and level lines are always perpendicular to one another.

Spirit Level. The most common tool used to test these qualities is the *spirit level*. A spirit level has two or three fluid-filled arched vials, each with a small air bubble inside. Hold the level against a horizontal or vertical surface to check if it is plumb or level; the bubble should be exactly between the gauge marks.

Water Level. A *water level* can be used to set a level mark at two distant points. It consists of a hose, filled almost completely with water, with transparent ends. If you hold both ends up, the waterline at one end will always be level to the waterline at the opposite end.

Laser Level. A *laser level* projects a horizontal or vertical beam of light. Some models are self-leveling, but on others you need to adjust the unit first with a vial gauge. Rotary models can project the beam on all four walls of a room at the same time. Once you have your level or plumb line established, you can place marks appropriately to guide your measurement or installation.

Plumb Bob. One of the oldest methods of gauging if something is plumb, or of striking a plumb line, is to use a *plumb bob*. This tool is simply a string with a pointed weight attached to one of its ends. Most bobs are fashioned of brass, and some of the old models can be quite decorative. If you suspend the bob from any point you can always be sure that the string will describe a perfectly plumb line.

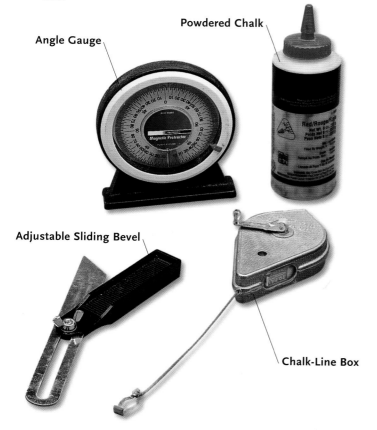

Powdered Chalk

Angle Gauge

Adjustable Sliding Bevel

Chalk-Line Box

smart tip GOOD MARKS

WHEN MARKING A BOARD TO BE CUT TO LENGTH OR DETERMINING A GUIDELINE ON A WALL, PLACE A "V" AT THE DESIRED MARK RATHER THAN A VAGUE LINE. USE THE POINT OF THE "V" TO INDICATE THE EXACT POINT OF MEASUREMENT; THEN USE A SQUARE, PROTRACTOR, OR STRAIGHTEDGE TO LAY OUT THE CUT OR LAYOUT LINE.

STUD FINDER

MOST TRIM CARPENTRY involves attaching pieces of wood to a wall or ceiling surface. Because most rooms are finished with drywall or plaster, it is important to fasten parts to the underlying framing members whenever possible. While you can always poke holes to locate studs or joists, a much neater and quicker technique is to use a *stud finder*. Older models relied on magnets to sense nails or screws driven into the framing. Most electronic models have sensors that detect difference in capacitance to locate the studs. The most recent developments use a type of radar technology to sense the framing inside the wall. Electronic stud finders use a series of sounds or lights to indicate when the tool is directly over a stud.

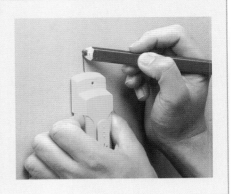

Levels:
A—2-ft. spirit level,
B—4-ft. spirit level,
C—6-in. spirit level,
D—water level with electronic level sensor,
E—plumb bob and string,
F—laser level, which can be attached to a standard level

smart tip   MAKE A MEASURING JIG

TAKING AN ACCURATE INSIDE MEASUREMENT—SUCH AS AN EXACT WINDOW OR DOOR OPENING—IS ONE OF THE CHALLENGES OF TRIM WORK. TO OBTAIN EXACT MEASUREMENTS, TAKE TWO STICKS, EACH SOMEWHAT LONGER THAN ONE-HALF THE OVERALL DIMENSION. HOLD THE STICKS TOGETHER, AND SLIDE THEM APART UNTIL THE ENDS TOUCH THE WALLS OF THE OPENING. USE CLAMPS TO LOCK THE DIMENSION; YOU CAN THEN USE THE GUIDE TO TRANSFER THE MEASUREMENT TO YOUR TRIM PIECE.

CUTTING TOOLS

For many specific jobs, as well as those times when an extension cord is not handy, a handsaw is the tool of choice. The saws most associated with the carpenter's trade are the traditional *crosscut* and *rip saws*. Each of these saws has a blade approximately 22 to 26 inches long that tapers from the handle toward the tip. A crosscut saw typically has 8 to 10 teeth per inch and a rip saw 4 to 5 teeth per inch. When using either of these saws, you should position yourself so that you can take long, straight strokes, with your arm and shoulder in line with the blade. If the saw is properly sharpened, you should not need to force the saw, but simply guide it back and forth, allowing the weight of the blade to determine the rate of cut.

A handy alternative to western-style handsaws is the Japanese *Ryoba*. This dual-purpose saw has fine crosscutting teeth on one edge and coarse ripping teeth on the opposite edge. All Japanese saws cut on the pull stroke, rather than the push stroke like western saws. This allows the saw blade to be thinner and therefore yields a smaller kerf, or width of cut. Using a Japanese-style saw takes some practice, but once you master the technique, you will find it a very valuable addition to your toolbox.

Backsaw. A *backsaw* has a rectangular-shaped blade with a steel or brass reinforcement along the top spine. The reinforcing spine allows the saw to have a thin blade that still stays straight. This type of saw comes in many sizes and tooth configurations, each with a particular use in mind. The smallest backsaws are called "dovetail" saws because they are designed to cut fine furniture joints called dovetails. Larger saws are handy for use in a miter box to cut molding to precise angles.

Coping Saw. A *coping saw* consists of a handle attached to a C-shaped frame. A thin blade is stretched between the ends of the frame. This configuration enables the user to make sharp turns with the saw to follow complex molding shapes. This tool is primarily used in the cutting of "coped" (or fitted) joints. Most carpenters install the blade so that the saw cuts on the "pull" stroke.

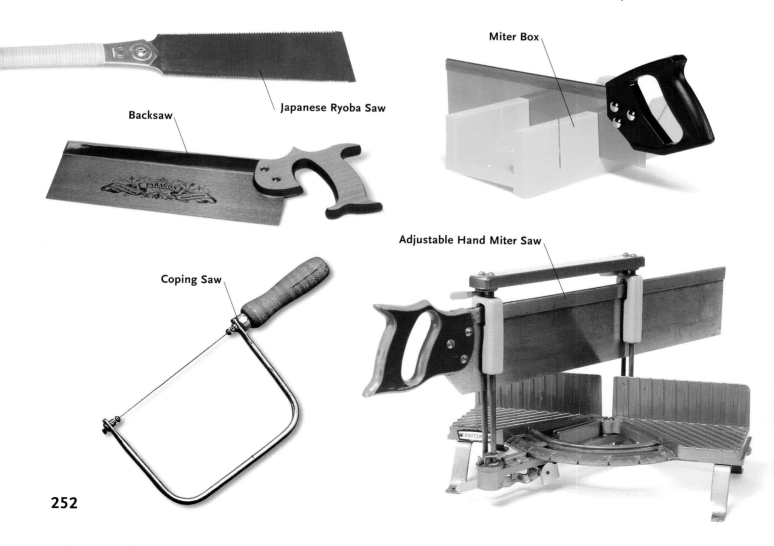

Japanese Ryoba Saw

Backsaw

Miter Box

Adjustable Hand Miter Saw

Coping Saw

Tools and Techniques

Miter Saws

If you only have a few miter joints to cut, it's hardly worth investing in a power miter saw. Fortunately, there are less expensive, and low-tech, alternatives—the wood or plastic miter box, and metal hand miter saw. The simplest tool for cutting simple miters is the *miter box*. A miter box has a U-shaped cross-section with saw kerfs cut at 45 and 90 degrees through the guide rails. These are meant to be used with a backsaw, which has a reinforcing spine along the top edge of the saw blade. You can find an inexpensive miter box, complete with back saw, at most home centers. Unfortunately, the miter box has the limitation of not allowing any adjustment in the angle of cut.

For more flexibility, you can turn to the *hand miter saw*. Some miter saws use a backsaw and some are designed to hold a saw that resembles a hacksaw. In either case, the saw is supported in a guide, and you have the ability to adjust the angle of cut from 45 degrees left to 45 degrees right, providing more flexibility than the miter box.

Power Cutting Tools

When you need a power saw for crosscutting or ripping solid lumber and sizing plywood panels, the *circular saw* is usually the first choice. Tool selection is based on the diameter of the cutting blade, and there are a number of sizes available. But for general use, pick a saw with a blade that is 7¼ inches in diameter, as this size should handle most cutting jobs. These models are adjustable for depth and angle of cut, and most will cut stock up to 2¼ inches thick at 90 degrees. Expect your saw to have a fixed upper blade guard and a lower retractable guard that operates by spring tension. Some saws offer an electronic blade brake that stops the blade when you release the trigger, and this is a great option for increased safety. If it does not come with the saw, you should purchase an accessory rip guide for cutting strips of uniform width from wide stock. There are a number of different types of blades available for circular saws. Initially, you should purchase a combination blade for all-around use and a crosscutting blade for fine work.

Saber Saw. Sometimes called a *portable jig saw,* this is an extremely versatile tool that is great for cutting curved or intricate shapes. These tools accept a wide variety of blades for rough and finish cutting of wood, as well as plastics and metal. Most saws have an adjustable base for bevel cuts and a switch to allow the blade to move in either an orbital (for wood) or reciprocating (for plastic or metal) motion.

HAND CHISELS

A BASIC SET of butt chisels, ranging in width from ¼ to 1½ inches, is a worthwhile investment for trim-work. You'll find them handy for fine paring of joints and cutting mortises for door hardware. In order to keep them sharp, purchase a good-quality sharpening stone and honing guide—and use them often.

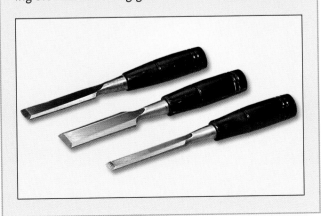

CIRCULAR SAW

SABER SAW

MAKING A MITER-SAW STAND

1 Build a frame for the table using 2x4s set on edge. Use wood screws to assemble the frame.

A MITER SAW is a great tool for cutting both flat stock and molding, but when the material is long, safety and accuracy concerns mandate that you provide more support than the saw table alone can offer. There are plenty of commercial miter-saw stands available for purchase; most have locking casters and folding outboard stock rests. However, it's easy for you to construct your own stand from a piece of plywood, some 2x4 stock, a piece of one-by pine, and a pair of sawhorses. Fashion a support platform in the shape of a ladder by nailing or screwing together some 2x4 stock. Cut a piece of ¾-inch plywood to fit over the top of the frame. Apply some construction adhesive to the top edges of the frame, and screw the ply-

2 Increase stability of the assembly by running a bead of construction adhesive on the 2x4s.

3 Cut the top using ¾-in. plywood. Set it in the adhesive and fasten with screws.

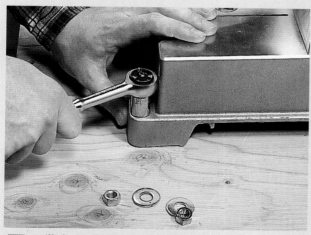

5 Drill through the plywood and secure the saw using lag bolts or lag screws.

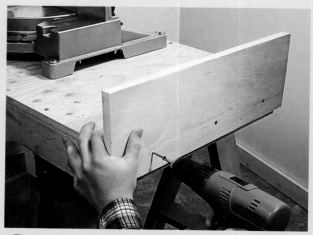

6 Attach a molding support to each end of the platform so that the top is level with the saw table.

wood to the base. Mark the location of saw mounting holes on the plywood surface, and drill pilot holes for mounting bolts. Fasten the saw base to the platform, and then add a support block at either end of the platform, making sure that the top edge of each block is level with the saw table. Clamp the saw platform to a pair of sawhorses to ensure stability of the work table.

TOOLS & MATERIALS

▌Power drill with screwdriver bit ▌Caulking gun ▌Pencil ▌Socket wrench ▌Clamps ▌2x4s ▌¾-inch plywood ▌Construction adhesive ▌Lag screws and washers ▌Utility screws

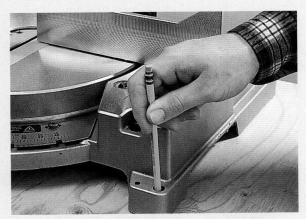

4 Place the saw in the middle of the platform, and mark the bolt-down locations.

7 Set up the bench at the work site, clamping it firmly to stable sawhorses.

Power Miter Saws

When your trim projects become more extensive, *a power miter saw* will undoubtedly become one of the primary tools on the job. These are essentially a circular saw mounted on a pivoting stand. The motor and blade can swivel from side to side over the table to cut the desired angle. Most saws have preset detents at 90, 45, and 22.5 degrees.

Compound Miter Saws. These tools have the added capability for the blade to tip to one side to cut a bevel angle, in addition to the miter. A *sliding compound miter saw* adds one more feature to the mix by providing guide rails that allow the blade to be pulled through the cut, toward the operator. With sliding capability, these saws allow you to cut wide stock, cut joints on crown molding with the material held flat on the saw table, and cut grooves or tenon joints by limiting the depth of cut with a stop. Saws are available in a variety of sizes which are determined by blade diameter—most fall in the range of 8½- to 12-inch sizes. When selecting a saw, pay particular attention to the capacity ratings of each particular model—both the thickness and width of stock it will cut. While sliding compound saws are the most versatile of all miter saws, they are quite expensive; some models can exceed $600.

Power saws increase your versatility. Shown left and below are a standard miter saw and a sliding compound miter saw.

SHAPING AND FINISHING TOOLS

Planes are one of the tools most often associated with carpentry. The image of the carpenter with shavings flying is almost an icon in woodworking. Aside from the image, however, the plane is a necessary part of your tool collection. While there are planes designed for many specific tasks, for a beginner approaching trimwork, a *block plane* will serve most purposes quite well. Block planes are about 6 inches long with a cutting iron approximately 1½ inches wide. The cutting iron is mounted, with the bevel facing up, at a low angle—this makes the tool especially well suited to trimming the end grain of a board, but it will also do a fine job planing the edge or face of a board.

You will find a block plane very handy for final fitting of a trim board to an uneven surface, or fine-tuning a miter joint. For best results, always keep the cutting iron razor sharp.

Block Plane

Sanders

For most people who work with wood, sanding is the least appealing part of any project—it is dusty and can be tedious—and it can seem hard to justify the effort. However, much of the final impression of a job lies in the quality of the finished surface, and sanding prepares the way for a first-class finish.

Belt Sanders. For the coarsest jobs, you can't beat a *belt sander* for fast stock removal. These tools usually accept 3- or 4-inch-wide belts in a variety of grits from very coarse (40 grit) to very fine (220 grit). A belt sander can be your best friend on a job, but it can also get out of control easily and do some damage. Make sure that you orient the sander so that the belt moves parallel with the grain, and always keep the machine moving down the length of the workpiece when the belt is running or you may gouge the surface.

Random Orbital Sander. A *random orbital sander* is a finishing sander that has a disc-shaped pad. The sanding pad turns on an eccentric spindle so that it creates tiny swirl marks on the wood surface. This type of tool has the ability to remove stock quickly, but it also can leave a fine finish

on the surface. Look for a model with a 5-inch-diameter pad because that size sanding disc is the most widely available.

Orbital Sheet Sanders. These tools have been the standard finishing sanders for many years. They are offered in ¼- and ½-sheet sizes and are generally the least expensive machine option for finish work. These sanders provide the best choice if you need to sand vertical surfaces.

Hand Sanding. Power sanders are great tools, but there are times when you just have to do the job by hand. For small flat surfaces, you can use a block of wood as a sanding block. Or you can go the commercial route and purchase a rubber or cork block. For sanding molded profiles, use a bit of creativity to fashion a sanding block or pad that matches the profile. You could use a pencil or dowel as a backer to sand flutes in a pilaster, or a small can, jar, or the cardboard core from a roll of paper towels as a backer to sand a cove molding.

BELT SANDER

RANDOM-ORBITAL SANDERS

ORBITAL SHEET SANDERS

PLATE JOINER

YOU COULD EASILY spend years mastering the art of cutting various joints in wood—and many people have done just that. To do trimwork, you really do not have to master those skills. However, there are situations when you will need to join materials without screws or nails, and a simple, flexible approach can be found in plate joinery. Joining plates are football-shaped wafers of compressed wood, about ⅛ inch thick, that come in a variety of sizes. (See "Joining Plate Sizes," right.) To use the plates, cut a semi-circular slot in each half of the joint with a *plate joiner*. The tool has a spinning blade that you advance into the wood to a preset depth. Location and alignment of the slot is controlled by two fences on the joiner, and there are adjustments that allow angle settings as well.

Once your joint is cut, spread a bit of glue into each slot and also on the surface of a joining plate. Push the plate into one of the matching slots, and assemble the joint. Use a clamp to hold the parts together while the glue sets. The glue causes the compressed wood of the plate to expand.

Joining plates have been dubbed "flat dowels" by some woodworkers, since they have largely replaced dowels as a means of joinery. Cutting a plate joint is

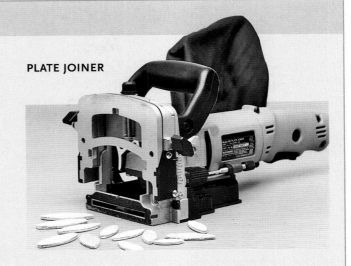

PLATE JOINER

much quicker than drilling matching dowel holes and has the added advantage of having some "play" in the joint. The slots are slightly longer than the plates, providing room to adjust a joint.

JOINING PLATE SIZES

#0: About ⅝ inch wide by 1¾ inches long (47 x 15 mm)

#10: About ¾ inch wide by 2⅛ inches long (53 x 19 mm)

#20: 1 inch wide by 2½ inches long (56 x 23 mm)

ROUTER TABLES

A ROUTER is a versatile tool, and you will want to explore its full capability. (See "Routers," page 258.) By mounting the router upside down in a *router table*, you can shape pieces that are too narrow or short to be cut with a hand-held tool. Commercial router tables are available in many configurations, some for tabletop use and others that are freestanding.

When you use a router table, the cutting bit is exposed, so you need to take extra precautions for safety. Always clamp a fence to the table so that no more than one half of the bit is exposed. And, whenever possible, use hold-down fixtures and guards to avoid kick back and to keep your hands away from the cutting edge. When cutting small parts, push sticks are a necessity.

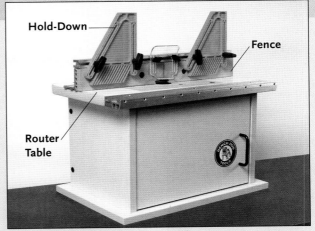

Hold-Down

Fence

Router Table

Since the router bit is inverted in a table, the direction of rotation is reversed. Therefore, when facing the table, you will need to feed the material from right to left.

Routers

A portable *router* gives you the ability to cut a wide range of molding profiles, as well as cutting grooves and trimming edges. Cutting bits are available in a dazzling array of profiles. Routers are rated by motor size and also by the size of the shank the collet (tool holder) will accept. For a first purchase, look for a model with a rating of 1½ to 1¾ horsepower with a ¼-inch collet. This is adequate for just about any task that you encounter and is a reasonable investment.

A basic router has a *fixed base* that requires you to set the depth of cut by turning a locking adjusting ring on the base; the depth must be set before turning on the tool. You will also see models that feature a *plunge base* that allows you to lower a spinning bit into the work surface. While a plunge-base router is the more flexible tool, it is a bit less stable than a comparable fixed-base tool. For molding edges, either type of base is fine, but for stopped internal flutes or grooves, you will need a plunge-base machine.

When using a router, always move the tool against the direction of rotation of the bit. As a general rule, this means that if you are facing the edge to be cut, the router should be guided from your left to your right.

If your router does not come with an accessory edge guide, you should certainly consider purchasing one. Many bits feature a ball-bearing pilot to guide the cut, but if you want to use other bits, the guide is almost a necessity.

ROUTER, GUIDE, AND BITS

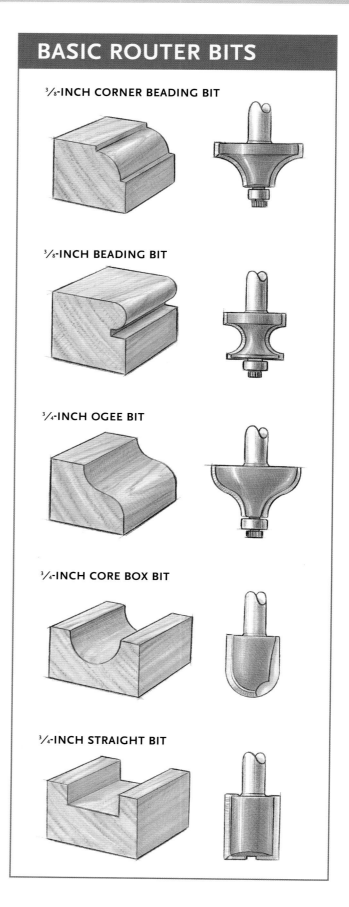

BASIC ROUTER BITS

⅜-INCH CORNER BEADING BIT

⅜-INCH BEADING BIT

¾-INCH OGEE BIT

¾-INCH CORE BOX BIT

¾-INCH STRAIGHT BIT

SETTING UP A ROUTER

PROFESSIONAL CABINETRY SHOPS create molding profiles using large cutters mounted in powerful shaping machines. The home workshop equivalent is a router. Thanks to a wide variety of bits, you can use the tool to shape your own custom profiles. When using a router, unplug the tool before changing bits, and always wear safety glasses.

TOOLS & MATERIALS
▌Router ▌Bits ▌Locking wrench ▌Safety glasses
▌1-by stock

1 Cutting bits have a mounting shank. Place the shank in a sleeve, called a collet, located under the motor.

2 Insert the shank, and tighten the bit in place using the wrench that came with the tool.

3 Test the setup on scrap lumber before moving on to the molding stock.

4 Adjust the depth of cut by turning the depth ring or the depth knob.

5 Plunge routers have a mechanism for adjusting the depth of cut.

FILES AND RASPS

Trimwork sometimes involves delicate fitting of two wood parts together, or one piece of wood against another surface such as plaster, drywall, brick, or stone. In those cases, the only true rule is to use the tool that works best—sometimes it could be a saw, others a knife, and still other times a *file* or *rasp* could be just right. Files and rasps come in a wide variety of shapes that make them perfect for the final fitting of coped joints, especially those that involve a complex profile.

One of the frequent challenges that can arise when casing a door or window is that the drywall will bulge out into the room, creating a hump in the wall surface. This situation is a natural by-product of taping a drywall joint, but it is a problem for the person applying the trim. One way to at-

tack the problem is to use a *Surform* tool to shave down the built-up drywall compound. The Surform has an expanded metal blade that is held in a frame so that it can be used like a rasp or plane.

Although you cannot sharpen files and rasps, you can, and should, keep them clean. The tool for this job is called a *file card*. Use the card like a brush to remove any built-up debris from file and rasp teeth.

Surform Tool

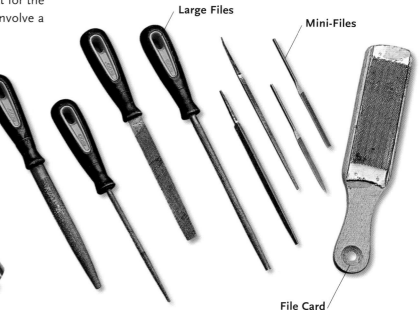

Large Files

Mini-Files

File Card

PRY BARS, END NIPPERS, AND LOCKING PLIERS

TRIM CARPENTRY is often a game of finesse. Many jobs require careful and patient fitting and re-fitting in order to achieve a tight fit between two parts. In that pursuit, many different tools can be brought into the mix, but some of the most effective, and necessary, are listed below.

When you need to remove an old molding, or coax a new piece into position, a *pry bar* is the tool for the job. These come in a wide variety of configurations, but the most useful for trim are the versions with flat ends, appropriately called flat bars. You will find some bars as short as 4 inches and some longer than 24 inches. If you select two different styles, usually those on the smaller side, you will be set for most jobs. In addition, it's useful to have a few different *putty knives* handy for scraping, gentle prying, and filling nailholes.

If your project includes removal of existing molding, you will need a way to remove the old nails from that stock. Two great tools for the job are *end nippers* and *locking pliers*. If you were to hammer the nails back through the face side, there is a great risk of chipping the material. With either of these tools, you can grab the protruding end of the nail and pull it through the back side of the board. This technique maintains the face side of the molding, allowing you the option of reusing it.

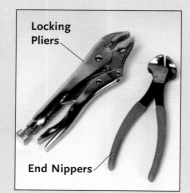

Locking Pliers

End Nippers

WORK-HOLDING TOOLS

Adjustable Clamping Worktable

Clamping Dog

VISE

WHEN YOU GET INVOLVED in almost any wood-cutting or shaping process, the issue of how to hold the workpiece will arise. You simply cannot do most woodworking operations safely and accurately if you are crouched on the living room floor. Of course, you can always hijack the kitchen or dining room table, but that's not always a popular, or practical, approach. The alternative solutions you can devise are endless, but some basic options will cover most situations.

Saw Horses. *Saw horses* are a simple and flexible support system for all types of work. You will find commercial models in steel and plastic, and you can always make your own from wood. Just about any horses that you buy will fold up for compact storage.

Clamping Worktables. Several manufacturers offer a folding worktable with movable top panels that function as a vise for work holding. These tables provide an ample top surface that can hold a miter saw firmly between its clamping dogs and can provide work-holding power for planing, sawing, routing, or chiseling. Their portability lets you take the worktable to the work site.

Clamps. The variety in styles and sizes of *clamps* is vast. And it is a traditional woodworker's refrain that "you can never have enough clamps." Clamps are used to hold a joint together while glue sets or while you drive a mechanical fastener. But they are also handy, when you do not have access to a workbench and vise, for stabilizing a board for sawing or planing. Small clamps are great for temporarily holding a molding in place or positioning a stop for repeat cuts on the miter saw. For a beginning tool kit, start with two or three of each of these types: spring clamps, C-clamps, lightweight bar clamps, and quick-release clamps.

Vise. If you have the luxury of having a dedicated workbench, one of the nicest modifications you can make is to add a *vise*. Vises for woodworking are available in many sizes, configurations, and prices. For most trim jobs, a lightweight vise that clamps to the top of a worktable will be sufficient. Whatever type you select, make sure that it has a provision for lining the jaws with wood so that you do not mar your workpieces when holding them.

C-Clamp

Spring Clamp

Lightweight Bar Clamp

Quick-Release Clamp

INSTALLATION TOOLS

The *hammer* is the most basic of hand tools—and probably the oldest. Primitive humans used some sort of hammering device at the dawn of civilization, and it is still a valued tool in the carpenter's tool kit. Although the popular image of hammer use in our culture is a rather crude one, in experienced hands a hammer can be a precise and subtle tool. For trimwork, look for a 16-ounce claw hammer. You will find models with curved and straight claws. Some "experts" will suggest that the curved claw model is preferred for trim; in fact, either style will be fine. Materials for the shaft include wood, fiberglass, and steel and, once again, personal preference rules. Of course, each manufacturer will offer their version of the "best" hammer, but you should choose one that feels comfortable and seems well balanced. If at all possible, test the hammer by driving some nails before purchasing it.

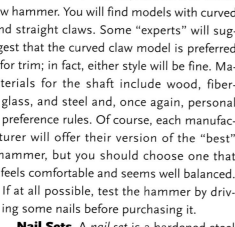

CURVED CLAW

STRAIGHT CLAW

Nail Sets. A *nail set* is a hardened steel tool with a tapered end that is used to drive a finishing nail below a wood surface. Sets come in various sizes to correspond to different size nailheads. To avoid hammer marks, drive the nail to within ⅛ inch of the surface and finish the job using the nail set. Make sure you use the appropriately sized set, or it could slip off the head and damage the wood.

Power Drills and Screwdrivers. These are tools that you will reach for frequently on most trim projects. You will use these to drill pilot holes for nails and screws, to drive screws for installing hardware or drywall, and to assemble jamb sets. This is a case where cordless models are certainly a worthwhile investment. Most tool companies offer combination drill/drivers with adjustable clutch settings. These can operate at high or low speeds, and you can set the torque for any job requirement—high for drilling in wood or low for driving small screws. You will find models rated from 7.2 to 24 volts, but as a nonprofessional, if you select a 12- or 14.4-volt unit, you will have plenty of drilling power. An additional attraction of the cordless models is that they all come with keyless chucks, so you don't have to worry about keeping track of the chuck key.

CORDLESS DRILL AND CHARGER

Finishing Nailer

Brad Nailer

Nail Clips

COMPRESSOR

USING A NAIL GUN

THE ABILITY TO DRIVE and set a nail in one step can save much time and effort even when applying trim to a small room. Look for a gun that will accept nails up to 2½ inches long. For fine work, a brad gun will shoot shorter and thinner fasteners. These tools are widely available from rental agencies, so you do not need to purchase one for a small job.

TOOLS & MATERIALS
▮ Air-powered nailer ▮ Compressor ▮ Nail clip

1 Pneumatic nailers use long clips of glued-together nails for easy loading.

2 For best results, make sure the firing head is perpendicular to the work surface.

3 For safety, most pneumatic nailers won't fire unless the tip is pressed firmly against the work.

In addition to having a power driver, you'll want to have an assortment of hand drivers, since there will always be those jobs where a power tool is too large or awkward. Try to include at least two sizes of driver in each common screw category: flat blade, Phillips, and Robertson (square drive).

Power Nailers

If your plans include extensive trimwork, the advantages of a *pneumatic nail gun* are obvious—increased speed and no hammer marks. But, even for a small job, there are reasons to consider a nail gun. First, the nails used in a finishing nail gun are thinner than those you drive by hand, so there is less chance of splitting the wood when nailing near an edge. You can adjust the pneumatic pressure that drives the gun, so with a simple pull of the trigger, you can drive and set the nail below the wood surface. When working with hardwood molding, you need to drill pilot holes for nails that will be driven by hand, but a pneumatic gun will shoot them home in one step.

Compressors. To drive a pneumatic nail gun, you will need a *compressor*. Look for an electric model in the range of 1.5-2.5 horsepower. These are available in designs that are either oil-lubricated or oil-less, and for occasional use in applying trim, either style will be fine. Make sure that you get an air hose that is at least 25 feet long, or you will find yourself moving the compressor every few minutes.

Tools and Techniques

USING SAFETY EQUIPMENT

TRIM IS NOT VERY DANGEROUS WORK, but there are two areas where it pays to be cautious. The first is with power tools, particularly saws. You should check the manufacturer's operating instructions and follow the rules for safe operation. The second is with wood chips and sawdust. Guard against injury by wearing safety glasses or goggles and, in some situations, by wearing a dust mask or respirator. Also, you will find gloves handy for sanding and finishing work, and you will come to appreciate kneepads when installing baseboard or wainscoting.

Safety equipment: A—rubber gloves, B—work gloves, C—knee pads, D—safety glasses, E—safety goggles, F—particle mask, G—respirator, H—ear protectors

DOWELING AND POCKET SCREW JIGS

IN COMMERCIAL FURNITURE and cabinet construction, dowels are still used as one of the primary systems to join lumber and plywood together. Those commercial systems rely on large machines with multiple drilling heads to bore the required holes in exact alignment. While the ease of plate joinery has made the use of dowels less popular for trimwork, a plate joiner is still a pretty expensive tool. If you only have a few joints to fashion, dowels are still a viable option, and a *doweling jig* is considerably less expensive. If you leaf through any tool catalogue or visit a home center, you will see any number of doweling jigs for sale. Just about any jig design will work well if you take care to accurately lay out the location of your holes. Follow the manufacturer's recommendations for operation of the jig, and use a sharp drill bit when boring the holes.

Pocket screws are another handy option for joining two pieces of lumber for a frame, extension jamb, or simple cabinet box. The system relies on a special jig that positions a drill bit to bore a shallow, angled pilot hole for specifically designed screws. These joints are quite strong and are easy to machine, but the screw holes are visible on the back side of the joint. Although there are proprietary plugs you can purchase for the screw holes, this system is best used where one side of the material will not be exposed—a wainscoting frame is a perfect use.

Doweling Jig

Bit Guides

Doweling jigs provide an easy way to use dowels to join two pieces of wood together.

Clamping Pliers

Tapered Bit

Pocket screw jigs position drill bits to bore angled pilot holes for special screws.

Tools and Techniques

STATIONARY OR BENCHTOP TOOLS

FOR ALL TRIM PROJECTS, accuracy is important, and when you are not a professional, it is hard to dedicate enough time to become proficient in every task. Even for the full-time carpenter, there are just some jobs that are easier and faster to achieve with a stationary tool than with a hand-held one. Straightening the edges of boards and ripping them to width are two such tasks. These jobs, among others, are easier and faster when you can use a tool that is specifically designed for the job, instead of adapting a hand tool. So, if your project budget permits, consider these as possible additions to your arsenal.

Table Saw

A small benchtop *table saw* can be extremely helpful on a trim job. If you need to rip strips for extension jambs or trim moldings to width, a table saw is the best tool for the job. Over the last few years, lightweight 8- and 10-inch saws have become very popular as alternatives to freestanding contractor-model saws. These saws offer a small miter gauge for square and angled cross-cuts, a fence for ripping stock to width, and a tilting arbor for bevel cuts. These saws are not the equivalent of floor model saws when it comes to power and accuracy, but for light-duty use they can do a great job.

Because a benchtop saw is intentionally lightweight, it is important that you clamp or bolt it to a heavy work-table before making any cuts. A stable base is important for safe and efficient operation. Also, make it a habit to check the rip fence setting at both the front and back of the blade because these accessories are notorious for not automatically locking parallel to the blade.

Jointer

A small tabletop *jointer* with a 4- or 6-inch-wide head can be very useful for straightening the edge of a bowed board or removing saw marks from ripped stock. These tools are scaled-down models of a cabinet-shop staple that is used in preparing lumber from rough stock. The jointer has two separate tables that surround the spinning cutterhead. To make a cut, hold a board against the vertical fence and push it across the infeed table, past the cutterhead and over the outfeed table. The depth of your cut is determined by the height of the infeed table—most benchtop tools use a hand wheel or lever to control table height. Safety note: The cutter heads are extremely sharp on this tool. Never joint material shorter than 12 inches long, and always use pushing paddles for stock that is less than 2 inches thick.

Planer

As your trim projects get more ambitious, you might run into situations where the thickness of stock materials does not suit your requirements. When that happens, you could bring your lumber to a custom woodworking shop or mill to have it planed, but you could also obtain a benchtop *planer* and do the job yourself. Many manufacturers now offer lightweight 12-inch-wide models, and most models do a very nice job. The best procedure with these tools is to always take a light cut, and work down toward your desired thickness with multiple passes.

TABLE SAW

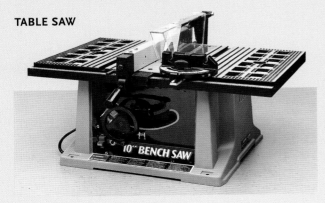

JOINTER

BASIC TRIM TECHNIQUES

Trim carpentry covers a pretty wide range of tasks and skills, and each particular discipline has an appropriate level of allowable deviation. At one end of the spectrum, a carpenter who is framing a house might work to a tolerance of ⅛ inch; anything more exacting could be construed as wasting time. However, a cabinetmaker could easily be concerned with measurements as fine as ¹⁄₆₄ inch or smaller, as gaps in a joint or irregularities in spaces around a door are readily visible and are signs of shoddy workmanship.

Applying interior trim falls closer to cabinetmaking than framing in the demand for accuracy. However, much depends on the type of trim that you are installing and the type of finish that will be applied. It's always nice to aim for perfection, and there is great satisfaction in putting together a tight miter joint or fitting a door with uniform margins all around. In practice, though, you will need to acquire your own sense for the appropriate level of accuracy on your jobs. It's rare for two carpenters to have the same approach to their work, and most have developed an intuitive judgment that operates in the background of each task.

In practical terms, you should not be able to see a space in a joint or a difference in the amount of overhang on opposite sides of a piece of trim. If your job is to receive a clear or stained finish, the demands are pretty high because any filler you use in a gap can easily be seen. When a painted finish is planned, you have a bit more leeway because fillers and caulk can correct many small problems. Keep in mind, however, that wide spaces in joints can telegraph through paint surfaces, and caulk does not cure all careless mistakes. In addition, if a joint depends on glue to keep it together, a tight fit is doubly important, as glue offers little strength when it must bridge a gap. It is much better to strive to develop good technique for measurement and fitting than to routinely rely on gap-filling measures.

Cutting Stock

Circular Saws. It's exciting to look over a neatly stacked pile of lumber waiting to be installed on the job. But before picking up a hammer, you will need to cut each piece to size, and you want to do it safely and accurately. To break down long pieces of stock into manageable length, as well as to make accurate finish cuts, a circular saw is likely to be one of your most useful tools. For all-around use, equip your saw with a combination blade; a 24-tooth, thin-kerf carbide tipped blade is a good choice. Carbide blades are more expensive than plain steel, but they maintain a sharp edge far longer. If you don't abuse the blade, or use it to cut through nails, it should last you for years. After prolonged use, a carbide blade will start to dull, but it is easy to find a shop to sharpen the blade.

To make fine finish cuts in solid stock, purchase a finish, or crosscutting, blade that has a 40-tooth configuration. Cutting plywood and other panel stock requires an even finer tooth blade. The thin veneer of a manufactured panel is very susceptible to chipping out where the blade

24-Tooth Combination

140-Tooth Plywood

USING CIRCULAR SAW GUIDES

TO MAKE RIP CUTS with a circular saw, use a rip guide. To use the guide, simply set the desired width of cut—measuring from the guide to the outside edge of the blade. Set the guide as shown right.

For short crosscutting jobs, you can use a square as a saw guide. First, mark your desired cut line across the workpiece. Measure the distance between the edge of the saw blade and the outside of the saw shoe, or foot. Place another mark that same distance away from your cut line, and align a square with that mark. Hold the outside edge of the saw shoe against the square. To cut panel stock, construct a simple cutting jig. (See "Plywood Cutting Jig," above opposite.)

exits the cut, and a finer blade minimizes this tendency. So if you have expensive panel stock to cut, consider a dedicated plywood blade with around 140 teeth. These are available in plain steel, so the expense is comparable to an all-purpose carbide blade.

Whenever you pick up a circular saw, give it your full attention. These are powerful tools, and careless or inattentive use can result in wasted materials or, worse, an injured operator. Begin by making sure that your work is properly supported. Place adequate support blocks under the piece being cut, so that the weight of the wood does not cause the blade to bind. Check to see that the blade guard operates properly—unplug the saw and clean any built-up sawdust from around the guard to prevent sticking. Set the depth of cut to be about ⅛ to ⅜ inch more than the thickness of your stock. Pull the saw trigger and let the blade come up to speed before starting your cut; then push it slowly and steadily, in a straight line, through the cut.

PLYWOOD CUTTING JIG

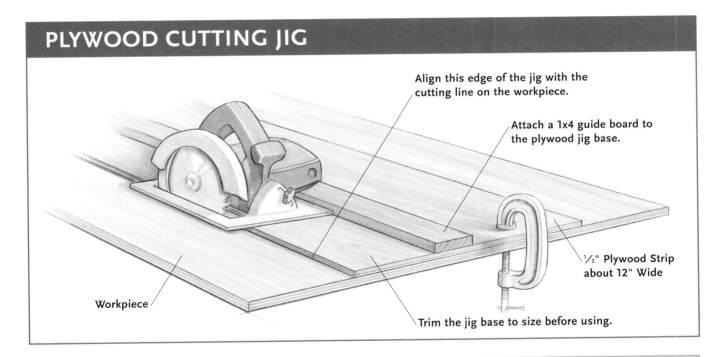

Align this edge of the jig with the cutting line on the workpiece.

Attach a 1x4 guide board to the plywood jig base.

½" Plywood Strip about 12" Wide

Workpiece

Trim the jig base to size before using.

Install a rip guide on the circular saw to rip strips of uniform width from a wide piece of stock.

A speed square is a handy guide for making crosscuts using a circular saw.

MITER SAWS

MOST PROCESSES in trimwork involve making joints in wood. Sometimes a joint could be as simple as butting two pieces of wood together, end to end or end to edge. At times, a joint will involve an angled cut. Miter cuts entail cutting an angle across the face of a board or piece of molding. Bevel cuts are angle cuts that run through the thickness of a piece of stock. Some joints require a cut that includes both a miter and bevel angle—these are commonly called compound miters.

In general, the angle that you cut on each half of a joint is equal to one-half of the total angle of the joint. For instance, for two pieces that will be joined at 90 degrees, each part needs to be cut at a 45-degree angle. Regardless of the specifics of the joint, in most cases, the best tool for the job is a miter saw. Whether you use a simple hand miter saw or a sliding compound saw, the basic principles remain the same. Adjust the saw to the desired angle of cut; hold the piece of molding against the saw fence; and align the cut line with the edge of the saw blade. Then slowly make your cut, keeping the molding steady so that the blade can move cleanly through the material.

Using a Hand Miter Box
TOOLS & MATERIALS
▮ Hand miter box ▮ Secure saw mount to bench
▮ 1-by stock

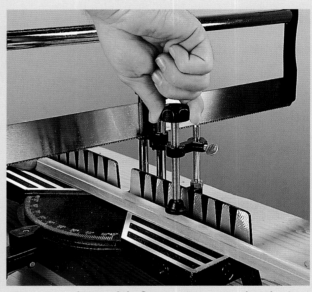

1 Secure the stock before cutting. Many hand miter boxes have a built-in clamp for holding thin stock in place.

2 Move the saw into the correct position by using the handle on the front of the miter scale. Move it left or right of the 0-deg. central setting.

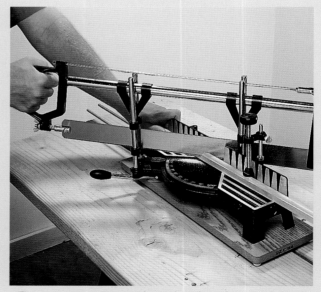

3 On most saws, such as this thin, fine-tooth blade built into this saw, the blade travels back and forth on a pair of guides.

POWER MITER SAW SETUP

IF YOUR PLANS include a good-size trim job, the investment in a power miter saw is well worth considering. These saws provide the ability to make quick and accurate cuts, as well as the ability to trim existing cuts for small adjustments—something that a hand miter saw cannot do. Miter saws generally have preset detents at common cutting angles: 15, 22.5, 30, 45, and 90 degrees.

Bevel and miter cuts can be described as either open or closed. If you look at the finished surface of a piece of molding, an open cut would expose the interior thickness of the material. Conversely, a closed cut would hide the interior thickness of the stock.

TOOLS & MATERIALS
▌ Power miter saw ▌ Secure saw mount to bench
▌ Adjustable sliding bevel ▌ 1-by stock

1 Release the locking button in order to free the saw arm. On most saws, the button is spring loaded.

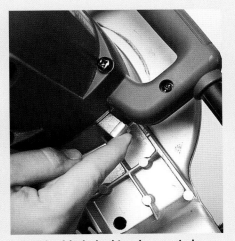

2 The blade locking button is located near the blade guard. It locks the blade in place so that you can change or tighten it.

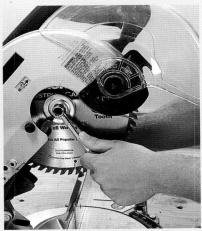

3 To change blades, mount a new blade on the arbor; then tighten it with the wrench that came with the saw.

4 Adjust the saw to the angle at which you want to cut. Release the handle to swing the saw left or right along the miter scale.

5 Set the degree setting using the handle on the scale. On most saws, the handle simply screws into position.

6 The lockout button (inset) is a safety measure found on saws. Depress the button before you can squeeze the trigger.

USING A PLATE JOINER

Plate Joinery

The plate joiner is a versatile tool that is extremely valuable for trim applications. You can adjust the blade to cut various-size slots in the mating surfaces of two pieces of stock. Then you apply a small bit of glue to each slot and the compressed, football-shaped joining plate. Slide the plate into one half of the joint, and assemble the parts.

Plate joints can be useful in a number of situations, including joining wide pieces of casing and wainscoting frame stock. All plate joiners have adjustable fences that can be moved to locate the slot at the desired height in the stock. You also have the option of using the flat bottom surface of the machine as a registration surface. Hold both the stock and the joiner tight to a flat tabletop while you cut.

TOOLS & MATERIALS

▌ Plate joiner ▌ Clamps ▌ Smooth, flat work surface
▌ Masking tape ▌ Pencil ▌ Joining plates ▌ 1-by stock
▌ Wood glue ▌ Glue brush

1 Place a mark to indicate the center of the joining plate slot on the surface of the board. If you want to avoid marking up your stock, use a piece of masking tape. Clamp the board to the worktable, and use both hands to control the plate joiner when cutting.

2 For slots in the edge of a board, lay out the center point of each slot; then clamp the board to the table. A flat work surface can function as a reliable registration surface for cutting the slots if both workpiece and plate joiner are held firmly to the surface.

3 All plate joiners have registration fences that you can use to locate the vertical position of a slot in the edge or end of a board. Flip the fence into position, and hold it firmly on the surface of the board while making the cut.

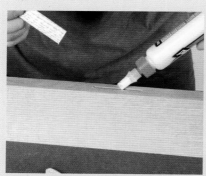

4 Use a thin wooden shim to spread a small amount of glue on the inside of each joining plate slot. The moisture in the glue will cause the plate to swell, further strengthening the joint.

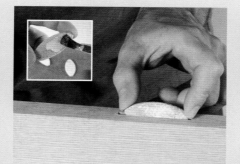

5 Spread glue on both sides of each joining plate before inserting it into its slot (inset). Insert the joining plate into its slot. The slots are intentionally sized a bit longer than the plates to allow for a small amount of lateral adjustment.

6 Assemble the joint; adjust the position; and pull the joint tight. Clamp the joint for at least one hour to allow the glue to develop a strong initial bond. Do not stress the joint for at least 12 hours.

MAKING SCARF JOINTS

Scarf Joints

Molding is usually available in lengths up to 14 or 16 feet, depending on your supplier and species of lumber. In larger rooms, or if your stock is of short length, you may need to splice together two or more pieces to cover a long wall. If you were to simply butt the square ends together, even the smallest bit of shrinkage would result in a visible gap between the parts, so the solution is to join the pieces with a scarf joint. In a scarf joint, the two parts are cut at an angle of 45 degrees, with one of the parts overlapping the other. The joint is typically glued and nailed together, forming an almost invisible joint. If there is any shrinkage over time, instead of an open gap, only more wood is exposed.

TOOLS & MATERIALS

▌ Power miter saw or hand miter box ▌ Power drill and bits ▌ Hammer and nail set ▌ Sanding block ▌ Baseboard molding ▌ Finishing nails

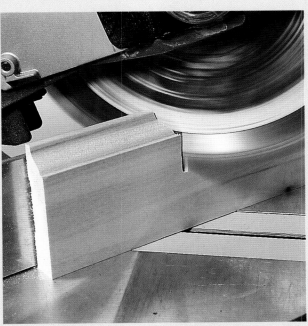

1 Plan the cut by locating the scarf joint over a wall stud. Using a miter saw, cut matching 45-deg. cuts on each piece that will form the scarf joint.

2 Attach the molding on the wall, overlapping the miter cuts. Strengthen the joint by first applying carpenter's glue to both sides of the joint. Drive finishing nails through the joint. Sink the nail heads below the wood's surface.

3 Fill the nailholes with wood filler. Sand the area smooth, and finish as desired. To further disguise a scarf joint in baseboard, add a shoe molding or a base cap. Offset scarf joints in built-up assemblies.

COPING CHAIR-RAIL MOLDING

Coped Joints

When two pieces of square, flat stock meet at an inside corner joint, the parts can simply butt together and the joint will stay tight. But when you need to make an inside corner joint with profiled stock, the situation is very different. In these cases, whether baseboard, chair rail, or cornice molding, the pieces should be joined in a coped joint. In a coped joint, the profile of one piece of molding is trimmed to fit over the matching profile of a second section of molding when the two meet in an inside corner. Baseboards, chair rails, and cornice molding can all benefit from coped joints.

The reasons for using a coped joint instead of an inside miter joint are twofold. First, not all corners are square, and a coped joint is forgiving of variations in angle. Second, even if an inside miter joint appeared tight at first fitting, the process of nailing it in place would tend to drive the joint apart, leaving you no way to remedy the situation except to fill the joint with caulk.

Cutting Coped Joints. To make a coped joint, install the first piece of molding square into the corner, and nail it in place. Cut a piece of stock to rough length (about 2 inches longer than finished dimension) for the next piece of molding. Use a miter saw to cut an open 45-degree bevel cut on the end that will receive the coped joint. An open bevel has its long point on the back surface of the stock, and it exposes the profile of the molded surface.

Use a coping saw to cut along the exposed profile, keeping the saw blade angled to provide a back-cut or clearance angle that is slightly greater than 90 degrees. The back-cut will allow you to easily adjust the coped profile without removing too much stock and ensures a tighter joint. For wide or thick molding, many pros use a combination of jig saw for straight cuts and coping saw for tightly curved cuts. (In many cases, it simply takes practice to trim the waste with a jig saw.) Feel free to switch back and forth between these tools to create the most efficient work flow.

Cutting Technique. When cutting a coped joint, it is a good practice to keep the saw blade about $\frac{1}{16}$ inch to the waste side of the profile line. Many people find it easier to stay to the waste side of the profile line by outlining the profile with a pencil to help it stand out. Once you have made the necessary cuts with the saw, it is then a simple matter to use a rasp or file to refine the cut to the line. Use a tapered half-round rasp to work the edges of rounded surfaces. Use a flat rasp on square edges.

This technique can be a true time saving measure, as it is easy to slip with the coping saw on an intricate profile and ruin a joint—something you are less likely to do when finishing the cuts with a rasp.

Test Your Work. When you're satisfied that the joint is snug, cut the other end of the molding to length. Expect your first few attempts at coping to be a bit frustrating, but with practice, the process becomes easier and should not take more than a few minutes per joint.

TOOLS & MATERIALS
▪ Clamps ▪ Measuring tape ▪ Utility knife
▪ Coping saw ▪ Flat and round rasps ▪ Sandpaper
▪ Chair-rail molding

smart tip

HELPFUL TOOLS

A GOOD COPING SAW MAY BE YOUR BEST FRIEND WHEN CUTTING COPED JOINTS, BUT DON'T FORGET THE MORE COMMON TOOLS THAT CAN HELP YOU ACHIEVE SUCCESS. A DARK PENCIL TO OUTLINE THE PROFILE CAN HELP KEEP YOUR CUTS ON TRACK, AND A GOOD SET OF FILES AND RASPS WILL GO A LONG WAY FOR MAKING THE FINAL ADJUSTMENTS TO THE CUTS. AND, OF COURSE, IT IS BEST TO BE PREPARED TO ATTEMPT TO MAKE THE JOINT FIT SNUGLY MORE THAN ONE TIME.

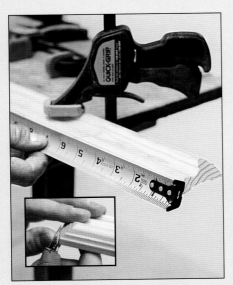

1 Make the miter cut, and measure the molding. Leave an extra inch or two to make adjustments. Use a utility knife to trim off the feathered edge of the miter cut, which is easily broken (inset).

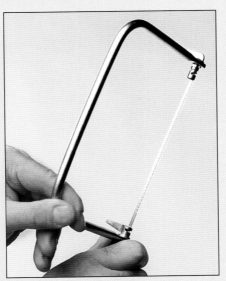

2 Turn the blade of the coping saw so that the teeth are facing at a right angle to the bow of the saw.

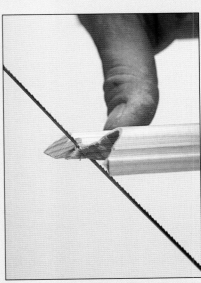

3 Back-cut the molding along the edge line of the miter. It is best to keep the blade of the saw about 1/16 in. to the waste side of the cut line.

4 After the initial cuts, it is time to make the final passes with a file or rasp. A tapered half-round rasp works well to clean up the edges of rounded areas.

5 A flat rasp works well on square edges where the molding will fit into place against the adjoining section of molding.

6 Test your work by placing the coped edge against the molding it will adjoin. In most cases, the piece with the straight-cut edge will already be in place.

MAKING MITERED RETURNS

Mitered Returns

As you move through the different tasks in trimming a room, you will usually encounter a situation where the end of a piece of molding will be exposed. This is a common condition at the ends of window stools, casing caps, aprons, or chair rail, but it also occurs with baseboard and cornice molding. Of course, the simplest solution would be to cut a square end on the stock, sand it smooth, and paint it. But this treatment has an unfinished look and indicates a lack of care in the job. Another approach would be to cut an open 45- or 30-degree angle on the end of the molding. This is an accepted detail on shoe molding, when it must end at door openings, but otherwise, it too looks incomplete. The preferred method is to fashion a mitered return on the end of the molding, creating a finished and intentional transition between the molding and the wall surface.

To create a mitered return, you will need to cut a small section of the molding profile and attach it to the end of the molding run. This will give the appearance of the shape of the molding wrapping around the edge of the molding.

TOOLS & MATERIALS

▮ Hammer ▮ Nail set ▮ Measuring tape ▮ Pencil ▮ Power miter saw or hand miter box ▮ Power drill and bits ▮ Small glue brush ▮ Chair rail molding ▮ Wood glue ▮ Finishing nails

1 Mark the edge of the dead-end piece about 1 in. back from the edge of the wall. In most cases, this is all the space you will need to expose the mitered return.

2 Cut the molding to length, allowing for a 45-deg. miter cut that will face the wall. If both ends of the molding will have a mitered return, plan accordingly.

3 Install the molding to a guide line for chair rails such as this. Attach the section by drilling pilot holes and using finishing nails to avoid splits. Sink nailheads with a nail set.

4 Cut the return from a piece of molding large enough to hold safely and securely against the saw fence. Apply glue to both surfaces.

5 Attach the return by pressing into place. You can set a small finishing nail in the return, or simply clamp the return piece until the glue sets.

MAKING A SIMPLE CUTOFF JIG

EVERY TOOL has its limitations. And even though a sliding compound miter saw can do many things, cutting a short piece of stock for a mitered return is not one of its best uses. In designing for flexibility, the fence on this type of saw is necessarily open around the cut, and does not provide good support for short cutoffs. A simple alternative for this particular job is to build a simple crosscutting jig that you can use with a backsaw. Screw two pieces of scrap 1x4 stock to the edges of a piece of 1x6. The entire assembly needs to be only about 18 inches long. Use a reliable square to mark across the top edges of the 1x4, and carry the guide marks down the outside faces. Use a backsaw to carefully cut down along your marks, stopping when the blade rests against the top of the 1x6.

To use the jig, simply place your molding in the box, resting against the back inside edge. Align your desired cut line with the kerf in the jig, and slide the saw back and forth in the kerf to make the cut. You can use the jig for both large and small moldings—anything up to 5½ inches wide.

TOOLS & MATERIALS

▌Power drill with screwdriver bit ▌Combination square ▌Pencil ▌Backsaw ▌1-by stock ▌Utility screws

1 Drill and countersink pilot holes; then screw a piece of 1x4 stock to either edge of a length of 1x6.

2 Use a square to mark cut lines across the top edges of the 1x4s and down the outside faces.

3 Use a backsaw to cut down along your layout marks until the saw teeth just graze the top of the 1x6.

4 To trim the molding, align the cut mark on your molding with the kerf on the jig.

CLEANING UP EDGES

EVEN IF YOU DON'T HAVE a home shop full of stationary power tools such as jointers and planers as you would find at a professional millwork company shop, you still can prepare trimwork so that your projects will have pro-quality results. There are a number of portable power tools and some hand tools that can help you prepare lumber for your trimwork projects. The tasks just take a little longer using these homeowner tools.

Use a belt sander, right, to smooth surfaces and to provide finishing touches on the edges of boards. Practice on scrap lumber first as a belt sander can gouge a groove in wood if it is not used properly. Use a power planer, below left, to reduce the width of boards in a hurry. These tools allow you to adjust the mount of wood you want to remove with each pass. Make a final pass with the rotating blade set to trim just a hair off the edge. Of course, you also can use muscle power and a hand plane, below right. Long planes are best for smoothing and straightening edges. Keep the blades on all of your power tools razor sharp.

A belt sander has two drums that spin and guide a continuous belt of sandpaper over the work.

A power planer has a small rotating blade that you can adjust to remove a little or a lot of wood.

A hand plane with an adjustable blade and a long bed can true up and clean the edge of a board.

USING A BELT SANDER

Sanding Basics

Some boards and stock moldings come from the lumberyard or home center ready to install. But that's more the exception than the rule these days due to a general decrease in lumber quality. As a practical matter, you often need to prepare your wood before you can cut and install it.

In professional shops, rough boards are cleaned up with a trip through large wood surfacing machines. The do-it-yourself equivalent is planing (in the case of very rough edges) and a lot of sanding. This is one area where you want the assistance of power tools, because sanding by hand with a block is difficult, time consuming, and not as accurate as power sanding.

The most efficient tool for cleanup work is a belt sander. It works like a floor sander, spinning a sandpaper belt over the wood. Working in line with the grain, use a medium-grit belt to remove material and a fine-grit belt to remove dirt and small surface scars. On smaller jobs, the best tool is a random-orbit sander. Its swirling motion erases most sanding marks and allows you to use the tool across joints where you can't always work with the grain.

TOOLS & MATERIALS
▌Belt sander ▌Sanding belts

1 Sanders have a mechanism (often a lever as shown above) that releases tension on the front wheel.

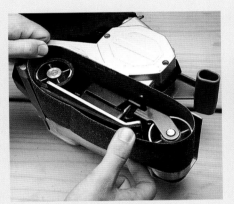

2 With the front wheel compressed, you have room to slide a belt over the sander wheels and base plate.

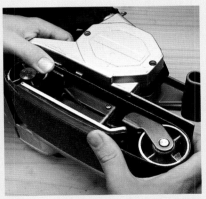

3 The next step is to extend the front wheel and apply tension to the sanding belt. (This lever locks to the left.)

4 Center the belt, turn on the sander, and adjust the tracking control to keep the belt centered as it spins.

5 Keep both hands on the sander, and keep the sander moving with the grain to prevent dig marks.

Resource Guide

This list of manufacturers and associations is meant to be a general guide to additional industry and product-related sources. It is not intended as a listing of products and manufacturers represented by the photographs in this book.

A & M Wood Specialty
357 Eagle St. N.
P.O. Box 32040
Cambridge, Ontario N3H 5M2
Canada
800-265-2759
www.forloversofwood.com
Domestic and exotic hardwood lumber—shipping available. Offers jointing, planing, and ripping services.

Alexandria Moulding
300 Lasley Ave.
Wilkes-Barre, PA 18706
800-841-8746
www.alexandriamoulding.com
Manufacturer of pine, cedar, hardwood, and MDF moldings.

Architectural Distributors, Inc.
162 Center St.
Grayslake, IL 60030
800-729-4606
www.archdist.com
Wood moldings, wood and fiberglass columns, and pilasters.

Architectural Ornament, Inc.
55 Bradwick Dr.
Concord, Ontario L4K 1K5
Canada
905-738-9459
www.architectural-ornament.com
Polyurethane moldings.

Balmer Architectural Mouldings
271 Yorkland Blvd.
Toronto, Ontario M2J 1S5
Canada
800-665-3454
www.balmer.com
Polyurethane moldings, medallions, door surrounds, and mantels.

Bloch Industries
140 Commerce Dr.
Rochester, NY 14623
585-334-9220
www.blochindustries.com
Manufacturer of stock and custom molding profiles.

Chadsworth, Inc.
277 N. Front St.
Historic Wilmington, NC 28401
800-265-8667
www.columns.com
Wood, composite, and PVC columns.

Fypon
960 W. Barre Rd.
Archbold, OH 43502
800-446-3040
www.fypon.com
Urethane millwork in hundreds of profiles.

Home Depot
For store locations check
www.homedepot.com
Or 800-430-3376
General building supplies, lumber, millwork, fasteners, finishes, and tools.

House of Fara
4747 W. State Road 2
LaPorte, IN 46350
800-334-1732
www.houseoffara.com
Wood moldings.

Lowe's
For store locations check www.lowes.com
Or 800-445-6937
General building supplies, lumber, millwork, fasteners, finishes, and tools.

M.L. Condon
248 Ferris Ave.
White Plains, NY 10603
914-946-4111
www.condonlumber.net
Hardwood and softwood lumber and millwork—shipping available.

Moulding & Millwork
1578 Sussex Tpk., Unit 5
Randolph, NJ 07869
973-584-0040
www.mouldingandmillwork.com
Pine, hardwood, and MDF moldings.

Ornamental Mouldings
3804 Comanche Rd.
P.O. Box 4068
Archdale, NC 27263
800-799-1135
www.ornamental.com
Wood moldings and architectural ornaments.

Resinart East, Inc.
201 Old Airport Rd.
Fletcher, NC 28732
800-497-4376
www.resinart.com
Polyester resin-based flexible moldings.

Rockler Woodworking and Hardware
4365 Willow Dr.
Medina, MN 55340
800-279-4441
www.rockler.com
Woodworking tools and supplies.

San Francisco Victoriana, Inc.
2070 Newcomb Ave.
San Francisco, CA 94124
415-648-0313
www.sfvictoriana.com
Architectural ornament for traditional and contemporary buildings. Traditional Victorian trim elements and custom molding services.

Sears
For store locations check
www.sears.com
Or 800-383-4814
Carpentry and woodworking tools, finishes.

ToolCrib.com
www.toolcrib.com
888-486-6527
Woodworking and carpentry tools.

Vintage Woodworks
Hwy. 34 S.
P.O. Box 39
Quinlan, TX 75474
903-356-2158
www.vintagewoodworks.com
Wood moldings and architectural ornaments.

West Penn Hardwoods
230 S. Clinton St.
Olean, NY 14760
716-373-6434
www.westpennhardwoods.com
Domestic and exotic hardwood lumber—shipping available.

White River Hardwoods Woodworks, Inc.
1197 Happy Hollow Rd.
Fayetteville, AR 72701
800-558-0119
www.mouldings.com
Hardwood and resin moldings, including flexible moldings. Carved architectural ornaments.

Windsor Mill
7950 Redwood Dr. #4
Cotati, CA 94931
888-229-7900
www.windsorone.com
Wood and MDF moldings.

Woodcraft
406 Airport Industrial Pk. Rd.
P.O. Box 1686
Parkersburg, WV 26104
800-225-1153
www.woodcraft.com
Woodworking tools.

Glossary

Apron The piece of trim at the bottom of a window, below the stool.

Back band Molding used to decorate the outer edges of flat casing. It can also be used as a base cap.

Back cut The technique of removing stock along the rear surface of a piece of molding to reduce the contact area of the joint. Back cuts are recommended in coped joints to allow maximum flexibility in fitting difficult joints.

Backsaw A handsaw with a rectangular blade that is stiffened by a reinforcing metal spine along the top edge of the blade. Available in a variety of sizes, these saws are used to cut precision joints and are the saw of choice for hand miter boxes.

Baseboard One-piece trim stock mounted at the bottom of a wall to transition between the wall and floor.

Base cap Molding applied to the top of base trim.

Base shoe Molding used to conceal any variation between the floor and baseboard. It is also used to cover edges of sheet vinyl flooring (when installed without first removing base trim).

Base trim Sometimes called base molding, base trim protects the bottom portion of walls and covers the transition area between the wall and the floor.

Bevel An angled cut, other than 90 degrees, into the thickness of a piece of stock.

Biscuits Football-shaped pieces of compressed wood that are glued into slots cut into the pieces of stock that will form a joint.

Blocking Wood stock applied between or adjacent to studs or in wall-ceiling corners to provide a solid surface into which molding and other treatments may be nailed.

Built-up trim Several profiles of trim combined to appear as one large piece of molding. Most often it is used to form a cornice or base trim.

Butt joint Two pieces of wood joined end to face using square cuts.

Casing The trim that is used to line the inside and outside of a doorway or window frame.

Chair rail Molding installed at a height that protects walls from being damaged by chair backs. It is also used to cover the edges of wainscoting.

Chalk line A string covered with powdered chalk used to mark a straight line between distant points. A chalk-line box opens to accept the powdered chalk in its cavity and has a reel of line inside. Chalk covers the line as you extend the line from the box.

Chamfer A shallow, angled cut along the edge or end of a board that is used as a decorative detail.

Clear grade A grade of lumber or trim that has no knots or other visible defects.

Compound miter A cut that angles across and with the wood grain simultaneously.

Coped cut Made with a coping saw, a curved cut that is made across the grain of a piece of molding to match the profile of an identical molding piece for a coped joint.

Coped joint A butt or corner joint, usually at a right angle, between two pieces of curved-profile molding using a coped cut.

Corner guard Trim that protects the outside corners of drywall or plaster in high-traffic areas.

Cornice Trim treatment at the top of a wall that transitions between the wall the ceiling.

Cove Usually, molding that covers the inside corners between sheets of paneling. It is also used with crown and other molding for built-up cornice treatments.

Crosscut A straight cut across the grain of wood.

Crown Molding that is used alone or with other molding stock as a cornice.

Drywall A panel composed of a gypsum core covered by heavy paper on two sides that is used to form the interior surface of walls and ceilings.

Finger-joint A means of joining short lengths of lumber together to form a long board or piece of molding stock. Interlocking "fingers" are cut in the matching ends, and the parts are glued together. Finger-jointed stock is suitable only for paint-grade applications.

Half-lap miter joint A joint that combines miter, cope, and butt cuts. Half-lap miters are used for moldings with full, rounded-over tops.

Jamb A frame that covers the inside surfaces of a window, door, or other wall opening.

Joist A horizontal member in house framing that supports a floor or ceiling.

Kerf The width of a saw-blade cut.

Miter cut A straight cross-grain cut made at an angle other than 90 degrees to join two pieces of wood.

Mitered return Used to continue the profile of trim back to the wall when the trim does not meet another piece of trim.

Miter joint A corner joint formed by cutting the ends of two pieces of lumber at an angle—often 45 degrees.

Molding Thin strips of wood that have a profile created by cutting and shaping.

Nail set A pointed metal tool used to drive the heads of finishing nails below the wood surface. Sets are available in various sizes to match nailhead diameter.

Paint-grade trim Trim made of many small pieces of wood finger-joined into one long piece. (See also *Finger-joint*.)

Picture molding Molding used to hang metal hooks to suspend paintings and wall hangings so that there is no need to put holes in the wall.

Plumb Vertically straight, in relation to a horizontally level surface.

Rabbet An open groove cut along the edge or end of a piece of wood. Rabbets are often used to join two pieces of stock at a right angle.

Rail The horizontal member of a wooden frame.

Reveal Amount of the jamb (usually ⅛ to 3/16 inch) that is allowed to show at the edges of the casing of a window, door, or wall opening (such as a passageway).

Rigid polyurethane molding Trim that is extruded into various profiles and sizes. It is lightweight, stable, and paintable.

S4S "Surfaced Four Sides," designating dimension lumber that has been planed on all sides.

Sash The framework into which window glass is set.

Double-hung windows have an upper and a lower sash.

Scarf joint A 45-degree miter cut that is used to join lengths of trim end to end.

Screen molding Half-round or flat molding used to protect the cut edges of screening nailed to a wooden screen door or wooden window screen.

Shelf edging Trim that covers the exposed edges of plywood or particleboard casework and shelving.

Shims Thin wood wedges (often cedar shingles) used for tightening the fit between pieces, such as filling the gap between the window frame and rough-opening sill when installing a window.

Stool The piece of window trim that provides a stop for a lower sash and extends the sill into the room.

Stops Narrow strips of wood nailed to the head and side jambs of doors and windows to prevent a door from swinging too far when it closes and to keep the window sash in line.

Stud Vertical member of a frame wall, usually placed at each end and every 16 inches on center.

Toenail To drive a nail at an angle, through one framing member and into another, to lock the parts together.

Trim General term for any wood used in a house that is not structural lumber. Also, ornamental enhancements that improve the appearance of buildings, both exterior and interior. Includes plain and shaped members.

Veneer A thin layer of wood that is sawn or sliced from a log. Inexpensive veneers can be glued together to form plywood, with a valuable lumber species displayed on the outer surfaces. Veneers can also be applied to composite cores such as MDF and particleboard.

Wainscoting Paneling, paint, fabric wallcovering, or other material applied to the lower half of an interior wall.

Wall frames Assemblies of panel molding applied to a drywall or plaster wall for decorative purposes.

Warp A descriptive term indicating that a board is not flat.

Index

Index

Index

Photo Credits

All photography by Neal Barrett/CH, unless noted otherwise.
All illustrations by Robert LaPointe, unless noted otherwise.

page 1: Anne Gummerson **pages 2–3:** *both* davidduncanlivingston.com **pages 6–7:** *both* Jessie Walker **page 8:** davidduncanlivingston.com **page 9:** *both* Gary David Gold/CH **page 10:** davidduncanlivingston.com **page 11:** *left* Eric Roth; *right* Gary David Gold/CH **page 12:** Jessie Walker **page 13:** *top* Jessie Walker; *center* Tony Giammarino/Giammarino & Dworkin; *bottom* Mark Samu **page 14:** Gary David Gold/CH **page 15:** M. Barrett/H. Armstrong Roberts **page 17:** *all* Gary David Gold/CH **page 18:** Brian Vanden Brink **pages 19–21:** *all* Gary David Gold/CH **page 22:** Mark Samu **page 23:** Anne Gummerson **page 24:** Gary David Gold/CH **page 26:** *top left* davidduncanlivingston.com; *top right* carolynbates.com, design & builder: Pat Pritchett, Vermont Vernacular Design; *bottom right* Tony Giammarino/Giammarino & Dworkin **page 27:** Lisa Masson, design: T.L. Knisley **page 28:** carolynbates.com, design: Kim Brown, builder: Roy Dunphy & Chris Dolan **page 29:** *top left* Jessie Walker, design: David T. Smith; *top right* Jessie Walker; *bottom right* Nancy Hill **page 30:** Jessie Walker, design: Diane Wendall **page 31:** *top & bottom right* Jessie Walker; *bottom left* Phillip H. Ennis Photography **page 32:** *top* Jessie Walker, architect: Paul Janicki; *bottom* Mark Lohman **page 33:** *both* Jessie Walker; *top* design: Glen Meidbreder Bath Designs; *bottom* design: Alan Portnoy **page 34:** Jessie Walker **page 35:** *top left* and *right* Jessie Walker; *bottom left* Tony Giammarino/Giammarino & Dworkin **page 36:** Jessie Walker, design: Jim & Jean Wagner **page 37:** *top left & right* davidduncanlivingston.com; *bottom* Jessie Walker, design: Chris Garrett **page 38:** Jessie Walker **page 39:** *top* John Parsekian/CH **pages 40–41:** *all* Gary David Gold/CH **page 44:** *all* Gary David Gold/CH **pages 45–50:** John Parsekian/CH **page 51:** *top left* John Parsekian/CH; *top right* Tria Giovan; *bottom right* K. Rice/H. Armstrong Roberts **page 64:** Brian Vanden Brink, design: Martin Moore, Coastal Design **page 72:** Brian Vanden Brink, design: Polhemus Savery DaSilva Architects **page 75:** *top* Gary David Gold/CH **page 78:** davidduncanlivingston.com **page 88:** *bottom left* Jessie Walker **page 104:** *left* carolynbates.com, architect: Sandra Vitzthum; *right* davidduncanlivinston.com **page 105:** *top left & bottom* Gary David Gold/CH; *top right* Tria Giovan **page 106:** davidduncanlivingston.com **page 107:** *top & center* John Parsekian/CH; *bottom* Gary David Gold/CH **pages 108–117:** *all* Gary David Gold/CH **pages 118–119:** *all* John Parsekian/CH **pages 120–130:** *all* Gary David Gold/CH **pages 132–134:** *all* John Parsekian/CH **pages 135–137:** *all* Gary David Gold/CH **page 138:** Jessie Walker **page 139:** *center* John Parsekian/CH **page 140:** Gary David Gold/CH **page 141:** *all* John Parsekian/CH **pages 156–158:** *all* John Parsekian/CH **page 161:** Jessie Walker **page 164:** Anne Gummerson **page 170:** *both* Jessie Walker; *left* design: Meidbreder Building Group; *right* architect: Stephen R. Knutson **page 172:** Lisa Masson **page 176:** Gary David Gold/CH **page 179:** Gary David Gold/CH **page 184:** Anne Gummerson **page 185:** *all* Jessie Walker; *bottom* design: Bob & Lorel McMillan **page 186:** *all* Jessie Walker; *top* architect: David Frankel; *bottom left* architect: Jim Tharp **page 188:** Jessie Walker, design: Jane Levy Designs **page 189:** *both* Jessie Walker **page 190:** *both* Jessie Walker; *top* design: Bob & Lorel McMillan **page 191:** *both* Jessie Walker **page 192:** Jessie Walker, architect: Gary Frank **pages 193–195:** *all* Jessie Walker **page 196:** Anne Gummerson **pages 197–200:** *all* Jessie Walker **page 201:** *all* Jessie Walker; *top right* design: Chris Garrett **page 202:** *both* Jessie Walker; *top* design: Jane Hopper, ASID **pages 203–204:** *all* Jessie Walker **page 205:** Jessie Walker, design: Jane Irvine **pages 206–208:** *all* Jessie Walker **page 209:** *both* Jessie Walker; *left* architect: David Raino **pages 210–212:** *all* Jessie Walker **page 214:** Mark Samu, design: Charles Reilly Design **page 216:** John Parsekian/CH **page 218:** Brian Vanden Brink **page 219:** carolynbates.com, design: Milford Cushman, The Cushman Design Group, Inc. **page 220:** Susan Andrews **page 221:** *top* Brian C. Nieves/CH **page 223:** *top* Jessie Walker **page 224:** *top* davidduncanlivingston.com **page 225:** *bottom* carolynbates.com, design: H.R. Thurgate & Sons, LLC **pages 228–229:** *illustrations by:* Mario Ferro **page 230:** *bottom* Tony Giammarino/Giammarino & Dworkin, architect: William Darwin Prillamin & Assoc. **page 231:** Tony Giammarino/Giammarino & Dworkin, architect: Fransis Fleetwood **page 232:** *right* Brian Vanden Brink, architect: John Morris **page 233:** *left* Tony Giammarino/Giammarino & Dworkin, design: Marge Thomas; *bottom right* Brian Vanden Brink, architect: Jack Silverio **page 236:** *bottom right* courtesy of Fypon **page 238:** Tony Giammarino/Giammarino & Dworkin, design: Beth Scherr Designs **page 239:** *top* Mark Samu, courtesy of Hearst Specials **page 240:** *top right* Jessie Walker **page 242:** *top left* Brian C. Nieves/CH; *right* John Parsekian/CH **page 244:** *bottom left* Brian C. Nieves/CH; *bottom right* courtesy of Solutions Miterless **page 246:** Mark Samu **page 247:** *center* John Parsekian/CH **page 248:** *left* Gary David Gold/CH **page 249:** *bottom* Gary David Gold/CH **page 250:** *left* Gary David Gold/CH **page 251:** *top & center* John Parsekian/CH **page 252:** *bottom left* Gary David Gold/CH **page 253:** *left* John Parsekian/CH; *right both* Gary David Gold/CH **pages 254–255:** *sequence* John Parsekian/CH; *right both* Gary David Gold/CH **page 256:** *left* John Parsekian/CH; *right all* Gary David Gold/CH **page 257:** *top* Gary David Gold/CH **page 258:** Gary David Gold/CH **page 259:** *all* John Parsekian/CH **page 260:** *right* Gary David Gold/CH **page 261:** *bottom* Gary David Gold/CH **page 262:** *left* John Parsekian/CH; righ *all* Gary David Gold/CH **page 263:** *all* John Parsekian/CH **page 264:** *top* John Parsekian/CH **page 265:** *both* Gary David Gold/CH **pages 268–269:** *all* John Parsekian/CH **page 271:** *all* John Parsekian/CH **page 273:** *all* Gary David Gold/CH **page 274:** *all* John Parsekian/CH **pages 276–277:** *all* John Parsekian/CH **page 286:** Jessie Walker

Metric Equivalents

Length

1 inch	25.4mm
1 foot	0.3048m
1 yard	0.9144m
1 mile	1.61km

Area

1 square inch	645mm^2
1 square foot	0.0929m^2
1 square yard	0.8361m^2
1 acre	4046.86m^2
1 square mile	2.59km^2

Volume

1 cubic inch	16.3870cm^3
1 cubic foot	0.03m^3
1 cubic yard	0.77m^3

Common Lumber Equivalents

Sizes: Metric cross sections are so close to their U.S. sizes, as noted below, that for most purposes they may be considered equivalents.

Dimensional lumber	1 x 2	19 x 38mm
	1 x 4	19 x 89mm
	2 x 2	38 x 38mm
	2 x 4	38 x 89mm
	2 x 6	38 x 140mm
	2 x 8	38 x 184mm
	2 x 10	38 x 235mm
	2 x 12	38 x 286mm
Sheet sizes	4 x 8 ft.	1200 x 2400mm
	4 x 10 ft.	1200 x 3000mm
Sheet thicknesses	¼ in.	6mm
	⅜ in.	9mm
	½ in.	12mm
	¾ in.	19mm
Stud/joist spacing	16 in. o.c.	400mm o.c.
	24 in. o.c.	600mm o.c.

Capacity

1 fluid ounce	29.57mL
1 pint	473.18mL
1 quart	0.95L
1 gallon	3.79L

Weight

1 ounce	28.35g
1 pound	0.45kg

Temperature

Fahrenheit = Celsius x 1.8 + 32
Celsius = Fahrenheit - 32 x 5⁄9

Nail Size and Length

Penny Size	Nail Length
2d	1"
3d	1¼"
4d	1½ "
5d	1¾"
6d	2"
7d	2¼"
8d	2½"
9d	2¾"
10d	3"
12d	3¼"
16d	3½"

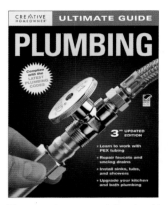
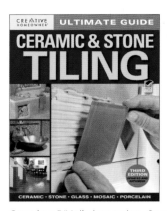
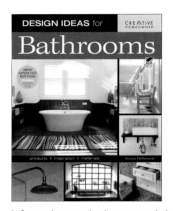
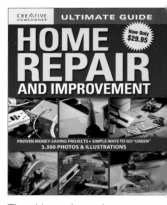

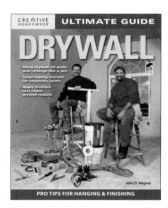
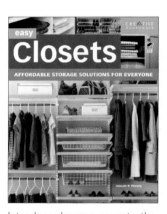
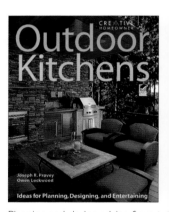
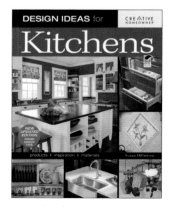
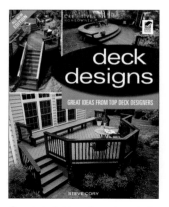
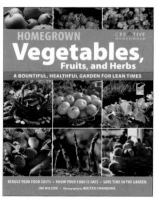
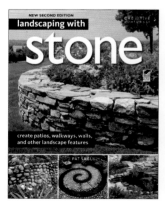